MESSERSCHMITT Bf 110
BOMBSIGHTS OVER ENGLAND

Also by John Vasco

THE STING OF THE LUFTWAFFE:
Schnellkampfgeschwader 210 and Zerstörergeschwader 1 "Wespengeschwader"
in World War II

MESSERSCHMITT Bf 110
BOMBSIGHTS OVER ENGLAND

Erprobungsgruppe 210 in the Battle of Britain

John Vasco

Schiffer Military History
Atglen, PA

Dust jacket and aircraft profile artwork by S.W. Ferguson, Colorado Springs, CO.

CROYDON'S COST

The dust jacket artwork show the fateful August 15, 1940 attack on RAF Croydon by ErprGr. 210 with *Gruppenkommandeur* Rubensdorffer and his gunner Ludwig Kretzer in the lead aboard their Bf 110D. *Letutnant* Horst Marx has just bailed out of his riddled Bf 109E *Jabo* as RAF assailant Flinders in his Hurricane closes in from the left. Seconds later, another Hurricane would attack the *Zerstörer* and send the crew down to their deaths.

Book design by Robert Biondi.

Library of Congress Catalog Number: 2001090727.

Printed in China.
ISBN: 0-7643-1445-9

Published by Schiffer Publishing Ltd.
4880 Lower Valley Road
Atglen, PA 19310
Phone: (610) 593-1777
FAX: (610) 593-2002
E-mail: Schifferbk@aol.com.
Visit our web site at: www.schifferbooks.com
Please write for a free catalog.
This book may be purchased from the publisher.
Please include $3.95 postage.
Try your bookstore first.

In Europe, Schiffer books are distributed by:
Bushwood Books
6 Marksbury Ave.
Kew Gardens
Surrey TW9 4JF
England
Phone: 44 (0)208 392-8585
FAX: 44 (0)208 392-9876
E-mail: Bushwd@aol.com.
Free postage in the UK. Europe: air mail at cost.
Try your bookstore first.

Contents

Karl-Fritz Schröder in the Bordfunker's position of a Bf 110.

Foreword

FOREWORD BY KARL-FRITZ SCHRÖDER
FORMER BORDFUNKER
3rd STAFFEL, ERPROBUNGSGRUPPE 210

Numerous books have been written in the last forty years about the air battles over England. In almost all cases, the course of the Battle is dealt with in a general way. What has been lacking up until now were descriptions of the events as seen by a single unit. The present book closes an important gap in this respect – reporting on a relatively small unit of the *Luftwaffe*, which played a decisive role in the battle over the British Isles. *Erprobungsgruppe 210* with its three *Staffeln* – in spite of its achievements this *Gruppe* was at no time in the public eye. On the German side at the time, that was left to the well-known fighter squadrons with their aces. It is a fair assumption that *Erprobungsgruppe 210* was better known by its opponents than it was within the *Luftwaffe*, at that time. Hopefully this book on this flying unit will help to complete the history of that air battle. In the name of the few survivors of the flying personnel of *Erprobungsgruppe 210*.

K.F. Schröder

Acknowledgments

A work of this nature is dependent upon the input of assistance from many differing people and organisations. First of all, I wish to record my grateful thanks to Andy Low and Andy Brown, who not only gave of their time, but also proved to be seasoned researchers during our many forays to the Public Record Office.

Many authors and researchers in the aviation field also provided valuable assistance, and special mention must go to Peter Cornwell, who was a constant source of encouragement and information during the course of the research. Many others gave help and it would be invidious of me to place them in any order of merit so I therefore thank them alphabetically for their respective contributions: Stephen Bungay; Pat Burgess; Christopher Elliot; Jean-Bernard Frappé; Chris Goss; Jim Kitchens; Dennis Knight; Ken Merrick; Alexander Mckee; Michael Payne; Peter Petrick; Cyril Russell; Andy Saunders; Hans Schliephake; Christopher Shores; Geoffrey Stephens; Hugh Trivett; Ken Wakefield and Ken West.

Staff of many institutions also provided generous help and I would like to thank Air Commodore Probert and Group Captain Flanagan and their staff at the Ministry of Defence (Air Historical Branch) for pointing me in the right direction on certain matters relating to the Battle of Britain; Chief Librarian D.W. Goode and the staff of the library section at the Royal Aircraft Establishment at Farnborough for making available the many and varied reports on some of the 'trade' which passed through their hands during World War 2; staff at the Public Record Office for their work in producing documents so necessary for the compilation of this work; and Herr Schonemann and Frau Busekow at the Deutsche Dienststelle (WASt) in Berlin for their assistance in the compilation of the loss table of the unit.

On the German side my thanks go to the following former flying personnel of Erprobungsgruppe 210: Otto Hintze; Wolfgang Schenck; Balthasar Aretz; Gerhard Schlee; Edmund Ernst; Karl Stoff; Helmut Ortner; Heinz Natzinger; Ernst Elfner; Willi Benedens; Ewald Schank; Werner Zwick; Peter Emmerich, Werner Neumann, Wolf Meyer-Erlach, Rolf Rohrschneider and Karl-Fritz Schröder. Special thanks are due to the last-named who very kindly acted as my interpreter during my attendances at the 'Wespentreffen', and who also wrote the introduction to this work. I would also like to thank Herr Horst Amberg of the 'Gemeinschaft der Jagdflieger' for the help he provided; the late Karl-Hans Trüdinger, former organiser of the 'Wespentreffen', who gave me the opportunity to meet many former members at their re-union, and Heinz Lüttmann who took over the running of the Wespentreffen in later years; Joachim Koepsell, formerly of Zerstörergeschwader 26 for his help concerning his unit's fighter escort for Erprobungsgruppe 210; the late Otto Bertram, formerly of Jagdgeschwader 2, for information on his brother, Kurt, who was killed in action on 11 August 1940; Victor Mölders for help with information on his former Staffel in the Battle of France (1st Staffel of Zerstörergeschwader 1) which formed the 1st Staffel of Erprobungsgruppe 210, and for assistance in the compilation of the appendix on the Bf 110 C-6, and to Leo Kabacinski, Werner Wulf and Willi Falkenroth for their help with ground crew matters. Thanks are also due to Frau Ruth Marx for making available the full details of the combat claim of 27th July 1940 lodged by her late husband, Horst Marx of 3rd Staffel. A special word of thanks must go to Dr. Hans Lutz who very kindly made available to me a copy of the 'Nachruf' sent by Generalfeldmarschall Albert Kesselring to the mother of Martin Lutz following the loss of her son in combat over England and gave permission for it to be included in this work.

On the RAF side I would like to thank the RAF magazine 'Airmail' for publishing my plea for assistance from former RAF personnel, and to Wing Commander N. P. W. Hancock who provided many contacts through the Battle of Britain Pilots' Association. I would also like to thank Air Vice Marshall John Worrall; Air Commodore John Thompson; Group Captain B. L. Duckinfield; Wing Commander Michael Crossley; Wing Commander Hugh Kennard; Group Captain John Bisdee; Squadron Leader R. H. Dibnah; Squadron Leader Antony Fisher; Squadron Leader Charles Cooke; Squadron Leader Henry Newton; Squadron Leader Robert Maltby; Flight Lieutenant John Burgess, and Sergeant Tom Townshend for their recollections of events over sixty years ago.

I would also like to place on record my thanks to Tom Anthem for the prodigious amount of translating he carried out on my behalf. Many times I was congratulated on my 'perfect German'; each time I had to advise that it was the work of a translator. He could receive no greater compliment than that. Thanks are also due to Mrs. Pauline McMillan who rendered typing assistance for part of the research period.

The many photographs contained in this work were received from various sources including: Pat Burgess; Andy Saunders; Michael Payne; Peter Cornwell; Geoffrey Stephens; Jean-Bernard Frappé; Chris Goss; Ron Mackay; Leo Kabacinski; Otto Hintze; Willi Falkenroth; Heinz Ludwig; Balthasar Aretz; Gerhard Schlee; Karl Stoff; Edmund Ernst; Heinz Natzinger; Ewald Schank; Werner Zwick; Peter Petrick; Otto Bertram and Karl Fritz Schröder. I am also indebted to relatives of former members of Erprobungsgruppe 210 who were killed in action while serving with the unit, or later in the war. In many instances painful memories may have been stirred after so long a passage of time, but they willingly loaned photographs for inclusion in the work: Frau Hilda Strobel and Frau Rena Strobel, wife and daughter respectively of Hermann Strobel; Herr Friedrich Weiss, brother of Christian Weiss; Frau Ingrid Wroblewski, niece of Ludwig Kretzer; Herr Werner Issmer, cousin of Walter Rubensdörffer; Frau Isolde Tratt, wife of Eduard Tratt; Frau Hedwig Avril, sister of Sigfried Tröppl; Herr Georg Wohlfart, brother of Martin Wohlfart; Frau Annemarie Kabon, niece of Karl Valesi; Frau Elsa Voltz, sister of Paul Hermann; Herr Hans Steding, nephew of Hans Steding; Herr Max Kopf, brother of Josef Kopf; Frau Hannelise Oedingen, sister of Fritz Heunisch; Frau Louise Henscheid, sister-in-law of Anton Henscheid; Josef Rüger, brother of Gerhard Rüger and Frieda Gieseler, sister of Richard Keilhaupt.

Finally, grateful thanks to my wife Anne, who for many years has had to endure the subject of Erprobungsgruppe 210 as part of her daily life. She now knows as much about the unit as I do!

1

Formation

When the German military juggernaut set forth on its campaign against Poland in September 1939, the air component of that military machine was considered to be the strongest and most modern in the world at that time and had, as an additional bonus, a core of flying personnel with valuable combat experience which would serve them well in the coming months. The course of the assault on Poland went as planned and the Luftwaffe played its part in the overall strategy, both in obtaining air superiority over the battle zone and in providing the necessary back-up for the ground forces, whether it be attacking troop concentrations and military targets in the field, or delivering a heavy blow to the industrial or population centres of that country.

Similarly, the campaign in the west in May 1940 followed an identical pattern with the Wehrmacht moving forward irresistibly with certain elements of the Luftwaffe providing the punch required to dislodge or destroy the more stubborn pockets of resistance in the path of the advancing army. It is true that the Luftwaffe met more cohesive resistance during the attack on France and the Low Countries than it had against Poland, but sheer weight of numbers and the daily changing situation on the ground conspired against the Advanced Air Striking Force (AASF) and Air Component squadrons being able to make a contribution sufficient to change the course of the war at that time.

Luftwaffe planning had not slackened, however, and a totally new concept of air warfare had germinated in the test centre at Rechlin: that of the fighter-bomber. It should be noted that the 'scout' aircraft of the First World War were fitted with bomb-racks and conducted missions against enemy positions but this type of bombing was, at best, of an indiscriminate nature and of nuisance value. The Luftwaffe had, by June 1940, developed the 'dive-bomber' concept to a fine degree with the Junkers 87, but the new emphasis was on an aircraft which would combine the accuracy of the Ju 87 with the speed of a conventional fighter. The obvious candidates for the testing and development of the advancing 'Sturkampfflugzeug' theory, for that is what it was in the days when the abbreviation 'Stuka' was considered by the Germans to embrace ALL aircraft which released bombs in a dive, was the Bf 109 and Bf 110. The Luftwaffe was already looking ahead to an aircraft which would be the successor to the Bf 110 and confidently expected the Messerschmitt 210 to fit the bill admirably. Unfortunately the development programme of the Messerschmitt 210 was to prove to be a continuous catalogue of problems of such gravity that ultimately production of the Messerschmitt 210 was abandoned with only a minimal number of aircraft reaching operational units.

It therefore fell on the Bf 110, in concert with the Bf 109, to bear the responsibility of implementing the theory of a tactical support arm to the land forces which could also be competent enough in combat to look after itself. The Ju 87 could not do that, for all its success in the Polish and Western campaigns. The passage of time would ultimately call into question the ability of the Bf 110 to fulfill such a role, but in June 1940 the 'Zerstörer' units were still considered by the Luftwaffe hierarchy to be a match for the Spitfires and Hurricanes ranged against them on the British mainland, although there was a more sober assessment of the true situation in the minds of those Bf 110 crews who had met stiff combat in the skies over Dunkirk.

On 1st July 1940 Erprobungsgruppe 210 (literally 'Experimental' or 'Test' Wing 210) officially came into existence. The formation took place at Köln-Ostheim airfield with Hauptmann Walter Rubensdörffer taking command of the unit. Rubensdörffer had previously been based at Rechlin and was given the opportunity to put into practise the 'Jabo' theory. He was a well-respected figure and quickly earned the respect and admiration of those who served under him. He was a fanatical flyer and had made arrangements for his ashes to be taken up in an aeroplane and scattered to the wind when he died. As we shall see, that wish was not to be fulfilled.

The 'Gruppe' consisted of a staff Flight (Stab) and three 'Staffeln', two with the Bf 110 and the other with Bf 109s. 1st Staffel with Bf 110s was formed from elements of the 1st Staffel of Zerstörergeschwader 1 (ZG 1) with Oberleutnant Martin Lutz as Staffelkapitän. 2nd Staffel, also with Bf 110s, was formed from 3rd Staffel, Stukageschwader 77, Oberleutnant Wilhelm-Richard Rößiger being Staffelkapitän. 4th Staffel, Jagdgeschwader 186 provided the nucleus of Erprobungsgruppe 210's 3rd Staffel with the experienced Oberleutnant Otto Hintze leading the sole Staffel equipped with Bf 109s.

Ground personnel were drawn from 4th Flughafenbetreibskompanie (FBK) of Kampfgeschwader 76 and from 2nd FBK of ZG 1, becoming 1st FBK under Oberleutnant Breitenborn and 2nd FBK under Oberleutnant Opkamp of Erprobungsgruppe 210 respectively.

It has been asserted in some previous publications that the formation of Erprobungsgruppe 210 was from a select band of elite flyers, but this is clearly not the case since the bulk of the flying personnel came from the transfer of three different Staffeln to a newly-constituted unit. Other personnel were posted-in with little or no previous combat experience. One such example is the Pilot/Bordfunker combination of Werner Neumann and Karl Stoff, who were posted to the unit upon completion of their training in early July 1940, joining 1st Staffel. Leutnant Erich Beudel. after completing a spell at Kopenhagen with the Ergänzungs Zerstörer Gruppe on 3 July, joined the unit at Köln-Ostheim soon afterwards with his Bordfunker, Obergefreiter Heinrich Diemer.

Provision of aircraft for the unit was made in different ways. It is known that at least five Bf 110 C-6s were brought by the former 1st Staffel, Zerstörergeschwader 1. These machines carried their former unit's identity code, '2N', until new aircraft were taken on charge in early August by the unit and all Bf 110s were given the official unit code, S9. During July 1st Staffel flew only the Bf 110 C-6 type aircraft – in fact their first mission with fighter-bomber Bf 110s was on 11th August. Otto Hintze recalls that when the pilots of his Staffel left their base at Wangerooge and moved to Köln-Ostheim, they left their Bf 109s behind and received new Bf 109 E-4/Bs on arrival at their new base. The Bf 109s had factory-fitted ETC 500 bomb-racks and the later-style 'square' cockpit canopy, but were not fitted with head armour for the pilot nor with armoured windscreens, as evidenced by the photographs of Hintze's 'Yellow 1' and Leutnant Marx's 'Yellow 3'.

Training commenced immediately at Köln-Ostheim with 3rd Staffel under the supervision of Hauptmann Karl Valesi, who was recognised as the foremost German aviation expert of his day in matters relating to the use of the Bf 109 as a fighter-bomber. Valesi was NOT Staffelkapitän of 3rd Staffel, Erprobungsgruppe 210 at any time. This erroneous assumption by previous authors was due no doubt to the fact that Valesi held a higher rank than Hintze and it was therefore believed that Valesi, holding the rank of Hauptmann, was Staffelkapitän. The truth is much simpler. Hintze had been Staffelkapitän of 4./JG 186 and upon transfer to Erprobungsgruppe 210 with his Staffel, retained his position. Hintze was Staffelkapitän of 3rd Staffel from its inception up to his being shot down on 29th October 1940. Valesi was 'seconded' to the unit because of his specialist knowledge and experience. Otto Hintze's Flugbuch records bombing practise in Bf 109 E-4/B, W. Nr. 6286 on 1st July, and three further practise flights on the following day.

Unteroffizier Heinrich Schultheis was involved in the supervision of the training programme for the Bf 110 crews, as was Oberleutnant Franz Fallenbacher. Training involved not only helping those Bf 110 crews from ZG 1 to adjust to the new idea of using the Bf 110 as a dive aircraft to place bombs on an allotted target, but also to train those crews who had transferred over from Ju 87s to handle an aircraft which was different in many respects to what they had been used to.

Balthasar Aretz's Flugbuch shows his first training flight with the unit on 6th July, accompanying Oberleutnant Franz Fallenbacher on the first flight in Bf 110, KE+US, W. Nr. 3336, then three further flights on the same day with Aretz at the controls in Bf 110, DE+CX, W. Nr. 3334. Further intensive flying took place for Aretz and his Bordfunker Gefreiter Rolf Schilleng on 8th and 9th July, with a total of 8 further practise flights in Bf 110, DE+CY, W. Nr. 3337. Leutnant Erich Beudel's training moved at a more leisurely pace, with one training flight on each of the 7th, 9th, 11th and 12th July. It was during training at Köln-Ostheim that the unit suffered its first casualty. Unteroffizier Volz of 3rd Staffel crashed to his death in a Bf 109 E on 8th July. The cause of the crash was never established. Volz was an experienced pilot, having been with 4./JG 186 and seen action during the Battle of France and the Dunkirk evacuation when that unit was involved in operations over France from their base at Antwerp.

At 05:00 hours on 10th July the supply columns of Erprobungsgruppe 210 left Köln-Ostheim with between 20-25 aircraft on charge and headed for their new base in France. Passing through Aachen, Liege, Namur, Charleroi, Mons and Valenciennes, they arrived at their new airfield at Denain at 18:00 hours. Not all had travelled by road, however. Some supplies had been transported by Ju 52/3m aircraft, and pilots and their aircraft left Köln early in the morning and arrived well in advance of the road party. Upon arrival at Denain there followed the usual settling-in of a military unit at its new base. Pilots and officers were billeted in the town of Denain, mainly in the houses of those French families who had chosen to move on in the face of the advancing German army. The rest of the personnel were billeted on the airfield.

Once settled in at Denain, the unit quickly found a place where it could carry out training without the possibility of causing great disruption to the civilian population. The place chosen was a small lake situated between Lille and Roubaix. In the centre of this lake a small wooden cross was anchored and training consisted of practise dive-bombing without any payload at first. The dive was started from a height of 13,000 feet and levelling-out occurred at 1,500 feet, the dive being carried out at an angle of 45°. There were usually ten practise dives of this nature per day. No ill effects were recorded as a result of this training, and practise then developed into diving with cement bombs to hit the target on the lake. The aircraft of Erprobungsgruppe 210 did not have a special sight for bomb-aiming and the lining-up of the target was carried out with the standard gunsight then fitted to all Messerschmitt 109 and 110 aircraft. As an additional aid some aircraft had a line drawn on the side of the canopy to help obtain the correct angle of dive.

Based at Denain, Erprobungsgruppe 210 came under the control of II. Fliegerkorps of Luftflotte 2, under the command of Generalfeldmarschall Kesselring. For the opening phase of the Battle of Britain, the attempt by the Luftwaffe to close the Channel to British shipping, it was directly subordinate to Oberst Johannes Fink, the Geschwaderkommodore of the Dornier 17-equipped Kampfgeschwader 2.

For operations against targets in the Channel, and later against land-based targets, the unit would take off from Denain and set down at a forward airfield near the French coast. Up to 8th August 1940 St. Omer-Arques was used as a forward base; thereafter Calais-Marck. Operations from mid-to late-September in the Luftflotte 3 sphere were undertaken from Cherbourg-Ost. Aircraft would be 'bombed-up' at Denain before the flight to the forward base. Upon landing, fuel tanks would be topped-up and a final check would be made on the aircraft before they set off for their intended target. If more than one mission was to be flown in a day, re-arming, refueling and all other servicing tasks were carried out at the forward airfield. It was only when the day's missions were completed that the unit returned to Denain. Ground crew toiled long hours to keep up the serviceability of the aircraft: radio engineers, airframe mechanics, armourers, engine mechanics, as well as administrative staff and others (e.g. canteen staff) who made up the unit. Otto Hintze estimated that it required a back-up team of over 100 to maintain his Staffel of 8 Bf 109 Es in an operational condition.

For the purposes of the combat section, the 'Battle of Britain' period is taken to be from 1st July 1940 to 31 October 1940, although latter day historians may assert with some justification that the Battle of Britain ended on 17th September, the date when, as a result of an 'Enigma' decrypt, the British Government knew that there would be no invasion that year. On the German side, the theory still persists that the Battle of Britain had no definite conclusion in 1940, and that the night offensive was a continuation of the overall strategy of the 'German Battle of Britain.' The Battle of Britain was effectively over by 17th September; after that date invasion was definitely out of the question. In conjunction with this point, it has been asserted in other works that the Battle of Britain was a draw. What a ridiculous flight of fancy! In the skies of southern England in the summer of 1940 there was a win-or-lose situation: if the Germans had gained permanent air superiority over southern England, together with the ability to nullify any Royal Navy threat if it materialised, the conditions would have been favourable for an invasion. As there was no invasion – they lost. That is not to say they did not come very close to gaining that victory. Just how close they came will be known by even the average reader on the period. In this section it is hoped to present the part played by Erprobungsgruppe 210 in that attempt to win victory over southern England in 1940.

As with every flying unit in the Battle of Britain, both British and German, there were days when no missions were flown. On such days crews would be released from duty and in the case of a German unit such as Erprobungsgruppe 210 the free time would be spent probably drinking and womanising, if what we are told about flying crews is correct at this time. To attempt to fill the gaps in combat days is almost impossible and has not been attempted. Concentration is therefore centred on the combats flown by the unit, and more precisely, bringing to the fore those combat missions which are well-known but on which fresh information can be presented, or on the lesser-known missions or sometimes missions which have never been previously ascribed to the unit. The combat account will, of necessity, therefore appear to 'skip over' days, but this will be due to the fact that no missions would have been flown.

In the account of combats and events, the intention was to avoid going 'overboard' on first-hand accounts of all that happened to the unit in 1940, although it has to be said that if the circumstances warranted it, particular accounts were included for their historical value. Therefore two accounts will be found by Sergeant Townshend of the unit's raids on Manston on 12th and 14th August because the one relates the first raid on Manston and the other tells of the shooting down of the first aircraft of the unit to fall on British soil (and into the bargain throws into the melting pot previous claims for the shooting down of those aircraft). On the other hand, Balthasar Aretz provided accounts of several combats, and his major contribution is that of events of 5th October, with accounts of other missions provided also. Hopefully a balance has been struck with quotes from combat reports and airfield Record Books. The combat reports provide a pilot's eye view of events, sometimes correct, many times incorrect, and the airfield accounts state graphically the damage caused by the unit's missions and the state of things in the aftermath of a raid.

Ultimately, however, it is hoped the book, and the Battle of Britain section in particular, will show that the individuals concerned, both German and British, were ordinary people caught up in the maelstrom of war who did not question the 'politics' of it; if you were a fighter pilot in Britain you flew the Spitfire or Hurricane, if you were born in Germany, the Messerschmitt fighters. 'Sailor' Malan, a South African, flew a Spitfire; Wolfgang Schenck, a South African by birth, flew a Messerschmitt.

Hauptmann Walter Rubensdörffer, first Commanding Officer of the unit.

Oberleutnant Martin Lutz, second from right, Staffelkapitän of 1st Staffel.

Oberleutnant Wilhelm-Richard Rößiger, Staffelkapitän of 2nd Staffel.

Right: Oberleutnant Otto Hintze, Staffelkapitän of 3rd Staffel.

Early days at Denain. The 2nd Staffel aircraft to the right has its fuselage sides prepared for the application of its full fuselage code, while a discussion appears to be going on in the background.

Groundcrew activity in the foreground with a partially camouflaged Bf 110 in the distance.

2

July 1940

13-18 JULY

After a settling-in period at Denain, Erprobungsgruppe 210 was ready for combat on 13 July. Roused early in the morning, the aircraft left Denain just after 06:00 hours and after a short flight of between 15 to 20 minutes duration, the unit landed at St. Omer-Arques, its forward base for operations against shipping for approximately three weeks. Although as yet untried in operations against shipping, the unit by no means lacked combat experience. The three Staffeln which made up Erprobungsgruppe 210 had all seen combat in the Western campaign. They were inexperienced only in the practical application of the fighter-bomber technique. Leutnant Erich Beudel flew over to St. Omer in Bf 108, KE+NU, to act as Communications Officer at Oberst Fink's headquarters.

Erprobungsgruppe 210 finally received orders for an attack against a convoy near the Thames estuary, which by the end of the year would be very much a hunting ground for the unit. A reconnaissance Dornier 17 had sighted the ships and at 11:45 hours eight Bf 109 E-4/Bs and 10 Bf 110 'Jabos' took off from St. Omer with four Bf 110C-6s of 1st Staffel as escort. Further escort was provided by the Bf 109 Es of I. Gruppe of Jagdgeschwader 52. Once in the Thames area, two convoys were sighted, about 65 ships in all, and the unit claimed to have scored four direct hits, one with a 500 Kg. bomb and three with 250 Kg. bombs, on a total of 20,000 tons of shipping. No British fighters were encountered and the unit suffered no combat losses. However on the return journey one Bf 110 developed engine trouble and force-landed at Gent. The fault was found to have been in the supercharger.

Erprobungsgruppe 210's first combat had been relatively successful according to their belief. No other missions were flown on this day and the unit returned to Denain in the early evening. As yet, it is likely that British Air Intelligence knew very little about 'bomb-carrying' Bf 109s and Bf 110s in general, and about Erprobungsgruppe 210 in particular; by the end of the Battle of Britain they would have amassed a great deal of information on both topics.

Erich Beudel's return to Denain in the evening proved to be something of an adventure, as he lost his way and had to force-land his Bf 108 in the yard of an ammunition works in Douai in pitch darkness at 23:00 hours!

14 July was a rest day for the unit – no combat missions were flown. 15th July saw Erprobungsgruppe 210 landing at St. Omer at about 05:00 hours and again the unit had to wait some considerable time before receiving orders for their second mission. In fact, because of the QBI (Instructions passed down to units, both German and British, consisted of a three letter code; QBI indicated that no missions were to be flown because of bad weather) issued to the unit on the morning of the 15th, 1st and 3rd Staffeln returned to Denain in the early afternoon and when the order finally came through for a mission, it was carried out by the Staff Flight and 2nd Staffel. Two aircraft of the Staff Flight and eight from 2nd Staffel (all Bf 110s) took-off at 14:00 hours and headed for a reported target of a convoy of 10 ships in the Thames estuary. Claims were for a 4,000 ton ammunition ship which was seen to have exploded and sunk, and a 3,000 ton ship which developed a list after being hit. A flight of Spitfires was seen but the unit suffered no losses on this mission also.

Following a respite of two days, Erprobungsgruppe 210 was back in action again on 18th July. Taking off from St. Omer at 10:15 hours, 1st Staffel Bf 110 C-6s of the unit set course for the Thames estuary and beyond on an armed reconnaissance mission. Flying at sea level, the formation sighted a convoy of about 10 ships off Lowestoft and immediately attacked. They encountered only slight anti-aircraft fire due to the speed of their attack. Claims were made for two 1,000 ton ships which were seen to catch fire. After the bombing run, two Bristol Blenheim fighters appeared and engaged the unit in combat. The Blenheims were outnumbered and one of their number was shot down into the sea by Staffelkapitän, Oberleutnant Martin Lutz and another pilot of 1st Staffel; the Blenheim was seen to go down with its starboard engine on fire and crash. It was almost certainly the one reported lost in combat at this time of day by 15 Squadron. After it was shot down, Erprobungsgruppe 210 continued its attacks on the ships, the unit finally returning to St. Omer at 12:00 hours. Leutnant Erich Beudel, with Obergefreiter Franz Öllers as Bordfunker, landed his Bf 110 C-6, 2N+PH, with .303 strikes in the port wing. 1st Staffel were not particularly happy with the performance of the 30 mm. cannon: three out of four aircraft carrying the cannon reported that it had jammed during combat. It was a situation which was to plague the Bf 110 C-6s of the unit which would lead eventually to 1st Staffel abandoning the C-6s and assuming a 'Jabo' role also.

Otto Hintze's Flugbuch shows a mission from St. Omer on 18th July taking off at 15:15 hours, and shown as 'Jagdschütz' – fighter escort. It is not known if this was escort to the Bf 110s of the unit, or to another attacking formation. In any event, it was of short duration, Hintze landing back at St. Omer 35 minutes later.

In the afternoon, personnel of the unit still at St. Omer received a taste of their own medicine when several Blenheims appeared at about 1,500 feet and bombed the airfield. Although the Bf 109 Es of 3rd Staffel were scrambled, they were unable to catch the bombers and 3rd Staffel then proceeded directly to Denain.

18th July also saw 3rd Staffel lose two members, one aircrew and one groundcrew. Over Antwerp, Gefreiter Ludwig Spreitzer was killed while flying a Bf 110, the cause of the crash being given as the right wing of the aircraft breaking off in flight. A member of 3rd Staffel groundcrew was also killed this day. The official version is that a member of the groundcrew was cleaning his pistol and it accidentally went off, the bullet hitting Hauptgefreiter Peter Neven but not seriously wounding him. As a precaution, however, he was taken to hospital at Valenciennes where an anaesthetic was administered prior to operating. However the medical staff did not notice that the anaesthetic had caused Neven to vomit and the unfortunate man choked to death as a result of it. At a subsequent inquiry, the medical staff of the hospital were exonerated of all blame; the groundcrew who had been cleaning his gun was court-martialled but the sentence was not carried out because of the war situation. Spreitzer was buried at Antwerp, Neven at Denain.

19 JULY

On 19th July 3rd Staffel was in action twice in the afternoon. The target on both occasions was shipping in Dover harbour. The first mission was carried out in concert with the two Bf 110 Staffeln and fighter escort was provided by III./JG 51 led by Hauptmann Hannes Trautloft. The unit attacked an armed trawler off the Dover coast without any loss to themselves, and were escorted back to the French coast by the Bf 109 fighter escort. The Bf 109s of III./JG 51 then returned for a 'Freie Jagd' and the Defiants of 141 Squadron had the misfortune to run into them.

The second mission of the afternoon was again against shipping at Dover, take-off being shortly after 15:00 hours. Squadron Leader John 'Baron' Worrall, leading 32 Squadron airborne from Hawkinge, sighted what he believed to be Ju 87s dive-bombing Dover harbour and led 32 Squadron in to intercept, but not before aircraft of Erprobungsgruppe 210 had completed their attacks on vessels in the harbour. The Admiralty oiler *War Sepoy* received a direct hit and sunk; the destroyer *Griffin* suffered damage following several near misses and required repair work, and the tug *Simla* and the drifter *Golden Gift* were also damaged. All aircraft of the unit returned safely to France. In the meantime the Bf 109 fighter escort tangled with 32 Squadron and shot one of the Hurricanes down.

In Admiralty reports compiled at the time, there is an interesting account of an attack by two aircraft identified as 'M.E. 110s' at 09:50 hours on 19th July 1940 on several Motor A/S Boats (A/S=Anti-Submarine). The account is of interest because it is probable that in describing the attack, the aircraft were almost certainly Bf 110 C-6s of Erprobungsgruppe 210. Amongst other things, the report stated: 'After passing M A/S B. 8, the M.E.s circled around to port and flew up astern of M A/S B. 8. The leading aircraft opened fire with 4 machine guns, of approximately .303 calibre A.P. bullets and two cannon firing explosive shells, assumed to be approximately 20 mm. when 3 cables astern. The planes came in at reduced speed, dropping to about 50 feet and preserving their formation. The second plane was not observed to fire. M A/S B 8 was proceeding at full speed with the wheel hard to port. The planes passed over number 8, turned a rapid circle to starboard, and attacked on the starboard bow, continuing over the boat turning hard to port (thus completing a figure of 8 movement) and repeated their first attack from astern'.

The reference to two cannons is only to be expected, since at that time it is very unlikely that the British Intelligence Services were cognisant of a 30 mm. cannon in combat use, but would have knowledge of the Bf 110 having 4 machine guns and two 20 mm. cannon.

20-28 JULY

Between 20th and 27th July Otto Hintze led his 3rd Staffel on 13 combat missions against shipping in the Channel and around the south-east coast of England. The number of combat missions flown by the Staff Flight and the two Bf 110 Staffeln is not known, but it is almost certain that they flew as many, if not more, missions than their Bf 109 counterparts. One matter which did intrude on operations was the burial ceremony at Antwerp on 20th July of Ludwig Spreitzer, which was attended by several members of the unit.

On 20th July Hintze recorded two 'Einsatz' (operation) in his Flugbuch (Flight Log Book), the second against ships in the Channel off Deal. This was certainly the convoy 'BOSOM' which had been subjected to Luftwaffe harassment all day. The results of the attacks are not known but once again all aircraft of the unit taking part returned safely to base. The 1st Staffel crew of Unteroffizier Werner Neumann and his Bordfunker Obergefreiter Karl Stoff carried out a reconnaissance flight in 2N+OH on this day, and it may have been their flight which triggered Hintze's Staffel into action.

The 3rd Staffel did not have any combat flights on 21st July, but the Bf 110 Staffeln did carry out missions. Ernst Elfner,

Bordfunker to Oberleutnant Alfred Habisch recalled: 'One event I remember very well. We had attacked a target on the English coast and were flying in the direction of Calais. Suddenly there were two Spitfires behind us. From about 250 feet one of them began firing at us (S9+CK). Hptm. Rubensdörffer, who was flying alongside, put his aircraft into a climbing turn, and came in behind the fighters. He fired at one of them. At once they dived away and did not attack again'. The result of the attack by the Spitfire is shown in the accompanying photograph after Habisch and Elfner returned to their base in France: they counted 78 hits on their aircraft as well as further damage caused by the collapsed starboard undercarriage leg and tail wheel. Such was the demise of the first 'S9+CK' to be flown by them.

As well as that attack, Elfner also recalled: 'A few days later, when we were flying home again, we (S9+CK) were attacked over the Channel by a fighter. We were hit by his gunfire and the right engine began to smoke. The English fighter flew beside us, at a distance of about 100 feet. We were waving to each other, and he flew with us until we reached the French coast. Waving once again, he turned around and flew back'.

Monday and Tuesday, 22nd and 23rd July, appear to have been rather uneventful days in the Battle of Britain in general, and in Erprobungsgruppe 210 in particular, although missions were definitely flown on 23rd July by 3rd Staffel. Air activity was minimal and the raids could not have made any great impression on British shipping, in particular, Convoy Pilot.

24th July saw Erprobungsgruppe 210 engaged once again in combat over the Channel and the south-east coast of England. The unit claimed 20,000 tons of shipping sunk (five ships) but also suffered its first combat loss during the Battle of Britain. 25 year-old Unteroffizier Paul Hermann, pilot, and his Bordfunker, 23 year-old Unteroffizier Heinz Meinhardt were shot down 30 Kms. east of Harwich by anti-aircraft fire from the convoy they were attacking. The Bf 110 received a direct hit and blew up in the air, giving the crew no chance of surviving. The Bf 110 was a 2nd Staffel machine and as a mark of honour to the first pilot of the unit to be shot down in combat, one 2nd Staffel machine had the name 'Uffz. Hermann' inscribed above the unit emblem. A photograph of the aircraft accompanies the text; unfortunately the full fuselage code of this machine is not known.

The Bf 109s of 3rd Staffel were in action on 25th July on three occasions, and it is almost certain that the Bf 110s saw action on this date also. A report of operations on 25th July by the Commanding Officer of *HMS Boreas* contained the following: 'At 1808 I was attacked from ahead by 8 Messerschmitt 110 dive bombers. They were sighted and engaged one minute before they turned to their attacking dive and as the first one turned I ordered starboard 20 with the idea of keeping my 3-inch and Pom-Pom in action and putting off the attackers.

'No hits were obtained by the enemy during this attack nor were there any casualties but there were a number of near misses which caused considerable damage and the ship was stopped for a short time. Perhaps the most remarkable of the near misses was two bombs which fell some ten yards ahead. Steaming at high speed into the resulting column of water was an astonishing sensation'.

The report goes on to mention a second attack by Junkers 87s several minutes later and *Boreas* was hit by two bombs during this attack. In summarising the action by the enemy aircraft during both attacks, the report went on to state: 'Both attacks were from ahead and were pressed right home. When first sighted the enemy were, in both cases, in loose formation but formed in line ahead just before they turned to dive. They dived at an angle of about 50 degrees, well above the maximum elevation of the 4.7 guns, and followed each other in quick succession. After dropping their bombs, they retired low over the sea'.

The reference to Messerschmitt 110 fighter-bombers encountered by the convoy identified the attackers as Erprobungsgruppe 210. The convoy did not escape unscathed on this occasion, five ships were sunk and four others damaged, including the destroyers *Brilliant* and *Boreas*.

26th July saw minimal activity over the Channel, a small number of ships passed through without incurring any losses.

27th July was, however, to prove to be an eventful day for the unit. In combat on this day the unit claimed to have sunk two large cruisers, but in the process also lost another Bf 110 of 2nd Staffel, crewed by Oberleutnant Franz Fallenbacher, the 28 year-old pilot, and his Bordfunker, Feldwebel Friedrich Oberland, aged 22, at a position 55 Kms. north-east of Harwich. Habisch and Elfner took part in this raid also, and Elfner remembered: 'In those days we attacked a big convoy. After we had dropped our bombs, I saw one of our planes attacking an anti-aircraft cruiser that drove into the middle of the convoy. I heard a voice in the R/T – "don't attack!", but it was too late. The aircraft of Oblt. Fallenbacher received a direct hit shortly before releasing the bombs. The plane exploded and the fragments fell into the water near the AA cruiser.

'At the time it was forbidden for us to drop bombs on England. Sometimes we would fly patrol over the Channel to search for ships. When we couldn't find a target, we were forced to release our bombs, because we could not land with such a heavy load. Therefore we did practise dives on a ship laying grounded on the coast in front of Calais, or we dived on a destroyer some miles from Dover'.

The 3rd Staffel carried out two attacks on Dover harbour in the afternoon of 27th July. At 14:30 hours the destroyer *Walpole* was damaged following near misses. A second attack towards 18:00 hours found the destroyer *Codrington* and the depot ship *Sandhurst* moored alongside each other. A near miss on *Codrington* was sufficient to break her back, and she sank. Sandhurst received damage from the same bomb, but survived the attack.

Leutnant Horst Marx of 3rd Staffel claimed a Hurricane shot down on this day, and it is almost certain that the aircraft which he shot down was the Hurricane of Flying Officer P.A.N. Cox of 501 Squadron, operating out of Gravesend. The loss of the Hurricane is logged at 17:45 hours over Dover harbour, and this tallies well with Marx's claim. Marx completed an 'Abschußmeldung' for his claim, which was witnessed by Oberleutnant Hintze and Feldwebel Büttner. Translations of the 'Abschußmeldung' and the witness statements are shown in Appendix 5.

One milestone occurred on 27th July which serves to illustrate the depth of experience within the Gruppe. On his second mission of the day, Otto Hintze recorded his 100th combat mission of the war. Otto Hintze embarked on a military career in November 1934 at the age of 20, breaking off architectural studies at the Technical University of Munich (he was to take up these studies again in 1948 and pass his final examination in 1950). In 1935, after basic military training, he passed to pilot's training school. From October 1936 he flew with various units, including JG 134, JG 234, and JG 135 before finding himself Adjutant of II./ZG 1 equipped with Bf 109 Es in September 1939 upon the outbreak of war. His combat service commenced with that unit in the brief fighting over Poland and it was during this campaign that he had a rather lucky escape – a bullet from a Polish fighter passed through the cockpit of his Bf 109 E missing his spine by an inch or so. The phoney war period found him with I./JG 333 at Westerwald and then from February 1940 he was with II./JG 186 based at Wangerooge, Oslo and Trondheim. By that time Hintze had flown a variety of aircraft: Arado 65s and 68s; Heinkel 51s and 70s; Bf 108s, before arriving on the aircraft which he was to fly for the duration of his war, the Bf 109 E. When the war in the west started in May 1940, II./JG 186 eventually found itself transferred to Antwerp to fly missions in support of the advancing German army. It was during such a mission in the early hours of 1st June that Hintze was shot down for the first time. Ever since, he has firmly believed that he was shot down by his own 'wing-man': the enemy fighters which his Staffel had seen were way out of range and there was nothing in the sky at the time remotely near them. While with II./JG 186 Hintze was appointed Staffelkapitän, and it was his 4th Staffel which formed the nucleus of the Bf 109 E Staffel of Erprobungsgruppe 210 upon formation. The above résumé gives an example of the type of experience which the Luftwaffe could call upon in the Battle of Britain.

By the end of 27th July, Erprobungsgruppe 210 claimed to have sunk 80,000 tons of British shipping, which included 4 warships, and to have shot down 3 RAF aircraft. While the veracity of this claim could be called into question, there is no doubt that the unit was beginning to prove to be a thorn in the side of the British, and although RAF Intelligence had no doubt come across the name of the unit through intercepting the 'Verluste' returns, it is probable that they did not know the exact role of the unit at this time.

28th July proved to be a day when the only event of note for the unit was a memorial service held for the two crews who had been lost in combat in the recent past.

29 JULY

After no activity for the unit on the morning of 29th July, a convoy sighting by a Dornier of KG 2 resulted in Erprobungsgruppe 210 being detailed to attack the convoy 'CAT'. Taking off from St. Omer at 16:35 hours, the formation consisted of 8 'Jabo' Bf 110s from the Staff Flight and 2nd Staffel, and 3 Bf 110 C-6s from 1st Staffel. Escort for the unit was provided by 30 Bf 110s of ZG 26. The convoy was sighted and the aircraft duly attacked, but during the attack the German formation sighted what they believed to be two British Hurricane squadrons; it was in fact two separate flights of 151 Squadron. The British squadron sighted the German bombers on the port side and curved into the attack. The German formation turned hard to port and sought refuge in the nearby clouds. However one aircraft of Erprobungsgruppe 210 did not make the clouds in time. One of the Bf 110 C-6s flown by Leutnant Erich Beudel, 2N+RH, received a full burst of machine gun fire from one of the Hurricanes on the starboard side. Beudel's 21 year-old Bordfunker, Obergefreiter Heinrich Diemer, was wounded in the attack, and the aircraft suffered damage to the starboard engine which resulted in the loss of oil, although the engine did not give out on the crew. Other damage was caused to the R/T apparatus and the lighting circuits by bullets passing through the cockpit, one or two narrowly missing the heads of Beudel and Diemer; other strikes had damaged the tyres and had holed both wings and the landing flaps, and one bullet had hit an ammunition drum and exploded the contents. Beudel and Diemer landed back at St. Omer at 18:05 hours, very fortunate not to have been shot down into the sea. A weapon of heavier calibre than .303 would probably have been sufficient to have brought down the Bf 110 C-6.

Although hit by the burst from a Hurricane, Beudel wanted to attack again with Lutz and 2 Bf 110s from ZG 26, but the state of the injured Diemer made it more prudent to return to base. The pilot of the Hurricane who hit Beudel's Bf 110 cannot be identified, since several pilots of 151 Squadron filed claims for damaged Bf 110s.

Because his aircraft was in no condition to fly back to Denain, Beudel spent the night in St. Omer. He returned to Denain the following day in a Bf 110 C-6, 2N+TH, flown by his Staffelkapitän, Oberleutnant Martin Lutz. Diemer was taken to hospital immediately, but later returned to flying duties and was posted missing in action with 1. Staffel, Zerstörergeschwader 1 on the Russian front on 19th September 1942.

On 30th July H.M.S. Guillemot filed a report from Harwich of "Air Attack on H.M.S. "Guillemot" and S.S. "Clan Monroe" on 29th July 1940". It ran: "At 1635 when acting as AA defence ship for the 12th Minesweeping Flotilla in approximately position 'X', a report of the mining of S.S. "Clan Monroe" about five miles away was received in "Guillemot". On my arrival at the scene H.M.S. "Hastings" informed me that S.S. "Clan Monroe" had not been searched for survivors although she had been abandoned, and it was found the Third Engineer and eleven Lascars were missing. A search party was sent in the whaler and "Guillemot" lay off. "Hastings" rejoined her convoy.

"The weather at the time was fine with wind force 3, blue sky three quarters covered with Strato-Cumulus cloud at a height of about 7000 feet. Sea Slight.

At 1714, just as the boarding party were returning, having found no one on board, nine British fighters were seen approaching to Starboard, and very shortly afterwards nine M.E. 110's were seen to port. The M.E. 110's split into two groups, the first, one of five machines, dived to attack crossing both "Clan Monroe" and "Guillemot" from port to starboard at a height of about 100 feet. The second, of four machines, remained high and were engaged by the British fighters.

"Eight bombs were dropped by the first group each machine dropping two, with the exception of one which was shot down by gun fire from "Guillemot" before he could release his bombs. Tracer shells from the Oerlikon were seen to burst on the target. The .5 and Lewis guns had very little tracer and the result of their fire could not be observed. This machine flew straight into the sea about 25 yards on "Guillemot's" Starboard quarter and sank without a trace. The eight bombs fell as shown in the attached sketch as near as could be judged by various observers.

"The enemy aircraft attacked singly but in rapid succession and apparently in quarter line. The whole attack was over in about thirty seconds from the time of sighting the enemy until the last bomb fell. The bridge Lewis gunner reported that he had put a good burst into another machine which was seen to fly low and disappear towards the horizon emitting black smoke. It was not, however, seen to crash.

"Fire was opened by "Guillemot's" short range armament at a range of about ten to twelve hundred yards about ten seconds before the first bombs were dropped. The enemy aircraft completely disregarded the fire and pressed their attacks well home. The first machine to attack "Guillemot" was shot down but drew the fire from the second attacker which dropped bombs number 3 and 4.

"Bomb number 4 caused a vast column of water to fall on board. The bridge was momentarily flooded to a depth of 18 inches and a large quantity of water entered the boiler room and engine room through fan downtakes and ventilators. A flow of water swept forward into the Galley flat and left 2 feet of water in the P.O.'s Mess on the lower deck".

The reference to an attacking Bf 110 being shot down is difficult to reconcile against the fact that no aircraft were lost on this mission. The report does, however, give testament to the fact that even at this early stage of their career, Erprobungsgruppe 210's young crews attacked in the face of fierce return fire without regard to their safety, which up to this point in the Battle had already resulted in the loss of two 2nd Staffel crews.

30 JULY

In the early stages of the Battle of Britain Erprobungsgruppe 210's role was not only one of evaluation of experimental weapons and assessment of new tactics in aerial warfare, but also tasks within the overall framework of the need to stop the movement of all British shipping around the southern coast of England. Consequently one of the additional duties allotted to the unit was armed reconnaissance missions seeking British convoys in order to report back the strength, size, course etc. of any convoys sighted. On 30th July Oberleutnant Martin Lutz and Leutnant Hans Herold of 1st Staffel took off in Bf 110 C-6s on an armed reconnaissance mission covering the Thames estuary and further north up the coast, in mid-afternoon. The two aircraft had located the convoy 'PILOT' and had carried out an attack on it when they were sighted by Red Section of 85 Squadron comprising Flight Lieutenant Hamilton and Sergeant Allard. The two Bf 110s were flying at sea level and were being fired on by a trawler at the rear of the convoy. The ensuing combat is graphically described in the combat reports filed by the two RAF pilots upon their return to base. Flight Lieutenant Hamilton reported: 'At 15:00 hours when on my way to patrol Pilot I sighted two Me 110 about 10 miles off Aldeburgh flying N at about 5 feet above sea level at about 280 mph. E/A put on speed, turned east and endeavoured to escape and we gave chase in line astern for 35 miles. I got abreast of the E/A to identify it and then delivered a stern attack firing a five second burst following with another stern attack firing another long burst. E/A opened fire at 1,500 yards and continued firing during attacks. I then broke away in order to gain height and speed for another attack and saw E/A lurch to the left and his nose drop towards the sea. I saw Red 2 close in and open fire and E/A hit the sea and broke up. I saw one man in the sea and pulled parachute about 10 yards away from him. Visibility was about 8 miles, clouds 10/10 at 1,200 feet. I chased 2nd E/A with Red 2 but he escaped into low cloud'.

Sergeant Allard reported in similar terms, describing his part of the action as follows: 'I closed in to about 150 yards firing continuously to about 25 yards. I saw starboard motor break into pieces and the E/A disappeared beneath me. I saw enemy tracer but received no hits. After I broke away, I chased the 2nd Me 110, which disappeared into low cloud. I reformed with Red 1 and returned to base'.

The Bf 110 shot down was a 1st Staffel machine flown by 23 year-old Leutnant Hans Herold with Obergefreiter Lotar Lilienthal, his 21 year-old Bordfunker. Martin Lutz made it back to base on this occasion.

One event of note to occur on 30th July was the visit paid to the unit by Generalfeldmarschall Albert Kesselring, who brought his personal congratulations to them for the amount of shipping which it had claimed sunk in the 16 days since they commenced operations (the claim was for 89,000 tons!). The photograph which accompanies the text showing Kesselring and Rubensdörffer in front of a Bf 110 C-6 was almost certainly taken during this visit, as there is no evidence of a further visit to the unit before Rubensdörffer was shot down on 15th August.

On 31st July Oberleutnant Werner Weymann was posted-in to the unit.

The nucleus of 3rd Staffel, seen here at Oslo in June 1940 when still 4th Staffel, Jagdgeschwader 186 (4./JG 186). Back row, left to right: Wienpahl; Büttner; Drawe; Volz; Rückert; Front row, left to right: unknown; Emmerich; Hintze.

Left: Horst Marx, seen here as an officer-cadet, flew with 1st Staffel, Zerstörergeschwader 1 during the campaign against France and the Low Countries, but transferred to 3rd Staffel and Bf 109s upon the formation of Erprobungsgruppe 210. Center: Georg Boxhammer, seen here as an Oberleutnant. Boxhammer flew with Erprobungsgruppe 210 during the Battle of Britain, and ultimately was Staffelkapitän of 3rd Staffel, Zerstörergeschwader 1 when he was killed on 29th May 1942 when his Bf 110 F crashed due to engine failure on a transfer flight. Right: Obergefreiter Ludwig Kretzer, Bordfunker, flew with the unit until his death on 15th August 1940 with his Gruppenkommandeur, Walter Rubensdörffer.

Unteroffizier Drawe joined 3rd Staffel from 4./JG 186 on 1st July 1940 upon the re-designation of his Staffel.

Leutnant Erich Beudel completed training with Ergänzungs Zerstörer Gruppe Kopenhagen on 3rd July 1940 and was posted immediately to 1st Staffel together with his Bordfunker, Obergefreiter Heinrich Diemer.

Gefreiter Christian Weiss had worked in the 'Versuchsabteilung' (Research Section) of the Heinkel works pre-war, and had volunteered for military service. A trained pilot, he was the lowest ranked pilot of the unit, but nevertheless one with a great deal of flying experience behind him when he joined 1st Staffel of Erprobungsgruppe 210.

Left: Unteroffizier Volz of 3rd Staffel was the first casualty of the unit when he was killed in a flying training accident on 8th July 1940.

Werner Zwick, Bordfunker of 2nd Staffel from the early days to the end of September 1940.

Balthasar Aretz, pilot with 2nd Staffel from the unit's inception to its re-designation in April 1941.

3rd Staffel pilots relax, from left: Vogel; Volz (in sunglasses); Rückert; Büttner and Hintze.

Right: Rolf Schilleng, Aretz's Bordfunker from joining the unit with him in July 1940 until Aretz was hospitalised on 5th October 1940 after being wounded in combat. Schilleng also remained with the unit until its re-designation, but was posted missing in action on 12 May 1941 flying with Schnellkampfgeschwader 210 on a nocturnal mission against England.

JAGUAR

Balthasar Aretz sits on the port wheel of a Bf 110 D freshly delivered to Köln-Ostheim airfield for the unit. The aircraft still carries the Stammkenn-zeichen on the fuselage, and the name 'Jaguar' (a reference to the propaganda-inspired name for the bomb-carrying Bf 110) is painted on the nose of the aircraft. Close examination of the demarcation line of the camouflage on the forward fuselage shows that it follows exactly the line taken by the fitment of the 'Dackelbauch' fuel tank. The only version of the Bf 110 to have either the 'Dackelbauch' or bomb-rack as an option was the D-2, which is the exact sub-variant, therefore, of this machine, although these aircraft were shown as 'D-0's or 'D-3's in the loss lists.

Officers of 3rd Staffel, from left: Leutnant Horst Marx, Oberleutnant Otto Hintze, and Leutnant Peter Emmerich.

Left: Some idea of the size of the 30 mm. cannon can be gained from this view of a ground mechanic standing under the muzzle of the weapon. Note the different panels riveted to the fuselage to hold not only the fairing, but also to accommodate the trough for the muzzle of the cannon.

Below: Leutnant Horst Marx in front of his Bf 109 E-4/B, 'Yellow 3'. The spinner tip is in the Staffel colour of yellow.

Leutnant Horst Marx climbs out of his 'Yellow 3'. This view shows to good effect the 20 mm. wing-mounted cannon and the underwing bulge to accommodate the rounds for it. Note also the square-style canopy and the lack of armoured windscreen.

Köln-Ostheim, 10th July 1940. Groundcrew wait on a wagon prior to starting the overland trip to their permanent base in France, Denain.

Relief at the roadside for 1st Staffel personnel during the trip between Köln-Ostheim and Denain.

Upon arrival at Denain the local fire station was found to be deserted. Ground personnel pose with a banner found on the premises.

Abandoned equipment was to be found all over France at the end of the campaign against France and the Low Countries. Here Oberleutnant Alfred Habisch, left, and Unteroffizier Horst Schramke of 2nd Staffel chat at the site of an abandoned gun in France.

The Erprobungsgruppe 210 'Oom-pah Band'! Groundcrew also found an assortment of musical instruments and helmets in the local fire station. An impromptu band was obviously set up, but heaven knows what it sounded like! The officer in the peaked cap is Leutnant Karl-Heinz Koch, Technical Officer of the unit, shot down on the Croydon raid on 15th August 1940.

Above and below: Some personnel were billeted in the town of Denain. These views show the Hotel Villars in Denain.

Gefreiter Rolf Schilleng sits in the cockpit of an abandoned French fighter, with an unknown colleague in attendance.

Otto Hintze with young Staffelhünde.

Peter Emmerich in similar pose.

The emblem of Erprobungsgruppe 210 carried on both sides of the nose of the Messerschmitt 110s. The British Isles was in red; the gun/bomb sight graticule was yellow.

Groundcrew pose with a Bf 110 C-6 of 1st Staffel. Note the multi-colored spinners, a feature unique to this Staffel. All the Bf 110 C-6s were allocated to 1st Staffel, and it is known that some, if not all, were brought by 1st Staffel, Zerstörergeschwader 1 when the unit was formed.

Guard is mounted over a Bf 110 C-6. The fairing for the 30 mm. cannon and the multi-colored spinner are in evidence.

3rd Staffel officers Horst Marx, left, and Peter Emmerich pose for the camera at Denain.

A smiling Leutnant Peter Emmerich of 3rd Staffel with children of Denain.

Otto Hintze's Bf 109 E-4/B, 'Yellow 1', which he flew as his personal aircraft from 8th July 1940 almost uninterrupted up to 17th October 1940, when it was taken off charge to have tests carried out after having completed 200 flying hours. What appears to be white stripes aft of the supercharger intake and on the rear fuselage are, in fact, shafts of sunlight through the gaps in the camouflage netting above the aircraft. Although fitted with the later-style square cockpit canopy, it does not have an armoured windscreen. The tip of the spinner is in the 3rd Staffel color of yellow. Sitting on the cockpit sill is a radio mechanic, distinguished from other groundcrew by his light colored overalls.

2nd Staffel Bf 110 fighter-bomber having its engines run up. This aircraft carries two-tone green camouflage on its upper surfaces. Note the unit emblem on the fuselage.

3rd Staffel land at Denain as groundcrew go out to meet the machines. Otto Hintze is seen climbing out of the cockpit of the Bf 109 E-4/B, 'Yellow 1', on the extreme left.

Leutnant Horst Marx in front of a 2nd Staffel Bf 110 fighter-bomber. The extended rear fuselage points to this being a 'D' variant, wearing early-style camouflage. The Werk Nummer appears on the rear fuselage, but is too indistinct for identification.

Unteroffizier Horst Schramke of 2nd Staffel enjoys a meal break perched on one of the tools of the unit's trade.

Leutnant Karl-Heinz Koch's dog, 'Grog', named after a popular German comedian of the 1930s, 'ready for take-off'!

Close-up of the nose of a 3rd Staffel Bf 109 E-4/B showing a distinctive lightly sprayed camouflage over the light blue fuselage sides. Note also the yellow spinner cap.

Otto Hintze in off-duty time at a local farm.

Right: Peter Emmerich mounted on the same horse as Hintze.

A good view of the fairing removed from a Bf 110 C-6 showing the MG 101 'Kanone'. Note that this aircraft has the early-style camouflage down the full length of the fuselage sides.

This view of a Bf 110 C-6 shows the clean lines of the fairing enclosing the cannon, and the under-fuselage conversion necessary on the change from two 20 mm. cannon to a single 30 mm. cannon.

Several members of 2nd Staffel are seen in this shot. From left, Hemmelberg; Rolf Kahl (Stab, Bordfunker of Leutnant Koch); Karl-Heinz Koch (in peaked cap, seated); unknown; Paul Hermann (standing); Oberleutnant Alfred Habisch (seated, below Hermann); unknown, and Hauptfeldwebel Völker.

Ground mechanics working on a Bf 110 C-6 of 1st Staffel. A rare feature in evidence in this photograph is the telescopic sight. Note also the aperture for the ESK 2000 camera just visible in the nose. This aircraft does not carry the unit emblem of the British Isles in a gunsight.

2nd Staffel lined up about to take off, S9+CK nearest the camera.

Otto Hintze, second right, giving instructions to ground personnel of his Staffel, with a Bf 109 E-4/B in the background.

A Bf 110 of the unit carrying the early-style two tone green camouflage down the fuselage sides, with the unit emblem clearly visible. The spinner tips are likely to be red, denoting a 2nd Staffel machine.

Opposite
Top: A mechanic fits back a panel to a Bf 110 of the unit. The camouflage and spinner marking would indicate that this is a 2nd Staffel machine. Note the open pilot's side window with a line drawn on it to act as a guide when in a dive to release the bombs. Contrast the camouflage of this aircraft with the Bf 110 in the next pen, which has solid two-tone green down the fuselage sides.

Bottom: Unteroffizier Ernst Elfner stands in front of a 2nd Staffel Bf 110 fighter-bomber. Heavy wear and tear can be seen on the propeller blades and around the area of the engines, indicating that this aircraft has seen a lot of use. It is not, however, the aircraft in which Elfner was shot down on 15th August 1940 – that aircraft had an aperture for a camera in the nose, this one does not.

Unteroffizier Balthasar Aretz of 2nd Staffel sits on the cockpit sill of a Bf 110 C-6 of 1st Staffel. Of interest is the hinge on the starboard side of the fairing which swung it down to allow access for maintenance.

2N (later S9)+SH, a Bf 110 C-6 of 1st Staffel in quite pristine condition. The pilot strapped in the cockpit is unidentified.

2nd Staffel at Denain. 3rd from left – Oberfeldwebel Hans Marx; 3rd from right – Unteroffizier Balthasar Aretz; 2nd from right – Gefreiter Rolf Schilleng; extreme right – Oberfeldwebel Roth.

Unteroffizier Ernst Elfner stands on the port wing of the first S9+CK after it was shot up following an attack on a convoy on 21st July 1940. Of interest are the early-style solid camouflage down the fuselage sides, the red spinner caps, and the word 'Jaguar' on the port side forward fuselage in two colours, an indication, perhaps, of a replacement machine gun cowling from another aircraft.

2nd Staffel aircrew, from left: Förster; Hemmelberg; Schramke and Meinhardt.

Unteroffizier Heinz Meinhardt (left), Bordfunker, and Unteroffizier Paul Hermann, pilot, of 2nd Staffel, seen here on their Junkers 87 when with 3rd Staffel, Stukageschwader 77. They were posted missing in action on 24th July 1940 after being hit by anti-aircraft fire while attacking a convoy.

Unteroffizier Paul Hermann of 2nd Staffel, killed in action on 24th July 1940.

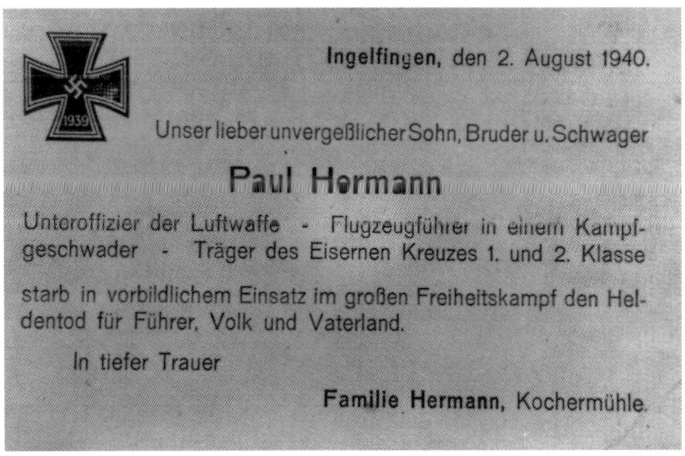

Ingelfingen, den 2. August 1940.

Unser lieber unvergeßlicher Sohn, Bruder u. Schwager

Paul Hermann

Unteroffizier der Luftwaffe - Flugzeugführer in einem Kampfgeschwader - Träger des Eisernen Kreuzes 1. und 2. Klasse

starb in vorbildlichem Einsatz im großen Freiheitskampf den Heldentod für Führer, Volk und Vaterland.

In tiefer Trauer

Familie Hermann, Kochermühle.

The obituary notice for Paul Hermann. It translates as: Ingelfingen, 2nd August 1940. Our dear unforgotten Son, Brother and Brother-in-law, Paul Hermann, Unteroffizier of the Luftwaffe – Pilot in a Bomber Geschwader – holder of the Iron Cross 1st and 2nd Class died the hero's death in an exemplary mission in the great freedom fight for Führer, People and Fatherland. In deep sadness, Family Hermann, Kochermühle.

A Bf 110 of 2nd Staffel with the name 'Uffz. Hermann' inscribed above the unit emblem. Paul Hermann was the first pilot of the unit to be killed in action on 24th July 1940, and his name was placed on one aircraft as a mark of honour. What appears to be striped camouflage is in fact the shadow of the camouflage netting in place above the aircraft. Note also the mascot inside the cockpit, extreme right.

Officers of the Gruppe pose for the camera at Denain. From left: unknown; Leutnant Horst Marx; unknown; Oberleutnant Wilhelm-Richard Rößiger; Oberleutnant Alfred Habisch; Oberleutnant Horst Fiedler; Oberleutnant Martin Lutz; Oberleutnant Otto Hintze; Leutnant Peter Emmerich and Oberleutnant Franz Fallenbacher.

Oberleutnant Franz Fallenbacher (left) and Oberleutnant Alfred Habisch, officers of 2nd Staffel, study something of great interest. Fallenbacher was killed in action on 27th July 1940 when his Bf 110 received a direct hit from anti-aircraft fire while attacking a convoy off the south-east coast of England.

Obergefreiter Heinrich Diemer, Bordfunker of Erich Beudel, badly wounded in 2N+RH on 29th July 1940. Diemer returned to flying duties later in the war on the Russian front with 1st Staffel, Zerstörergeschwader 1, and was missing in action on 19th September 1942.

Leutnant Erich Beudel, pilot of 1st Staffel, who managed to get his damaged Bf 110 C-6, 2N+RH, back to St. Omer on 29th July 1940 after combat with Hurricanes of 151 Squadron.

Leutnant Horst Marx, extreme right, and Unteroffizier Drawe next to him, study a map in preparation for a day out in Paris, a rare treat not granted to all.

On the way to Paris Horst Marx relaxes on the back seat of the car.

Above: Bf 110 C-6, 2N+RH, which was damaged while providing escort to fighter-bomber Bf 110s of the unit on an attack on a convoy on 29th July 1940 when crewed by Beudel and Diemer.

Right and below: Two views of 2N+RH after it crash-landed back at St. Omer. The damage is consistent with that sustained as described in the text.

30th July 1940. Albert Kesselring, 3rd from right, talks to Walter Rubensdörffer at Denain in front of the starboard wing of a Bf 110 C-6. The muzzle of the 30 mm. cannon and the fairing enclosing it can be clearly seen. Note the multi-colored spinners of 1st Staffel.

During his visit, Kesselring takes time to talk to Oberleutnant Martin Lutz. The senior officer obviously gets the best chair!

Kesselring poses for photographs before boarding his personal aircraft, a Siebel Fh 104 "Hallore", with a 'Balkenkreuz' in the unusual position of full-on the nose, and a single lightning flash.

3

August 1940

1-9 AUGUST

Between 1st and 9th August there was very little combat activity undertaken by the unit. However there appears to have been a fair amount of training taking place, as well as the take-on of fresh aircraft. On 1st August Leutnant Erich Beudel was a passenger in a Ju 52/3m on a flight to Liegnitz with his 1st Staffel colleague, Leutnant Otto von Steinhart, to collect Bf 110 fighter-bombers for 1st Staffel. Together with other pilots they were to collect a total of 4 Bf 110 D-0s and one Bf 110 C-4/B. A stop was made in Erfurt due to engine trouble. On 2nd August Beudel and Bordfunker Feldwebel Schulze flew Bf 110 D, CG+OT, to Neuruppin via Gorlitz, Karlsbad, and Juterbog. On the following day they completed the journey to Denain via Köln-Ostheim.

1st Staffel had not been very happy with the performance of their Bf 110 C-6s; problems were always occurring with the 30 mm. cannon installations and they were finding that the gun was jamming before it had fired anywhere near the full set of magazines carried on a combat mission. Another frustration for the 1st Staffel crews flying the Bf 110 C-6 was that the fitment of the 30 mm. cannon precluded the aircraft from carrying bombs; underwing bomb racks had not been introduced at this stage of the war for Bf 110s, and so the aircraft only had one 30 mm. cannon and four rifle-calibre machine guns with which to attack British shipping. The chances of sinking a ship with that kind of offensive weaponry were practically nil - they could at best be of nuisance value.

On 4th August 1st Staffel crews commenced bombing training for the first time. Their initiation into the technique of dropping bombs should have been relatively easy, since 1st Staffel had been formed from a 'Zerstörer' Staffel; the biggest transition was probably for 2nd Staffel, having to change from the slower single-engined Ju 87 to the much faster twin-engined Messerschmitt 110. Erich Beudel, with a new Bordfunker, 19 year-old Obergefreiter Otto Jordan, began bombing practise. Unteroffizier Balthasar Aretz with Bordfunker Rolf Schilleng, of 2nd Staffel, also carried on bombing training on this date in Bf 110, W. Nr. 3377, which would later carry the code S9+EK. Training also continued for both pilots on the following day.

1st Staffel got through its training without mishap but on 6th August two training accidents occurred in 2nd Staffel. First of all Leutnant Kurt Prokop, with Gefreiter Herbert Dust as Bordfunker, pulled out of his practise dive too late and both were killed in the crash which followed. Then later in the day, Unteroffizier Heinrich Schultheis took off on a test flight with an engineer from the Daimler-Benz works. The engineer was visiting the unit because an engine on one of the recently-delivered Messerschmitt 110s from the Messerschmitt works in Augsburg had been giving trouble and when it was stripped down by mechanics, it was believed that sabotage by foreign workers at the Augsburg plant was to blame. The engineer wanted Schultheis's normal Bordfunker, Gefreiter Werner Zwick, to check on the engine's in-flight performance, but Zwick suggested that the engineer himself take part in the test flight to obtain accurate details. During the flight the aircraft got into difficulties and the engineer bailed out successfully; Schultheis bailed out only to hit the aircraft and was killed. All three crew were buried in a local cemetery.

The following day the unit suffered a further loss in training. Hauptmann Karl Valesi, attached to 3rd Staffel for training purposes as previously stated, crashed in his Bf 109 E after not pulling out of a dive. One theory was that his control column broke off as he attempted to pull out of the dive; another was that the angle of dive was too steep and when he released the cement bomb it simply fell into the propeller blades and the aircraft crashed out of control. Whatever the reason, the loss of such an experienced officer was a severe blow to the unit.

This particular period of 9 days had not been totally bereft of combat missions, however. Otto Hintze's Flugbuch shows two missions on 2nd August, one taking off at 16:10 hours and lasting 55 minutes, and another commencing at 18:30 hours also lasting 55 minutes. At this time the target would have been shipping and it is likely that 3rd Staffel of Erprobungsgruppe 210 were responsible for the sinking of the trawler *Cape Finisterre* which was sunk off Harwich when part of a convoy was attacked. Another mission was flown in the afternoon of 5th August but the outcome of it is unknown.

By 10th August 1st Staffel had 10 Bf 110 D-0s and 5 Bf 110 C-6s on charge. One Bf 110 C-6 had already been lost on 30th July. From the entries in the Flugbuch of Erich Beudel for July, it is clear that four Bf 110 C-6s carried the individual aircraft letter of 'G', 'N', 'O', and 'P'; from the photographs accompanying the text it is clear that other Bf 110 C-6s of the unit carried the identity letters of 'R', 'S' and 'T'. From this it can be deduced that at least six, probably seven, Bf 110 C-6s were in service with 1st Staffel. In the hectic combat days to follow they would be grateful for every combat-ready aircraft on charge as the tempo of the battle rapidly increased.

On 10th August Leutnant Willi Benedens was posted to Erprobungsgruppe 210. After 'Zerstörer' training at Oberschleissheim, he had worked at the Erprobungsstelle at Rechlin. His time with the unit would be brief, but very eventful, as shall be seen.

COMBAT - 11 AUGUST

11th August opened for Erprobungsgruppe 210 with a raid over Dover and the Bf 109s of 3rd Staffel despatched three barrage balloons before the Bf 110s of the unit bombed the harbour without causing any great damage. All the aircraft returned to Calais-Marck, no British fighters having made an interception.

A reconnaissance aircraft had reported a convoy off Felixstowe and Erprobungsgruppe 210 was detailed to attack it. Taking off at 11:20 hours, the unit, consisting of 15 Bf 110 'Jabos' and four 1st Staffel Bf 110 C-6s, met its escort of Bf 110 fighters from ZG 26 over Gravelines at 1,500 feet and the complete formation headed north-west to seek out the convoy. Whereas Balthasar Aretz still awaited his first 'Feindflug' with the unit. Otto Hintze was on his 105th of the war in his Bf 109 E-4/B, 'Yellow 1', and Erich Beudel was on his third in Bf 110 D, S9+DH. Patchy clouds were over the convoy which made a concerted attack difficult, but Erprobungsgruppe 210 was able to attack without interference. Following the attack, however, things became pretty hot indeed. Three Hurricanes of 85 Squadron led by Squadron Leader Peter Townsend, six Hurricanes of 17 Squadron led by Flight Lieutenant Harper and eleven Spitfires of 74 Squadron led by Pilot Officer John Freeborn (in the absence of 'Sailor' Malan) all attacked the German aircraft. Some Dorniers of KG 2 were also involved in this attack and it is likely that the Hurricanes of 85 Squadron tangled with them; Squadron Leader Townsend identified one of his quarry as a Do 17 and his aircraft recognition appears to have been better than most during the Battle of Britain. With so many aircraft involved on both sides it is impossible to state with any certainty which British pilots shot down which German aircraft and vice-versa. What can be stated with certainty is that Erprobungsgruppe 210 lost two aircraft from 1st Staffel, both Bf 110 C-6s. One Bf 110 was crewed by Leutnant Kurt Bertram, aged 20, the pilot, and his Bordfunker, Obergefreiter Gerhard Mertins, a 22 year-old Berliner. Kurt Bertram's brother, Otto, at that time Staffelkapitän of 1st Staffel, Jagdgeschwader 2, recalled that: 'What they (his comrades) told me was – "When I last saw him in the air over the mouth of the River Thames, he was chasing a Hurricane and was himself chased by two Spitfires". I, at that time was Squadron Leader of 1. Staffel, Jagdgeschwader Nr.2 Richthofen, and for me this information was equal to a death sentence. My brother was a man without fear. This was his first mission with enemy contact, and his last'.

The other Bf 110 C-6 was crewed by 27 year-old Gefreiter Christian Weiss, pilot, and Obergefreiter Richard Keilhaupt, his 21 year-old Bordfunker. One German source states that the aircraft of Weiss and Keilhaupt was seen to glide down with the starboard engine on fire onto the sea and a rubber dinghy was thrown to them by Feldwebel Stütz of the unit, but they were never picked up. The only British combat report which in any way tallies with this incident is that of Pilot Officer John Freeborn who reported attacking two enemy aircraft and 'in one case the E/A dived straight into the Sea and in the other case the E/A pancaked on the sea and then sank'.

This had been 1st Staffel's first mission with a combined force of Bf 110s fitted with the 30 mm. cannon and others with bomb-racks, a mixture of Bf 110 C-6s and the newer 'Jabo', the Bf 110 D-0. Some crews had only been retrained on 'Jabos' a few days earlier, having only flown the 'C-6' since the formation of the unit. Three C-6s had been lost in action following this mission, with another having to make a forced-landing badly damaged on 29th July. ZG 26 suffered the loss of two aircraft and, like their British counterparts, overclaimed their combat victories. ZG 26 also had two aircraft damaged in combat who made it back to France, and KG 2 had three damaged Do 17 Zs on return to base. Matters had not gone all the way of the British, however. Sergeant Allgood of 85 Squadron returned to Martlesham Heath with damage to his Hurricane, but was himself unwounded. 17 Squadron suffered the loss of Pilot Officer Kenneth Manger, DFC, shot down into the sea and posted as missing, and two other pilots, Flying Officer D. Hanson and Pilot Officer L. Stevens, both returned with damaged Hurricanes to Debden. 74 Squadron were hit hardest in lost pilots. Pilot Officers D. Cobden and D. Smith were killed when their aircraft were shot down into the sea.

Erprobungsgruppe 210 claimed to have sunk one 8,000 ton ship as a result of this action. The next day it would switch from shipping to land targets, as the Luftwaffe altered course in their attempt to gain the upper hand and wrest control of the skies over southern England from the RAF. Regarding the attacks on shipping, Karl Stoff of 1st Staffel recalled: 'At the beginning of the Battle of Britain, about the middle of July 1940, the orders from above were that no missions were permitted over the British Isles. So Erprobungsgruppe 210 were limited to armed reconnaissance flights over the Channel and also the English coast. Close to the English coast, Hptm. Lutz, to whom I was assigned, succeeded in sinking an English armed look-out ship with his 2 cm. cannon after several passes. As proof, there was film from the automatic camera (ESK 2000) installed in the Me 110. As a result, until we were shot down, we considered it essential that one was carried on all missions.'

COMBAT - 12 AUGUST RADAR STATIONS, MANSTON AND HAWKINGE AIRFIELDS

Just after 07:30 hours on Monday 12 August the crews of Erprobungsgruppe 210 left Denain for Calais-Marck and one of their most intense days of the Battle of Britain. Otto Hintze leading 3rd Staffel was in his familiar mount, 'Yellow 1'; Erich Beudel, with his Bordfunker Otto Jordan touched down at Calais-Marck in Bf 110 D, S9+EH. Their first mission on this day was against the radar stations at four points on the south coast of England. Slated for attack were Dunkirk, Pevensey, Rye and Dover. At 09:30 hours, Erprobungsgruppe 210 was taking-off from Calais-Marck fully bombed-up and briefed as to their targets. Rubensdörffer would take the inland station at Dunkirk; Hintze with his Bf 109s would take the nearest at Dover; the two Bf 110 Staffelkapitäne would take their formations further along the coast: Lutz and his 1st Staffel to Pevensey and Rößiger with his 2nd Staffel to attack Rye.

The unit headed out over the Channel and turned west parallel to the English coast. Otto Hintze then led his Bf 109 E-4/Bs to the Dover radar station and the 8 Bf 109s managed to cause some damage to huts within the radar compound and noted that the masts swayed but were not demolished!

At Rye, the radar station which first picked up the track of Erprobungsgruppe 210 over the Channel, the station personnel were puzzled when the Filter Room at Fighter Command HQ at Stanmore only gave their track an 'X' designation (unidentified). Rößiger's Bf 110s claimed ten direct hits on the radar complex and it went temporarily off the air.

Martin Lutz led his aircraft furthest west and his 6 Bf 110s, with two 500 Kg. bombs under the belly of each aircraft, attacked Pevensey. They claimed eight hits on the station, one of which severed the electricity cables with the result that the station also went off the air.

Rubensdörffer led the last formation several miles inland and claimed many strikes on his allotted target: huts were hit but Dunkirk continued to function – the only one to do so of the four stations attacked. However within a few hours, the other three stations had recommenced transmissions. Further attacks by Erprobungsgruppe 210, or other units, may have resulted in the permanent disablement of the radar stations but no such follow-up attacks occurred. Ventnor, which was hit by Ju 88s of KG 51, was put out of action for three days on this date, but the defences managed to get by without it. It must remain a matter for speculation as to what would have happened in mid-August had the radar stations received continual attacks. The course of the Battle of Britain and the fate of Fighter Command could have decisively changed.

All the aircraft taking part in the raids against the radar stations returned to Calais-Marck, and groundcrew there set about preparing the machines of the unit for their next mission of the day: the airfield on the south-eastern tip of England in a very exposed position, Manston.

14 Bf 110s of the Staff Flight, 1st and 2nd Staffeln and 7 Bf 109s of 3rd Staffel took off shortly after mid-day and headed for Manston. On the way they joined up with a group of Dornier 17s from KG 2 at 11,000 feet, Erprobungsgruppe 210 leading the complete formation. On approaching Manston the unit dropped down to 3,000 feet and then ran in to the target without interception from any RAF fighters. The bombs hit the intended target and the Dornier 17s followed up with their payload. The Operations Record Book of Manston recorded the raid in a very laconic manner, viz.: 'The aerodrome was attacked by approximately 15 Me 110's and some HEINKELS (sic) and bombed at low altitude. Some 150 HR bombs were dropped. The aerodrome was pitted with approximately 100 craters, and rendered temporarily unserviceable. Two hangars were damaged, and Workshops were destroyed. In the latter building a civilian clerk was killed, this being the only casualty. The raid lasted approximately five minutes'.

During the raid, 600 squadron personnel were on the ground and one of them, a Sergeant Gunner, Tom Townshend, recalled the first raid on Manston thus: 'As an air gunner with 600 Sqdn. operating as night fighters, we also had other jobs of work to perform, and with regards to Manston, we were trying to operate out of one of the hot spots from the German point of view.

'As air raid warnings were the order of nearly every day, part of our job was also to man the Field Telephone which was positioned on top of the firing butts.

'On the morning of the 12th August 1940 my turn of duty was at 10:00 a.m. to man the Field Telephone, which was a direct line to Sector HQ which I believe came under Hornchurch, and my job was to keep in contact with Sector Control by telephone and report every movement of any aircraft flying either across or in the vicinity of Manston. I was to give a running commentary. I also had an armourer with me whose job it was to operate the .303 machine guns in the event of an attack. At Manston the Armoury section had made up a tripod with mounting for four fixed .303 Browning Machine Guns as part of a defence system. The two of us would be standing inside the small confined square on top of the firing butts with the tripod and four guns. We also had stacked sandbags on top of the four brick walls and it was on top of one of these sandbags that I was operating the Field Telephone.

'It was around 12:30 to 12:40 as I remember when the telephone rang to say that a raid was approaching Manston, believed 20+ – could I see or hear anything? The station was on "Red Alert" and below me spread out in "V" formation were 12 Spitfires with engines running and waiting for the signal to scramble. Weather conditions were near perfect with slight haze in the upper level. I spotted a long nose Blenheim painted all black which flew past very low, and reported this. This aircraft was a constant visitor every time a raid was imminent. It was disclosed later that it was one which the Germans had got hold of and were using, perhaps trying to fool us. I could hear plenty of noise but could not pick up any raiders. What seemed like hours must have been minutes as when I turned to my right looking over the aerodrome boundary I spotted two rows diving down in line astern. I must have spotted them at about 3,000-4,000 ft., screaming down to pull across the drome with one line across the hangar and the nearside line of them coming for the firing butts. I screamed through the telephone "Hell, here they come, they're coming for us, must be at least 20 of them". All in seconds it happened. A "Very" cartridge shot up over the drome and the Spits opened full throttle. The Me 110s had by now reached the drome and bombs were falling at random. The blast from some of the exploding bombs had stopped the engine of the last Spitfire at the rear of the port side formation, and the pilot in white drill flying outfit ran like hell to take what shelter he could below the wall of the firing butts. There were Army personnel manning some Bofors guns and these chaps had run for it leaving their guns. I was holding the Field Telephone in my hand one moment when a blast from a nearby bomb took the lot from my hand. My Armourer, who should have been trying to shoot them down, went into near hysterics and crouched into a corner. All hell had broken loose and I believe on that particular raid not one gun was fired. The Army had left their posts, my eyes were transfixed on what I saw; I just could not believe it all. As I turned to look left beyond the drome, I took a dive for the floor, joining the armourer. The yellow-nosed 109s were sweeping in nearly at ground level and all I remember was seeing this one particular fellow coming straight at the butts with flashes coming out of the nose and wings. As quick as it started so it stopped and when we had regained our senses I remember F/Lt. Pritchard, with others, walking below my position and calling out asking how many rounds fired. The answer was nil. Although I was within my rights in carrying out my duty assigned to me, I was torn off a strip and was then and there instructed that Armourer or no Armourer I was to take over the guns. Such was the shambles and red tape going on at Manston.

'The pilots of the Spits certainly showed their true colours in getting off at all. It states in one book that only one Spitfire got airborne and it was Geoffrey Quill. This is not true and in fact 11 Spitfires got airborne. If the German leader of the attacking formation had had the presence of mind to have swung his line of attack at a slight angle, he would have cut right across the path of the Spits taking off, and without doubt he would have blown the whole eleven out of existence. For all that I think it was an attack well executed and with surprise'.

The pilot of the Spitfire of 65 Squadron which had stalled, and who 'ran like hell' for shelter was Pilot Officer K.G. Hart who was unscathed on this occasion but was to lose his life later in the war.

600 Squadron's Operations Record Book recorded that in the raid, one of their aircraft was seriously damaged and one slightly. As a result of the attack, 600 Squadron was unable to operate out of Manston and it henceforth operated from Hornchurch.

Erprobungsgruppe 210 completed their bombing of Manston and headed for Calais-Marck. However their return flight was not to be as easy as their outward journey. On the way back across the Channel they were engaged by Spitfires and Hurricanes. 54 Squadron, led by Flight Lieutenant Al Deere, had been alerted about the raid on Manston but were not in a position to prevent the attack from taking place. Deere led his section towards the bombing force but had to engage the Bf 109 Es which intercepted and prevented any effective combat with the Bf 110s and Do 17s which had bombed Manston. Deere claims to have shot down a Bf 110 into the Channel and claims to have seen one of the crew climb into a rubber dinghy, but this was not any of the Manston raiders.

Leutnant Horst Marx of 3rd Staffel claimed a Hurricane shot down into the Channel and this is likely to be Hurricane P3803 flown by Flying Officer K. Lukaszewicz of 501 Squadron, reported as missing following combat with enemy fighters at 12:55 p.m.. The aircraft of Erich Beudel suffered engine failure on touching down at Calais-Marck due to a single bullet puncturing the starboard radiator but he and Otto Jordan were uninjured. Other .303 strikes had hit the propeller and starboard wing.

Erprobungsgruppe 210 had no mission in the afternoon of 12th August but in the late afternoon, shortly before 17:00 hours, the unit left Calais-Marck for their third mission of the day, without Beudel and Jordan due to their S9+EH being 'hors-de-combat'. The target this time was the airfield at Hawkinge. Accounts of the Battle of Britain have previously ascribed this first large-scale raid on Hawkinge as having been undertaken by Ju 88s; in fact it was Erprobungsgruppe 210.

The raid was carried out without loss to the unit and the Hawkinge Record Book recorded the raid as follows: 'Bombing attack by Ju 88s (sic) against the Station was carried out at 1730 hours and lasted for approximately 10 minutes. One hangar, No. 3, was almost completely wrecked whilst one other, No. 5, was partially wrecked. A number of bombs of heavy calibre, including incendiary, were dropped. The aerodrome and buildings were machine-gunned during the attack. The main stores were partly damaged by fire, the clothing store almost completely. The fire was quickly brought under control by RAF personnel aided by local AFS. The Station Workshops were wrecked. Two houses in the Airmen's Married Quarters, occupied by airmen, were destroyed. Twenty eight craters were made on the aerodrome, the longest being 76'x72'x28' deep and the smallest 10'x10'x8' deep, but the aerodrome was not rendered completely unserviceable. Repairs to the surface were immediately commenced by REs already attached for such work. Ground defences were surprised and no guns, except two Hispano, were fired. The altitude of the attacking aircraft was such that it was impracticable for the PACU to be brought into action. Two civilians employed by contractors of the Works Directorate were killed, and three airmen were killed. Six airmen received severe injuries and were admitted to the Kent and Canterbury Hospital, Canterbury. The casualties occurred to personnel employed in No. 3 hangar. Two Spitfire aircraft, under repair, were damaged, whilst one or two others were struck by splinters. The two non-operational aircraft on charge were damaged but repairable'.

Although not put out of action, the airfield received a fair amount of damage. Thus ended a day of three missions for the unit, which were carried out with a great deal of success given the total bomb-load available to the Bf 110s and Bf 109s, and the difficulty presented by the structure of the first of the day's targets. With hindsight it could be stated that for Erprobungsgruppe 210's attacks to be deemed a total success it was necessary for the targets to be put out of action completely, but at the time, both of the combatant air forces were breaking fresh combat ground. For the Luftwaffe, the campaigns since September 1939 were of a style whereby airfield strikes were followed very quickly by advance by the ground forces and so Luftwaffe thinking had not considered what the ramifications of a static ground war would be on their overall planning. For the RAF, there was to be no headlong retreat such as happened in France. They simply had to take whatever pounding came along and then set about making good the damage as quickly as possible. The result was that the RAF quickly came to realise that it took continual bombardment to put an airfield out of commission, and when a landing ground was pitted with craters they were simply filled in, in order to allow aircraft to land again. In 1940, the Luftwaffe had not fully appreciated that lesson; in 1940 the RAF appreciated the lesson sufficiently to ensure that when they went over to the offensive in the later war years, enemy airfields would have to live with continual bombardment, the last six months of the war being an object lesson in how to conduct such an operation.. Given the above constraints, therefore, it can be placed on record with almost total certainty that 12th August 1940 was the day of greatest success for Erprobungsgruppe 210 in its entire history. The day closed for Erich Beudel with him being ferried back to Denain by his Staffelkapitän Martin Lutz in S9+CH.

COMBAT - 13 AUGUST 'ADLERANGRIFF'

Erprobungsgruppe 210 were roused early on the morning of 13 August. By 05:30 hours they were climbing away from Denain and had landed at Calais-Marck by 06:00 hours. Balthasar Aretz and his Bordfunker Rolf Schilleng were part of the formation in S9+EK, as was Erich Beudel and Otto Jordan in a new Bf 110 'Jabo', S9+JH. What has never been previously stated is that the first mission for Erprobungsgruppe 210 on this day was to have been Eastchurch aerodrome. This raid was to have been carried out in conjunction with the Dornier 17s of Oberst Johannes Fink's KG 2. It is not known whether the instructions to abort the mission were received by the unit when it was airborne or when it was still on the ground. What did happen was that the Bf 110s of the unit took no part in the raid, but Otto Hintze's 'Flugbuch' shows a combat mission with take-off from Calais-Marck at 06:15 hours which lasted one hour thirty five minutes. Previous accounts of the Battle of Britain have stated that the reason why the bombers of KG 2 carried out the mission was because they did not have the correct crystals in their radio sets and the Bf 110s of ZG 26 received the cancellation order in the air. It is likely, therefore, that Hintze's 109s did not receive the cancellation order and carried out their mission. It is not known what their target was, but it is reasonable to assume that it was Eastchurch also. One book, 'Battle over Britain' by Francis K. Mason, states that the Spitfire pilots of 74 Squadron, who intercepted the Dorniers of KG 2, claimed that the Dorniers were escorted by Bf 109s, and this could indeed have been true if Hintze's Staffel carried out their mission in concert with Fink's raiding force. In any event, all 3rd Staffel Bf 109s returned safely to Calais-Marck and the unit awaited its further instructions for 'Adlerangriff'.

Before leaving this particular raid, it is interesting to note that the postponement orders had not reached another Bf 109 unit – I. Gruppe of Jagdgeschwader 2 carried out a Freie Jagd mission early in the morning, losing one of their number to RAF fighters. It would appear that Bf 110 units received the order, but that other units did not and carried their allotted tasks without questions.

Erprobungsgruppe 210 finally got the 'Go-ahead' for a combat mission in the early afternoon of 'Eagle Day' and were off from Calais-Marck at about 15:15 hours. Aretz and Schilleng remained behind, still awaiting their first 'Feindflug' with the unit. Erich Beudel was involved in S9+JH, his 6th enemy flight. The target was Southend aerodrome (Rochford) and escort for the unit was drawn from the Bf 110 fighters of ZG 26. The unit flew over the Channel at 11,000 feet but once over England they encountered 10/10ths cloud at 3,700 feet which meant they would not be able to carry out their attack on the intended target. The bombs were released over Canterbury with no particular target aimed at, and Erprobungsgruppe 210 returned to Calais-Marck without any losses. An example of the kind of conditions experienced on this mission can be given by considering the fate of one of the ZG 26 escort pilots. Joachim Koepsell, flying in Bf 110, U8+HH, a 1st Staffel machine, lost his way over England and with two other aircraft of his unit, attempted to regain his home base. Such were the problems encountered that Koepsell finally managed to land at 'sHertogenbosch in the Netherlands after a combat flight lasting 2 hours 45 minutes!

This was the sum total of Erprobungsgruppe 210's contribution to 'Adlertag'. After the missions of 12th August, this day must certainly have been an anti-climax for them. However things would soon be hotting-up!

COMBAT - 14 AUGUST

Although the unit was at Calais-Marck before 07:00 hours on 14 August, it received the signal 'QBI' – no missions to be flown – bad weather. At 11:30 hours however, having received the necessary clearance to do so, the unit took off, and was ordered to attack Ramsgate airfield (1st Staffel) and Manston (2nd Staffel). 3rd Staffel did not fly on this occasion. The airfield given to 1st Staffel was a tiny peacetime civil airfield, the military value of which is unknown but which must have made the Luftwaffe Intelligence authorities think that aircraft could have operated from it. Two barrage balloons protecting Ramsgate harbour prevented 1st Staffel's eight Bf 110 D-0s from carrying out their mission and so they joined with their 2nd Staffel colleagues in the attack upon Manston. Before going in to attack Manston, two aircraft of 1st Staffel had to return to Calais-Marck due to engine trouble. Beudel and Jordan, this time in S9+CH, were paying their second visit to Manston. Unteroffizier Ernst Glaeske, posted-in to 2nd Staffel in early August after a spell as an instructor, flew his first mission on this raid.

Manston's Operations Record Book logs the time of the attack as 12:10 hours and the unfortunate Sergeant Townshend was once again perched precariously on top of the firing butts in touch with Hornchurch Sector Control by telephone. His account of the raid is given in its entirety as an excellent example once again of being on the receiving end of a Luftwaffe airfield raid at the height of the Battle of Britain.

'Once again we were blessed with good weather. With the bombing of two days previous the aerodrome was in fairly poor shape with craters filled in as best as could be to allow the fighter squadrons operating by day to get in and out.

'I was once again detailed for duty on top of the firing butts to keep a look-out for any movement of aircraft whether friend or foe that should happen to be in the area, and keep Sector Control informed. I also had an Armourer detailed to be with me. The Army were also on duty down below with their Bofors guns, and also in a field nearby. It must have been around 12:15-12:30 p.m., I cannot recall the exact time, when my phone rang. Amber alert had turned to Red and an enemy formation which was given to me as fifteen-plus was approaching Manston from offshore between Margate and Ramsgate. No squadrons were on the deck this time - squadrons were up already. I could hear faint aircraft engines in the distance which was more of a drone but I could sight nothing. I had, in the meantime, checked all four .303s to make sure they were cocked and on 'fire' position. The telephone line to Sector Control was open all the time and information was being fed to me direct. "Formation appears to be thirty-plus and has turned to swing along the coast flying up and down between Margate and Ramsgate. Keep a sharp watch-out, we believe they are feinting this raid". What they were up to they only knew, as we were left guessing. Once again the all-black long-nosed Blenheim showed up and flew low parallel with the 'drome. The same as two days previous. Then suddenly over the phone – they are turning and heading across the coast line. Manston was about three miles or so from the coast. "Could I see them?" – No, I could hear them and the noise was increasing. The last message I could remember was: "They must be nearly on top of you". They were. The identical attack as on 12th August. I picked the two long lines up through the haze, identical in detail as before. I grabbed the mounting with the four Brownings fixed to it and had the leader of the nearest formation to me in my sights. Both lines of the formation swept past between myself and the hangars. They were that close that I still think today that I could have thrown a stone and hit one or other of them. As it was, I opened fire and to my utter amazement watched a row of bullet holes ripping through the port wing right along the aileron section, the bullet holes travelling towards the fuselage. The formation was pulling out at just above hangar height. This particular Me 110 rolled slightly, never pulled out, and went straight in, I would say about fifty to seventy five yards from my position. At the same time the Bofors guns were firing away and between my watching the one I was going for, the leader of the starboard formation of Me 110s broke in two at where the Gunner/Radio Operator sat. This happened just over the hangar which had been hit. Think I can say I witnessed the most amazing escape I was ever to see throughout my war service. As the aircraft broke in two so a body shot out horizontally and a parachute opened. How, I would never know because it was impossible for this gunner to have opened it. The 'chute opened that fraction of a second long enough for him to save his life as he fell to the ground in front of the remains of one of the hangars. The forward portion of the aircraft hit the ground and scattered bits and pieces all over the 'drome. This I would say was a definite Bofors gun hit. Once again F/Lt. Pritchard came across to speak to me on top of the firing butts. His question was: "How many rounds did you fire Townshend?" I started to count the spent cartridge cases on the floor. I could not count all but estimated to him that it was in the region of 250-300 rounds. It was a rough guess. There was also an armoured car with a scarf-ring mounting fitted with, I believe, a .303 Vickers gas-operated gun somewhere behind the hangar area. I did read that a Corporal Clark was in this and shot one of the Me 110s down. This I would disclaim.

'In summing up these particular raids I would say that the vast majority of Station and Squadron personnel were under cover in shelters etc. I was in the grandstand seat and think without doubt that I must be one of the very few who can give the exact details of what happened on the 12th and 14th August 1940.

'I was on first readiness that night of the 14th August. I went across to the crew-room to put my flying kit on and as we were not taking off for some time, I strolled across to where the Me 110 had gone straight in. The breakdown cranes were put in position to lift the tangled heap out. Our squadron doctor was on the scene along with others and on seeing me dressed for flying, asked what I was doing gazing at this lot. I told him that I wanted to see what was going to be pulled out. His reply was that I should not see it as it was not going to be a pleasant sight. I had to face up to the life we were leading and I had to harden myself to it all. I told him this and he understood. The crane had winched the wreckage up and it was hanging in mid-air. The doctor and some medical orderlies were busy cutting through the harness which was holding the remains of the pilot in his seat. When they had cut through, they got the pilot's body out. After it was put on a blanket, they opened up the flying suit and from one of the pockets they found what I believe was a diary. I think I am correct in saying that there was an entry to the effect that this was the pilot's first trip leading a formation. Yes, it did harden me, but I could not help but feel sad. I have often thought back, even these days. They were doing their job as we had to do ours'.

Another member of 600 Squadron, R. Brookes, recalled the raid of 14th August, particularly the shooting down of Steding and Schank's aircraft: "The Sergeant Armourer of our Squadron, 600 City of London Fighter Squadron, obtained permission to install a gun emplacement on top of the butts, which consisted of seven or eight, maybe more, I cannot recall the exact number, of .303 Browning machine guns. The Sergeant shot the tail off of the twin-engined aircraft; the tail section fell to earth. The aircraft must have released its bombs because the upward blast of the bombs cushioned the descent of the tail section. To my utter amazement a figure appeared from the tail section. Very confused and dazed, he had a pistol in his hand held by the butt. He was saying over and over 'Kamerad'. I think he was trying to say to us that at that moment he had no hostile intention towards us, but he appeared to believe that he would be ill-treated by us. We were undecided what to believe: the 'Kamerad' or the pistol pointed at us. We believed he was so confused that he did not realise that he was pointing a gun at us. Anyway we led him away to a dug-out air raid shelter which lay behind our control room just off of the Margate road. Our officer took charge of him, relieved him of his pistol, and that was the last we saw of him. I had the worst time of my life at Manston, but remember I feel a great affection for the airfield. I cannot explain why, but it is so".

Brookes also shed light on the so-called 'Manston Mutiny'. "Another thing was that we had a mutiny at Manston which I have never seen published anywhere. What happened was the airfield Commander, the aerodrome Commander, he inspected our huts when we were on duty, issued orders that we had to keep our huts tidy. We all got a rocket for that because you can imagine, there was no working shifts, we were all out there sometimes 16 hours a day re-fuelling, re-arming. Because there were 2 Spitfire squadrons there when we were there with our Blenheims, and squadron associations went by the board, you just helped if some Spits wanted re-fueling. You used the appropriate tankers, cos I believe they used a different octane. Our Blenheims used 90 I believe it was, I'm not sure, but I believe Spits used 100. I don't know whether that's true or not. But anyway, we always used to muck in, so there was no demarcation lines: 'Oh I can't do that, I'm 600 Squadron'. You used to muck in and help the armourers under their instructions and all that sort of business. Anyway the aerodrome Commander decided that all bed space had to be polished and beds made and everything. Well, when you're doing a 12-14 hour and sometimes longer day you don't feel like getting back home and cleaning up your bed space. So this went on and we moaned to the officers of the aircraft, and they had a moan, and eventually they refused to fly, and they said they'd got no confidence in the ability of the crews, through weariness, to service the aircraft properly and they were not happy flying. Anyway, to the best of my knowledge and I can't swear to this, a high ranking officer came down, and eventually got it sorted out, and eventually we were relieved the duty of polishing but we had to detail one bod to do the lot, but that was an actual instruction. Call it a mutiny or whatever you like, I believe the word mutiny was used at the time". So, the 'Manston Mutiny' was not about cowardice in the face of the enemy, but rather the irksome problem of keeping the area around the men's beds tidy while most of Manston was being blasted on a regular basis. Small wonder that some stood their ground on this issue, and challenged what they saw as a ludicrous instruction in the prevailing situation. While it may be argued that discipline had to be maintained, of paramount importance was the servicing and turn-around of the aircraft that landed there, and a corollary of that was the fitness of those carrying out those duties to continue to do so. In stark terms, 'spit-and-polish' came a poor second to keeping front-line fighters flying.

After the raid was completed Erprobungsgruppe 210 reformed and returned to Calais-Marck. Oberleutnant Werner Weymann, only recently arrived and flying with 1st Staffel, landed back at Calais-Marck on one engine due to loss of oil. The Bf 110 which 'went straight in' was that of 23 year-old Leutnant Heinrich Brinkmann, pilot, and his Bordfunker, 24 year-old Unteroffizier Richard Mayer. Both had no chance of surviving the crash. Their aircraft was coded S9+NK, a 2nd Staffel machine. The other aircraft to be shot down was also from 2nd Staffel, coded S9+MK, crewed by Unteroffizier Hans Steding, aged 23, and his Bordfunker, Gefreiter Ewald Schank, aged 24, who had 'the most amazing escape' of almost anybody's life. Schank's recollection of the events surrounding his first and last combat mission over England are vivid: 'At 7 o'clock on 14.8.40 we left our airfield with our Staffel for Marck airfield near Calais. From there we were supposed to take off for a mission at 1100 hours. Because of bad weather, take-off was put back until midday. Two Staffeln took off, about 7-9 machines, Me 110, with Me 109s as escort. Our aircraft carried two 500 Kg. incendiary bombs. During the flight over the Channel two aircraft had to turn back with engine trouble.

'At a height of about 3,000 m. the Staffel began a diving attack in order to hit the target. After the bombs had been dropped, we pulled our machine higher. In the same instant, our aircraft received a heavy blow from below, probably a hit from the 'Flak'. Because of this, the aircraft was damaged and crashed. I was thrown out of the machine, but remained attached to the aircraft by a boot. Without thinking, I freed myself from the boot. When I was free of the aircraft, I operated my parachute. Shortly after the parachute opened, I landed heavily on the hard red tarmac. I quickly released my parachute, as it was pulling me towards a large fire. When I stood up, I realised I was missing a boot, and was wounded in the head. As I looked around, I noticed pieces of aircraft, undercarriage, a wheel, and bits of the fuselage. The rest of the aircraft was smashed into the red tarmac not far away.

'I dragged myself through the wreckage to search for the pilot, but could see nothing. As I was all alone and helpless on the runway, three men in blue uniforms came. I did not know, or understand, any English words at that time. I said to the soldiers in German: "My friend is in the aircraft". They took me in their midst and led me to a shelter, in which there were soldiers in brown uniforms and steel helmets, with guns. A soldier spoke to me in German, but I no longer recall what he said. I asked him: "When will I be shot?" "You will not be shot", he replied, "you will go to a prisoner camp with many others". I probably said: "Ich bin glücklich, daß mich Gott gerettet hat" (I am lucky that God has saved me). I fainted shortly afterwards.

'When the raid was over, I was taken in a car by two soldiers to a hospital, and was immediately attended to by a doctor. I was in hospital for approximately 10 days. The following day (15th August) I was told that the remains of the pilot had been recovered from the wreckage. After the shooting-down, I was presumed dead, as no-one had made a note that I was still alive'.

The bodies of the three dead crew from Erprobungsgruppe 210 were interred at Minster cemetery, but were all later re-interred in the German War Cemetery at Cannock.

Manston's Record Book once again described the raid in a concise manner, although for some reason the date entered for the raid is given as the 15th instead of the 14th. The entry ran thus: 'The station was again attacked by nine M.E.110's. They were heavily engaged by ground defences and two e.a. were destroyed - one by a R.A. post (Bofors) and one by a RAF post (Hispano). Two hangars on the east camp were partially wrecked and damage was caused to a Bellman and Bessonneau hangar. One large crater made in the centre of the aerodrome'. 600 Squadron's Operations Record Book recorded: 'More bombing, which destroyed one of our hangars, and three aircraft, certain damage was done to the aerodrome. The only casualty was the COMMANDING OFFICER who received a black eye from a stone that rocketted off the ADJUTANT'S steel helmet'.

This was the only combat mission undertaken by Erprobungsgruppe 210 on 14th August. Their most testing time was yet to come.

COMBAT - 15 AUGUST

Thursday 15th August came to be known later in Luftwaffe circles as 'Black Thursday' because of the heavy losses inflicted by the RAF. Equally, by the end of the day, Erprobungsgruppe 210 would have good cause to say it was a 'Black Day'.

According to Karl-Heinz Koch's narrative, given with the account of the raid on Croydon, Erprobungsgruppe 210 carried out five missions on 15th August. However only two have previously been logged for them, the raids on Martlesham Heath in the afternoon and Croydon in the early evening. What is frustrating is the fact that the 'Flugbuch' of Joachim Koepsell of 1st Staffel, Zerstörergeschwader 26 records for 15th August: 'U8+DH, combat mission, Take-off 9:30. Landing 9:40, escort to Erprobungsgruppe 210, landed again due to loss of oil'. From that brief entry, and making the necessary adjustments to reconcile the difference in times between the two countries, it would appear that Erprobungsgruppe 210 had a combat mission which would have been crossing the English coast sometime between 09:00 and 09:15 a.m. Unfortunately no trace has been found of any raid at this time of day on 15th August. Additionally, no information has come to light to indicate other raids by Erprobungsgruppe 210 on this date and so we are left with the Martlesham Heath and Croydon raids, the only two recorded in Otto Hintze's and Erich Beudel's 'Flugbucher'.

Otto Hintze led his 3rd Staffel off from Calais-Marck at 14:20 hours, formed up with the Staff Flight, 1st and 2nd Staffeln Bf 110s of the unit, and the complete formation set course for Martlesham Heath. Among them were Beudel and Jordan with 1st Staffel, and Aretz and Schilleng with 2nd, finally flying their first enemy mission, in S9+EK. The sixteen Bf 110s and nine Bf 109s were detected by British radar and tagged 'Raid 22'. Three Hurricanes of 17 Squadron were scrambled from Martlesham Heath just before the raiders arrived (Flight Lieutenant Harper, Pilot Officer Pittman and Sergeant Griffiths), and three other pilots managed to take off during the raid (Flying Officer Hanson, Pilot Officer Stevens and Sergeant Bartlett). From North Weald nine Hurricanes of 1 Squadron took off to intercept the incoming raid, but both formations of British fighters were too late to prevent Erprobungsgruppe 210 from carrying out their attack on Martlesham Heath airfield. This was the first attack suffered by the airfield and the raid was recalled by Squadron Leader (then Flight Mechanic) Robert Maltby:

'In 1940 I was 19 years of age and a flight mechanic at Royal Air Force, Martlesham Heath, near Woodbridge, Suffolk. Daily tasks were plentiful in my unit, 'D' flight performance testing, later Special Duty Flight, where the aircraft types varied from the tiny Avro autogiros to Blenheims and giant (in those days) Harrow bombers. Despite the operational role of Martlesham – experimental work and a forward fighter base – we enjoyed a remarkably quiet (that is war-free) albeit busy hectic daily routine in that sunny summer of 1940. By and large, therefore, we had come to ignore the moanings of the Air Raid siren on top of a hangar near the Watch Tower (Air Traffic Control) - until that afternoon in mid-August.

'Suddenly the air was full of rattling machine guns and the ominous whine of small high trajectory missiles. In this unfriendly atmosphere I was caught up a ladder with my head in the engine bay of a Blenheim – not for long. Some micro-seconds later and 200 yards away found me crouched in the muddy bottom of a slit trench and thankful to have a buddy drop in on top of me. In my progression 'twixt Blenheim and trench I recall a glimpse of two attacking twin-engined aircraft, one of which, or so it seemed to me, was directing all of its menace in my direction. He missed.

'The raid was quickly over, the main damage centred in the area wherein were grouped the watch tower and hangars. An aircraft on the hard standing, a Fairey Battle, was set on fire and there was damage in the domestic area near the Sergeants' Mess, Officers' Mess and sick quarters. There were few casualties to personnel as I remember and those aircraft dispersed on the airfield perimeter seemed to escape serious damage.

'Erprobungsgruppe 210 were fortunate on the 15th to set the Battle alight because the bomb damage in that area was considerable. I went over to see it on my way to tea and it was quite chaotic around there.

'The Hispano gunners were rather exposed on top of the hangars, which in those days had great convex roofs.

'I think it is fair comment to say that apart from the duration of the raids themselves, few, if any, working hours were lost.

'Such are my memories of a brief acquaintanceship with Erprobungsgruppe 210 in August 1940'.

The Battle of Britain, Then and Now, in the chapter on Martlesham Heath, states: 'Emerging from slit trenches in which they had rapidly taken shelter, airmen were met with the awesome sight of the aftermath of a precision hit-and-run raid and it was obvious to all that the station had been badly clobbered'.

The airfield Operations Record Book recorded: 'Exactly half a minute before the siren was sounded, the aerodrome was attacked by approximately 12 Ju 87s and Me 110 (Jaguar) Dive Bombers. It is stated that there was an above guard of about 20 ME 109 aircraft. The attack was divided into two – the Ju 87s concentrating on the uncompleted Signal Station two miles to the West of the aerodrome and the Jaguars dealing with the aerodrome. Large bombs were dropped – estimated at 500 lbs. each – and in addition a considerable number of incendiary bombs were dropped. The Signals Station suffered no damage other than shattered windows and a burst water tank. The bombs aimed at the aerodrome were widely dispersed although they were dropped in pairs. Two craters on the aerodrome were filled in by 1900 hours. Two fell in the main camp road and wrecked the Guard Room, Coppersmiths' Shop, Joiners' Shop and burst the water main. Two shattered almost every pane of glass in the Officers' Mess and severely damaged all the roofing. Doors and window frames suffered very considerable damage. The Vegetable Garden was smothered in debris – much to the distress of S/Ldr. Brice. The Refrigerator Plant was wrecked. A visiting Fairey Battle, carrying 1,000 lbs. of bombs and parked on the tarmac close to the Watch Office was set on fire (presumably by machine-gun fire) and blew up. The explosion did far more material damage than the enemy bombs. Two hangars were rendered completely U/S and the Watch Office and the Night Flying Equipment Sheds were blown to bits. The remainder of the bombs landed in heathland and did no damage.

'The attack started at approximately 15.10 hours and lasted about 5 minutes. There were seven casualties, but only two were serious, and there were no fatalities. Although the Aerodrome was taken completely by surprise, the quick action of personnel in using makeshift shelter such as slit trenches in addition to normal shelters, undoubtedly saved loss of life and large numbers of injured.

'The height from which the attacks were delivered will never be proved, but the Hispano gunners claimed that the aircraft were too high, and the Bofors blamed the smoke.

'There was no panic although naturally everyone was badly scared'.

The reference in the above account to Ju 87s is misleading; the 'Jabo' Bf 109s of the unit were almost certainly mis-identified as Ju 87s, an easy mistake to make during a sudden air raid. It should also be remembered that at this point in the Battle of Britain, RAF Intelligence had not discovered any crashed Bf 109 Es with bomb-racks, so although they may have suspected that such an aircraft existed, they did not have conclusive proof, and it is likely that ordinary personnel on an airfield did not connect with the single-engined Bf 109 at that time.

Erprobungsgruppe 210 completed the bombing of Martlesham Heath without any loss to themselves and then set about making the return journey to Calais-Marck. Before being able to do so, they were engaged in combat by three Hurricanes of 17 Squadron and the nine Hurricanes of 1 Squadron. On this occasion the British fighters definitely came off second best. Flight Lieutenant Harper of 17 Squadron crash-landed on marshland near Laurel Farm by Felixstowe after having his engine stopped by enemy action; he was admitted to Felixstowe Hospital with wounds to his face – his aircraft was damaged but repairable. 1 Squadron fared badly. Pilot Officer D. Browne and Sergeant M. Shanahan were shot down into the sea and killed; Flight Lieutenant M. Brown bailed out of his Hurricane injured over the sea and was rescued by a trawler. Another Hurricane flown by Pilot Officer J. Elkington was slightly damaged but returned to base safely. The combat claims for shot-down German aircraft cannot be substantiated for this raid, since Erprobungsgruppe 210 returned to base without loss, although Leutnant Eric Beudel of 1st Staffel got back to Calais-Marck in a 'Jabo' which suffered sufficient damage that it was not serviceable for further operations that day.

The aircraft of Erprobungsgruppe 210 landed back at Calais-Marck at about 15:45 hours; the day had gone well so far.

Ernst Elfner recalled one particular event which is relevant at this point: 'One day when we came back from England there was a Spitfire near our airfield. This plane had been hunted by four of our Me 109s. Two Mes had blocked the route back to England while the other two Mes hunted him. In the dogfight the Spitfire was hit and it was forced to set down near our airfield. As far as I remember, the pilot was not wounded. For a short time I saw him sitting in the command room with Rubensdörffer'. This could only relate to Spitfire SH-W flown by Pilot Officer Roberts of 64 Squadron which forced-landed near Calais-Marck airfield on the afternoon of 15th August. No other Spitfire came down near Calais-Marck airfield from the time Erprobungsgruppe 210 began operating from it, to Rubensdörffer's death on 15th August.

COMBAT - 15 AUGUST - CROYDON

In the early evening the unit took off from Calais-Marck to attack Kenley. Hintze's 'Flugbuch' shows him leading off 3rd Staffel at 18:15 hours. Fighter escort was provided by a Gruppe of Bf 109 Es from JG 52. The formation, losing one of their number because Balthasar Aretz in S9+EK returned to base with a damaged airframe, crossed the English coast and continued its incursion inland without interception from RAF fighters. During the flight to the target the escort fighters flew in a position 200 m. above Erprobungsgruppe 210 but on the way became detached and consequently returned to base and took no further part in the action. The reason for their becoming separated has never been satisfactorily explained. One theory is that due to the haze on the approach run they simply lost visual contact with their charges and therefore carried out the most prudent course of action by returning to base; another was that they had to turn back because fuel was beginning to run short. Either way, the loss of the JG 52 fighter escort was to prove crucial to the ultimate fate of Erprobungsgruppe 210 on the Croydon raid.

Flying in over Sevenoaks, Rubensdörffer, leading his Gruppe in his Bf 110 D coded S9+AB, W. Nr. 3338, turned on a south-westerly course to commence his run-up on Kenley. By this time airfields in the immediate vicinity had been alerted and at Croydon 111 Squadron were scrambled at 18:50 hours with orders to patrol at 10,000 feet over the western boundary of the airfield – 'A mistake in my opinion. We saw the bombers just after they had entered their dive just east of the airfield' commented the then Squadron Leader (who would later rise to the rank of Air Commodore) John Thompson, leading 111 Squadron.

At Biggin Hill, 32 Squadron took off between 18:50 and 18:55 hours led, on this occasion, by Flight Lieutenant Michael Crossley on their third scramble of the day. Crossley was leading 32 Squadron because, as Squadron Leader John Worrall recalled: 'I had just returned from leading 32 Squadron to intercept Ju 88s over Selsey Bill, I believe part of a raid on Portsmouth or Southampton. I knew I was due to do something else on my return and instructed F/Lt Crossley to take charge of the Squadron. Just as I set off by car around the perimeter track, 32 was scrambled to 12,000 feet over Croydon. Immediately I took off, caught the squadron up and fell in behind Crossley'.

Two Hurricanes of the Station Training Flight also took off from Biggin Hill with Pilot Officer 'Polly' Flinders and Flight Lieutenant 'Humph' Russell at the controls of them.

What happened next is one of the most famous, and controversial, raids of the Battle of Britain. For a reason known only to Rubensdörffer, Erprobungsgruppe 210 dived to attack Croydon. Leutnant Karl-Heinz Koch, Gruppe Technical Officer, believed it was the haze which led Rubensdörffer to attack the wrong airfield; Otto Hintze believed 'maybe the mist and the presence of English fighters over the area of the aerodrome, who began to attack E.G. 210, is the reason that Rubensdörffer suddenly attacked the aerodrome which was laying below him. In this situation, and from this height – about 3,000 m. – it was difficult to decide whether this aerodrome was Kenley or Croydon'.

The 'English' fighters mentioned by Hintze were the 9 Hurricanes of 111 Squadron who were still climbing to their patrol height when they saw the attack of Erprobungsgruppe 210 commence. 111 Squadron turned immediately and attacked the fighter-bombers. Squadron Leader Thompson (Blue 1) selected the leader of the formation and caught him climbing vertically after his attack. 'I fired a five second burst at a Jaguar climbing vertically from astern and observed bits of cowling, fuselage etc. flying off in all directions. This was observed by P/O Walker, No.2 of the section. This aircraft was probably destroyed, but I was forced to break away due to my low speed' – thus ran Thompson's combat report for the interception of a Bf 110 during the Croydon raid. A hand-written note at the end of the report states: 'Jaguar confirmed ground observation', but this is clearly incorrect as all the Bf 110s brought down in the immediate vicinity of Croydon can be allocated to specific RAF pilots, as will be subsequently shown. Previously published accounts crediting the shooting down of Rubensdörffer and his Bordfunker, Obergefreiter Ludwig Kretzer to Squadron Leader Thompson are erroneous.

As 111 Squadron was engaging Erprobungsgruppe 210, 32 Squadron arrived on the scene and entered the fray. Although intercepted, Erprobungsgruppe 210 completed the bombing of Croydon airfield and set about attempting to extricate itself from a very grave situation. The 8 Bf 109 Es of 3rd Staffel, bringing up the rear in the bombing run, had a difficult task trying to protect the Bf 110s of the unit from the two RAF squadrons. 'After the attack I made a so-called 'defence-circle' between the English fighters. In this position I saw 2 or 3 Me 110s below us who soon disappeared in the thin mist' recalled Otto Hintze. On this occasion 3rd Staffel were not to be very successful.

Over Croydon Sergeant Dymond of 111 Squadron latched onto a Bf 110 which broke from a defensive circle – 'One a/c broke and headed due south. I engaged it 4 miles N of Redhill aerodrome and he crashed in flames on 'drome (Redhill)'. However Sergeant Dymond was not alone in pursuing his quarry. Sergeant Pearce of 32 Squadron recorded – 'I selected a Do 17 flying south from Croydon district and when about 600 yards from it saw another Hurricane level with me. I dived and came up below it, firing into front fuselage mainly, while the other Hurricane attacked from astern. Port engine caught on fire and aircraft dived on fire probably at Redhill'. Although Pearce had mis-identified the aircraft attacked (a frequent occurrence during the Battle of Britain, and particularly so of the bomb-carrying Bf 110s of Erprobungsgruppe 210, who were often identified as Do 17s or Do 215s), he shared with Dymond the destruction of Bf 110 D, S9+BB, W. Nr. 3374, crewed by Erprobungsgruppe 210's Adjutant, Oberleutnant Horst Fiedler, and Bordfunker Unteroffizier Johann Werner. Fiedler died in hospital three days later; Werner became a prisoner-of-war.

The Gruppe Technical Officer, Leutnant Karl-Heinz Koch, also found himself in trouble over Croydon. After the war he placed on record his recollections of the Croydon raid as follows: 'On 15th August 1940 around 06:20 p.m. we took off from Calais-Marck in order to attack Kenley airfield. Our formation consisted of:

3 Me 110 Staff
8 Me 110 2nd Squadron
7 Me 109 3rd Squadron

It was our 5th mission on that day. For the first time we had decided to stay overnight in the village of Marck after the mission, since it would be too late in the evening to return to our home base, Denain, near Valenciennes, after a stop-over with re-fuelling at Calais-Marck. Our fighter cover (3 Squadrons of Me 109s) returned shortly before we reached the target area; they claimed afterwards that they became short on fuel! In the target area we encountered a rather poor vertical visibility due to haze caused by the declining sun. Because of this our lead missed the target and we attacked Croydon airfield instead of Kenley airfield. We attacked with a 45° dive in a south-westerly direction. When somebody called over the radio to break off it was too late since it was shortly before bomb release. I personally realised during the dive that it must be the wrong target, however I, as No. 3, had to follow No. 1 and 2. At our pull-out altitude (about 2,400 ft.) we were met by RAF fighters – I guessed 24 aircraft – closing in from the west at exactly this altitude. We formed immediately a left 'defence circle' (after becoming PoWs we used to call it an attack circle!). Within this circle, in which every one of us had in front as well as in the rear 1 or 2 RAF fighters, we tried to climb up. At the beginning of this airfight my No. 1 and 2 (Commander and Adjutant) were shot down. During this circling and climbing my left engine was hit – presumably by AA – and shortly afterwards my rear gunner was also hit and became unconscious. After reaching about 6,000 feet I decided to leave this unfriendly area and found myself on my own. My left engine was less than windmilling and therefore the airspeed lower than normal; my rear gunner was partly conscious. Approaching the coast west of Hastings I was suddenly attacked by two fighters without any counteraction by my rear gunner. Both engines died immediately. I dived simultaneously to the right to break off from the fighters and looked for a reasonable belly-landing field in order to save my rear gunner's life. I crash-landed the aircraft on a waste land between smaller and larger pools filled with some water and was received by the Home Guard. My rear gunner was taken to hospital and I was taken by the Police to the Police Station at Hastings. That was the end of my 100th mission'.

Although there are minor inaccuracies in the account (7 instead of 8 3rd Staffel Bf 109s; No. 1[Rubensdörffer] was not shown down over Croydon but much further south), it is an interesting insight into the interception over Croydon from the German side.

Humphrey a'Becket Russell had taken off in a Hurricane of Biggin Hill's Station Training Flight, as described earlier, and saw Erprobungsgruppe 210 on their approach to Croydon but they were too far above him to engage so he continued to climb up-sun and eventually saw 6 aircraft flying south-east from Croydon about 4 miles away. He caught up and attacked the rearmost straggling aircraft from astern with the sun behind him. His combat report stated: 'I fired 3 bursts of 1 second each and the enemy aircraft hobbled badly and the starboard engine smoked badly' continued his combat report. 'I broke away below and to port and then steep turned back and attacked the same enemy aircraft from astern again. I fired 3 more bursts of 1 second and the enemy aircraft turned onto its side, began to smoke very badly and lost height rapidly and I last saw it 1 mile south of Bexhill turning inland about 1,000 feet off the water. A Searchlight Site confirm this as having crashed near Pevensey at R.1326. The Searchlight Site identify this enemy aircraft as a Me 110'.

Russell has also set down a further account of this combat as follows: "I had been posted from No. 32 Squadron, Biggin Hill, to the Operations Room in September 1938, and when the Battle of Britain began I was still in this post. However, on 15th August my posting back to the Squadron came through. This was my last day of duty in the Operations Room. By tea time I was off duty but I went to Operations to see what was happening and I saw heavy German raids being plotted, and they appeared to be coming well inland. This was the first occasion, I believe, on which the Germans attacked inland targets and one appeared to be heading for Croydon airfield.

"32 Squadron was already in the air, so I got permission from the Station Commander to take off in a Hurricane of the Station Training Flight. I was off the ground in about 5 minutes.

"The sun was already low in the west. I realised that the Germans would be flying directly into it, and I didn't envy them. Being entirely on my own I kept out of trouble whilst I gained height and I could see the raid over Croydon being intercepted by our fighters. I decided to position myself between Croydon and the coast at about 15 to 20 thousand feet.

"I guessed that the Germans would soon be beating it hot foot for the coast by the shortest possible route so I circled waiting for them. After about 10 minutes I began to think that I had made a mistake because I could not see a single aircraft, friend or foe, until I looked directly below me and there they were. About 20 to 30 M.E. 110 twin engined fighters flying due south, probably having been separated from their bombers. They were going so fast that the aircraft at the rear of the formation was plainly having difficulty in keeping up, in fact there were several stragglers.

"I positioned myself up sun and I am convinced none of them saw me because I was able to dive down and come up directly behind a straggler without any reaction from the enemy formation. I gave him a 3 second burst and immediately his port engine went on fire. He went down in a diving turn to port, so I gave him another 2 to 3 second burst. I was satisfied that this aircraft would not be able to get back to France, so I broke away and returned to Biggin Hill.

"Confirmation that this M.E. 110 had crash-landed on Pevensey Marshes was obtained from the Army who reported that they had taken the crew prisoner and that the pilot was wounded but the rear gunner unharmed. A good wheels up landing by a wounded pilot with one engine on fire.

"This enemy aircraft destroyed was credited to 32 Squadron".

This aircraft claimed by Russell could only be that of Koch and his Bordfunker, Unteroffizier Rolf Kahl, coded S9+CB, W. Nr. 3339, although Russell is wrong as to who was wounded and who was uninjured. Kahl was seriously wounded and was repatriated to Germany later in the war. For some unknown reason, Russell's combat report is filed with those of 501 Squadron at the Public Record Office at Kew, which perhaps accounts for the fact that his claim has never been tied in with Erprobungsgruppe 210's raid before.

Upon landing, Koch was apprehended by Commander Coussens of the LDV Ninfield, and his badly wounded Bordfunker was attended to by Dr. Wood of Catsfield. Upon the arrival of an ambulance, Kahl was transported to the military hospital at Hellingly. Koch was handcuffed and taken to Battle Police Station from where, following advice from Intelligence staff at Hawkinge airfield, he was passed into custody of the Devonshire Regiment at Battle Abbey shortly before 21:00 hours.

Over Croydon, Flight Lieutenant Connors, who was to be killed in action 3 days later, led Green Section of 111 Squadron in combat against 3 Bf 110s. 'I was able to give the third Me 110 a very long burst and a great deal of smoke started to come from his starboard motor. Green 2 went in and fired at aircraft which dived straight into the ground, bits falling off it on the way down – enemy aircraft crashed south of Redhill'. The 111 Squadron Operations Record Book gives no clue as to who 'Green 2' was, and as the file in the Public Record Office contains only 5 combat reports for the interception, those of Squadron Leader Thompson, Flight Lieutenant

Connors, Sergeant Craig, Sergeant Dymond and Sergeant Wallace, it is possible that in the heat of the action Connors believed his 'No. 2' attacked the 110 with him, when it was another pilot of his squadron. It could possibly have been Sergeant Wallace, who 'followed one Jaguar that broke away from the right. He dived slightly, I gave two short bursts from astern, and he went straight into the ground'. The Bf 110 shot down by Connors, and perhaps Wallace, was Bf 110 C-6, S9+TH, of Leutnant Erich Beudel and his Bordfunker, Obergefreiter Otto Jordan. Their luck had finally run out: both died in the crash. Eyewitness accounts state that the pilot was seen to have climbed out of the cockpit as the aircraft came in low and appeared to be reaching back for something. RAF crash investigators were very interested in this 30 mm. cannon-armed Bf 110, details of which are given in Appendix 2.

While Sergeant Pearce had joined Dymond in bringing down Oberleutnant Fiedler, Flight Lieutenant Michael Crossley led Red Section of 32 Squadron in an attack on a Bf 110 over Croydon and reported - 'I attacked a Do 17 from astern and opened fire at 200 yards, setting the port engine on fire. I broke away and Red 2 closed in and knocked some pieces off it. He then gave way to Red 3 who also hit it. We followed, and the fire appeared to go out, giving place to two streams of white. Red 2 and 3 went in and knocked it about so badly that it crashed east of Sevenoaks, the pilot escaping by parachute'. Crossley has since acknowledged that his aircraft recognition was at fault, and concedes that the aircraft in question was a Bf 110. Squadron Leader Worrall, flying No. 2 to Crossley, reported the shooting down of this aircraft in similar terms, but with the following additional information - 'One of the crew baled out. Enemy aircraft crashed near Plaxtol (south of Borough Green) in a wood. The baler-out landed to the south of the a/c on the north side of a wood, the parachute being caught by a tree'. The identity of 'Red 3' has not been established since, of the 7 combat reports on record, 5 relate to 'B' Flight and those of Crossley and Worrall are the only ones for 'A' Flight.

The aircraft brought down by Crossley, Worrall and 'Red 3' was that of Leutnant Helmut Ortner and his Bordfunker, Obergefreiter Bernhard Lohmann, which crashed at Ightham. Ortner recalled that his Bordfunker was killed following the attack by the British fighters and the only course of action left to him was to bail out as a crash-landing was out of the question. Ortner was detained by the Military Police at Biggin Hill for a time before taking the usual PoW route to captivity via the interrogation centre at Cockfosters in London.

For some reason previous publications have stated that Ortner's Bf 110 was a 'C-6' variant, but that is not consistent with the facts that Ortner and Lohmann were 2nd Staffel crew (C-6s were only operated by 1st Staffel), and the only recorded C-6 to crash on land was that of Beudel and Jordan: had Ortner's machine been a C-6 the fact would certainly have been placed on record. Furthermore, in an interview with Ortner, he categorically stated that he had never flown the 'C-6' on an enemy mission, only fighter-bomber Bf 110s.

Another Bf 110 brought down on the Croydon raid was that of Oberleutnant Alfred Habisch and Unteroffizier Ernst Elfner, a Bf 110 D, coded S9+CK, W. Nr. 3341. Photographs accompanying the text show relatively little damage to the machine, and Elfner recalled: 'After leaving the defence circle we flew south alone at low altitude, without any contact with fighters or AA (in the defence circle we had been hit by gunfire). Suddenly the aircraft began to shake violently. After that it was difficult to control, so we came down at Hawkhurst. I was slightly wounded in the right hand by a bullet. We were encircled by the Home Guard. Then I was brought to a big barbed-wire fence. I thought it was built and prepared for prisoners, waiting for the invasion, but I was the only one who sat in it while the sun was setting. I was eventually brought to Oldham. On the passage to Canada, on the ship *Duchess of York*, I saw Habisch, Koch and Ortner for the last time'. As well as being the most photographed Bf 110 of the period, S9+CK was also the subject of a newspaper article whilst on display at Hendon at the end of August 1940. It was later passed to the United States for evaluation, arriving at Los Angeles on 5th April 1941 aboard the freighter *Montanan*. It was examined at Vultee Field but unfortunately its ultimate fate is not known; it was most probably scrapped when it had served its purpose.

The Bf 110 of Rubensdörffer, claimed damaged by Thompson over Croydon, managed to head south with the Bf 109 E-4/B, 'Yellow 3' of Leutnant Horst Marx in attendance. Pilot Officer Flinders, who had taken off with Russell from Biggin Hill, climbed to 12,000 feet, but in the process lost contact with Russell. Noticing AA bursts in the direction of Croydon he went to investigate and saw that the airfield had been bombed. Seeing what he believed to be two Ju 88s flying in a south-easterly direction about four miles away and 3,000 feet above him, he gave chase and was catching them up 'when an Me 109 came towards me from the starboard side. I throttled back completely and he passed in front of me and into my sights. I fired for about two seconds and a stream of white smoke came from his engine. The aircraft dived towards the ground, I realised that he could not get home and continued to chase the bombers. A minute later I saw a parachute open at about 6,000 feet south of Sevenoaks'. Flinders had incorrectly identified the bombers as Ju 88s, but it is likely, although by no means 100% certain, that the 109 he attacked was that of Marx. What is certain is that the only parachute to be seen in the area south of Sevenoaks at that time of day on 15th August 1940 was that of Marx: Rubensdörffer and Kretzer, Koch and Kahl, and Habisch and Elfner, the three crews to come down south of Sevenoaks, all remained in their aircraft. Flinders witnessed briefly the descent of Marx, who landed at Mark Cross with only a cut on his left thumb. His 109 crashed at Lightlands Farm, Frant, a short distance away. RAF crash investigators found so little of Marx's 109 identifiable that they were unaware that it had operated in a bomb-carrying capacity. The first time RAF Intelligence had concrete evidence of a bomb-carrying 109 was when the 109 E of Feldwebel Gottschalk of II./LG 2 force-landed on Hawkinge airfield on 6th September 1940.

Pilot Officer Duckenfield, airborne with 501 Squadron since 17:25 hours, closed in on an enemy formation heading south from Croydon and latched onto a Do 215 (sic). Duckenfield chased the aircraft for several minutes and managed to hit it with the last of his ammunition, observing that one engine caught fire. The aircraft crashed in the vicinity of Tunbridge Wells but Duckenfield was unable to check the exact location of the crash as he was very low on fuel by then. It cannot be stated with complete certainty that the aircraft claimed by Duckenfield was that of Rubensdörffer and his Bordfunker Obergefreiter Ludwig Kretzer, but it is interesting to note that the only twin-engined aircraft shot down in the Tunbridge Wells area at that time on 15th August was Rubensdörffer's.

On the ground, Marx stopped a police car travelling to the scene of Rubensdörffer's crash and surrendered, informing the police that he had been in radio contact with Rubensdörffer who had told him that his Bordfunker was dead and he was wounded. In one of Rubensdörffer's pockets was found a telegram from Kesselring congratulating him on the award of the Iron Cross, First Class for 'courageous leadership of your Gruppe'. That Iron Cross became a treasured possession of Otto Hintze and on the reverse it bears the simple inscription 'Rubs 19.7.40'. On 19th August 1940 he was awarded the Knights Cross of the Iron Cross posthumously, the first Zerstörer pilot to receive it.

One further casualty of the Croydon raid remains to be reported. Leutnant Willi Benedens had joined the unit on 10th August. On 12th August he flew his first combat mission in the raid against the radar stations, and later in the day flew in the first attack against Manston. Two days later he was involved in the second raid against Manston, and in the afternoon of the 15th, took part in the attack on Martlesham Heath airfield. Upon joining the unit Rubensdörffer told him that he would be attached to the Staff Flight as z.b.V. (zur besonderen Verwendung = for special duties, but more likely to mean supernumerary) and Benedens flew with the Staff Flight on the Croydon raid. He recalled the raid thus: 'In the early evening we flew a further mission, it was to be the most fateful undertaken by Erprobungsgruppe 210. This time our target was Kenley airfield. We were accompanied by machines of JG 52 as fighter escort, who lost us, however, before we reached the target area. As Hauptmann Rubensdörffer gave the order to attack and we dived down onto the target, we were already being attacked by Hurricanes. I think every pilot was as nervous as I was. A terrible dogfight started, during which I was wounded, but I did not realise I was wounded until I was in the 'Abwehrkreis'. In the awful confusion after the combat everyone had so much to do, in order not to be shot down. I reached Calais-Marck totally exhausted. We learned later that we had attacked, not Kenley, but Croydon. I will never forget this raid on Croydon in my entire life'.

Benedens spent two months in hospital following his return to Calais-Marck. Several small pieces of metal were removed from his left foot and thigh. Curiously his Bordfunker Unteroffizier Mass was unwounded. When he recovered, Benedens was posted once again to the Erprobungsstelle at Rechlin.

So much for the action in the air, how was the raid viewed from the ground? Sergeant Henry Newton of 111 Squadron, who was to be shot down and badly burned three days later, was at Croydon during the raid and recalls that the attacking aircraft were first of all identified as Blenheims, but that was quickly amended as they commenced their diving attack! The blast from the first bomb threw him to the ground and he very quickly joined others in a shelter. He did not hear any fire from the Army soldiers situated on the roof of a nearby hotel (sited there to in order to shoot enemy paratroopers should a landing be attempted at Croydon airfield), nor from ground level. There was reply from ground level, however, Flinders stating so in his combat report. The parachute and cable device installed at Croydon was not operated simply because the attack came from such an angle that they were rendered impotent.

As well as damage to the airfield, there was damage caused to property in the immediate area around the airfield. In 1949 Croydon Council produced a book entitled 'Croydon and the Second World War' and it deals with the 15th August raid in some detail. It was moved to record that: 'From the cold military point of view the attack was an enemy success. Bombs fell upon the airfield but it seems not to have received major damage and this and such casualties as may have occurred there were not revealed. The neighbourhood suffered certainly. At right angles to the airfield, running along its edge, were the several hangars and workshops of aircraft companies; and beyond them to the north the main factory area of Croydon lying along Purley Way; while on the opposite side of the Way lies the large Waddon housing estate. The bombs that overshot the aerodrome these received; they hit the Redwing Aircraft Factory and the NSF factory which were destroyed, and in the latter the Board of Management, which was meeting, had all its members killed. The premises of the Bourjois scent factory and of Philips', Mullards' and of other firms were also hit. On the housing estate bombs fell in Crowley Crescent and Coldharbour Way with fatal casualties, and in Foss Avenue and Waddon Way. The human results of the raid were the deaths of sixty-two persons, serious injury to thirty-seven and lighter injuries to 137'.

John Southall, a 12 year-old at the time who lived in 55 Crowley Crescent set down his memories of the raid: "Although I frequently visited Croydon's many cinemas, usually in the school holidays or on a Saturday afternoon, my father had never previously taken me to a performance on a week-day evening. The feature film - Richard Tauber in 'Blossom Time' – was certainly not to my taste (I preferred cowboy or war films!) but also showing was a documentary about the scuttling of the German Grand Fleet in Scapa Flow in 1919. As my father had been serving in the Royal Navy when the event took place he particularly wanted to see it - hence our visit. So after cycling home from school followed by a hurried tea my father and I walked the half mile to the Classic Cinema in Brighton Road, south Croydon in time for the start of the programme at 6.15 p.m..

"We had seen the inevitable cartoon, news plus the Scapa Flow documentary and were about 15 minutes into 'Blossom Time' when mysterious thuds began convulsing the building for about three minutes. Fellow patrons were beginning to exchange anxious glances when the screen suddenly went blank and the manager jumped onto the stage to say that Croydon airport was being bombed and would everyone remain in their seats. For a minute or so no-one moved but inquisitiveness and/or fear soon had people heading for the foyer, despite appeals from the usherettes to "keep away from the glass". My father and I were no exception and as we reached the street we could see black smoke from the fires at the airport billowing into the sky behind the Whitgift Public School.

"As there were no longer sounds of bombs or any aerial activity (the latter having moved rapidly away southwards as the RAF fighters chased the fleeing attackers towards the Channel) my father and I walked briskly home. Smoke was still pouring from the shattered hangars and factories on the northern side of the airport and we had not proceeded far along our street before we encountered evidence of local destruction – shattered windows and tileless roofs. Two bombs falling in the gardens of houses at the eastern side of our street were responsible for these initial signs of damage but, 200 yards further on, we could see similar damage and the road carpeted in mud. As 55 Crowley Crescent came into view I excitedly remarked "Cor, look what they've done to our house, dad!". The roof was mainly devoid of tiles which lay in broken heaps on the ground and all the windows were shattered. As we opened the garden gate the air raid sirens wailed the alert - 15 minutes too late.

"We were relieved to discover my mother and four year-old sister crouching in our Anderson shelter but they too had miraculously been absent when the bombs fell. Because my father and I had been going out my mother had decided to take my sister to Croydon's Surrey Street market to do the week's shopping a day earlier than the usual Friday. Their mission completed they had been walking back across Duppas Hill – a local park – when my sister pestered to be allowed to play on the swings and slide. She was thus engaged when the German formation appeared overhead at about 3,000 feet diving towards the airport. My mother saw the bombs released before she and my sister hid in the bushes to escape the machine gun fire which was coming from the Messerschmitts and their pursuing Hurricanes.

"It soon became evident from an examination of the interior of our house that it would be impossible to sleep indoors as with the ceilings down and most of the tiles gone, the bedrooms were covered in plaster and exposed to the sky. So as darkness fell we took four canvas deck chairs into the Anderson shelter and tried to settle down for the night. However it was impossible to sleep properly as it was too uncomfortable and the experience of the past few hours had been so traumatic."

One final incident remains to be recorded regarding the Croydon raid. Otto Hintze vividly recalled that on the way back to Calais-Marck he heard over the radio: 'Please fly slowly, pilot is wounded' and discovered a Bf 110 about 200 m. below being followed by three Hurricanes. 'I turned with my squadron behind the Me 110, the 3 Hurricanes disappeared and we escorted the Me 110 to Calais'. The Bf 110 escorted back to Calais-Marck could well have been that of Unteroffizier Werner Neumann and his Bordfunker Obergefreiter Karl Stoff. Although it has never been recorded before, Karl Stoff and his pilot counted 57 hits on their Bf 110 when they landed. Hintze and his 3rd Staffel did not escort the Bf 110 of Benedens, since he returned to Calais-Marck in the company of several other Bf 110s of the unit. It must remain a mystery as to who Hintze heard over the intercom on the return to Calais-Marck.

Each Luftwaffe unit was required to report the injury to, or death of, or loss in action of, every member of their unit. This took the form of a typed return completed at unit level on a document called 'Namentliche Verlustmeldung' – Loss List of Names. This was completed in addition to the aircraft loss return which was for the benefit of the Luftwaffe Quartermaster in order to make good aircraft losses to units. The completed Namentliche Verlustmeldung was normally signed by the Adjutant of the unit; on this day Horst Fiedler had been shot down and the task of signing the list fell to Martin Lutz. Lutz is given as 'Oberleutnant u. stellv. Gruppenkommandeur'. 'stellv.' is an abbreviation of 'stellvertreter', which would translate as deputy. Lutz therefore became Acting-Gruppenkommandeur on the loss of Rubensdörffer. It should also be noted that after the Croydon raid, the only casualties set down in the Namentliche Verlustmeldung return were those members who did not return to base. Although wounded and hospitalised for two months, there is no mention of Benedens in the return.

One final statistic should be considered concerning the Croydon raid. All previously published accounts have stated that 23 aircraft of the unit carried out the Croydon raid. 23 aircraft took off for the raid, but with the return of S9+EK to base when part-way across the Channel, the correct number of aircraft attacking Croydon was 22.

COMBAT - 20 AUGUST

Weather conditions were not particularly good over southern England on the morning of Tuesday 20th August, but that did not deter Erprobungsgruppe 210 from sending aircraft on a mission up the east coast of England. Following the raids against land targets of the previous few days, this was a reversion to the anti-shipping role previously undertaken by the unit. The exact number of aircraft sent is not known; the intercepting British aircraft sighted only three.

'A' Flight of 66 Squadron, comprising Red and Yellow sections, were airborne from Coltishall at 10:35 hours, Red Section of Flight Lieutenant Gillies (Red 1), Sergeant Cameron (Red 2) and Pilot Officer Bodie (Red 3) in the lead with Pilot Officer Kennard (Yellow 1), Pilot Officer Cooke (Yellow 2) and Pilot Officer Cruickshanks (Yellow 3) following. Three aircraft, identified as Me 110s, were sighted by the six Spitfires at 10:44 hours about 5 miles south of Lowestoft at a height of 11,000 feet, approximately 4,000 feet above the British fighters.

The combat which then followed is vividly described by the surviving combat reports of the six RAF pilots. 'A' Flight of 66 Squadron and the three aircraft of Erprobungsgruppe 210 approached each other head-on, the German aircraft having the height advantage. Flight Lieutenant Gillies reported: 'After passing underneath enemy we did a climbing turn to port in order to engage from the rear and below. Enemy first saw us when we arrived in astern position. They were flying in wide vic formation on course 340° M. On sighting us enemy went into a steep diving turn to starboard in wide line astern'. Gillies then led his section in a No. 1 attack upon the rear German aircraft. After firing two 3-second bursts he noticed that the starboard engine of the Bf 110 began to slow up and it was unable to keep formation with the other two aircraft. Sergeant Cameron then attacked the same aircraft and with his second burst noted the starboard engine had caught fire. Pilot Officer Bodie also observed that the starboard engine had caught fire, but was unable to see what ultimately happened to the Bf 110, as it dived down through clouds.

Pilot Officer Kennard then led Yellow Section into the attack, and with the starboard engine of their Bf 110 D already virtually useless, the fate of 25 year-old Feldwebel Martin Wohlfahrt, piloting the aircraft, and his Bordfunker, Gefreiter Albert Dietrich, aged 22, was sealed. Pilot Officer Kennard attacked an enemy aircraft 'which another Spitfire was firing at and noticed when he broke away the starboard engine was alight. I carried on with my attack, and followed E/A through clouds after my attack, and one of the crew jumped in his parachute at about 1,000 feet. E/A crashed in the sea and sank, and the parachute landed in the water about 500 yards away. He abandoned his parachute and started swimming'. Hugh Kennard, who eventually rose to the rank of Wing Commander, later recalled that another aircraft was damaged and the third aircraft 'was only saved by the fact that we had then run out of ammunition and I recall that we formated on it and waved him a fond farewell and returned to base'.

Pilot Officer Cooke, following his Section No. 1, also carried out an astern attack on the same aircraft, broke away to starboard and turned in and then delivered a quarter attack. He too followed the stricken aircraft down, saw one crew member bail out and witnessed the crash of the Bf 110 in the sea. He also remembered the combat and recalled that 'the rear firing gunner continued to fire during the whole of the descent from 10,000-12,000 ft. down to sea level when it finally ditched. I was much impressed by the actions of the German crew. One at least of the crew, I think the pilot, escaped from the a/c and started to swim, in what direction neither he nor I could know precisely, but as I flew over him he looked up and shook his fist at me! I reported by radio and rescue services were alerted, but neither a/c nor crew were found. They were a brave crew. I admit I was impressed and sorry they could not be saved. I would like to record my admiration for the bravery of the enemy crew'.

Although none of the British aircraft were shot down, Flight Lieutenant Gillies aircraft received hits in the oil tank, port wing and rocker box but there was no engine failure and he returned to base safely.

There is mention in the 66 Squadron combat reports of another Bf 110 being damaged, but the damage must have been of minor importance as there is no record in the German loss returns for this date of a damaged Bf 110 of Erprobungsgruppe 210 returning to base.

Just as the Namentliche Verlustmeldung for 15th August betrayed who was Acting-Gruppenkommandeur, so the list for 20th August tells us that Oberleutnant Werner Weymann of 1st Staffel became acting-Adjutant of the unit. Weymann would ultimately become Staffelkapitän of 1st Staffel when Lutz finally became Gruppenkommandeur.

COMBAT - 22 AUGUST
CONVOY 'TOTEM' and MANSTON

The convoy 'TOTEM' passed through the Dover straits on the morning of 22nd August and after ineffective shelling by German artillery batteries near Cap Griz Nez, the two Bf 110 Staffeln of Erprobungsgruppe 210 were despatched against the convoy, with a Gruppe of Bf 109s as escort. On the British side, 610 Squadron from Biggin Hill and 'B' Flight of 54 Squadron from Manston intercepted the attacking force and succeeded in preventing the 'Jabo' Bf 110s of the unit from inflicting damage on the convoy. One of 610 Squadron's Spitfires crash-landed near Hawkinge, the pilot being unhurt; 'B' Flight of 54 Squadron suffered the loss of one Spitfire also, in this case the pilot was killed when the aircraft crashed into the Channel. Unteroffizier Ernst Glaeske and his Bordfunker Konrad Schweda of 2nd Staffel, Erprobungsgruppe 210 had a lucky escape on this mission. Glaeske formated on what he believed to be a Bf 109 only to find that it was a Spitfire! The starboard engine of their Bf 110 was shot-up by this Spitfire and they returned to Calais-Marck on the power of the port engine only. 610 Squadron were attacked by the Bf 109 escort fighters and their Operations record Book makes no mention of combat with Bf 110s. 'B' Flight of 54 Squadron also tangled with the Bf 109s, but Pilot Officer Hopkins reported: 'Whilst on convoy patrol (cloud base 1500 feet) I encountered a Me 110 (Jaguar) approaching it head on. I opened fire some distance away and saw my bullets entering cockpit and pieces fell off. E/A commenced a steep dive but I did not see him entering water as I had to pull up into the clouds to avoid e/a. I am sure e/a must have crashed into the sea'. A hand-written note beneath Hopkins' signature by 54 Squadron's Intelligence Officer, Patrick Shallard, states that a Searchlight Post confirmed the destruction of the Bf 110, but they may, in fact, have unwittingly confirmed the crash of Sergeant Collett who, as stated above, was shot down into the Channel during this engagement.

In the early evening Erprobungsgruppe 210 paid a further visit to Manston. However by now all 600 (Blenheim) Squadron personnel had moved to Hornchurch and those ground personnel still remaining at Manston had become very adept at taking cover in the face of an incoming raid.

Although bombs once again struck hangars, stores and offices and depleted the station even further, there were no casualties to personnel. Manston's Record Book, which must have been one of the few things left intact on the airfield by this time, recorded precisely: 'A further attack was made by a squadron of Me 109s and Me 110s. About seven bombs were dropped, and hangars in the

East Camp damaged. There were no casualties'. The unit returned to Calais-Marck without loss.

COMBAT - 24 AUGUST

Erprobungsgruppe 210 flew two missions on 24th August, both in Gruppe strength. The unit had flown to their forward base at Calais-Marck by 08:00 hours but carried out no combat missions in the morning. They finally took off at 14:15 hours and headed for Manston. Balthasar Aretz and Rolf Schilleng were on their 2nd 'Feindflug' in S9+DK, W. Nr. 3370. Despite Erprobungsgruppe 210's attacks of 12th, 14th and 22nd August, and attacks by other units also, Manston continued to have RAF squadrons operating from it. 264 (Defiant) Squadron had a lucky escape just after mid-day when an incoming raid on Manston almost caught them on the ground. That raid had given Manston a further hammering. Erprobungsgruppe 210 were about to put the final nail in the Manston coffin. Their raid left Manston a complete shambles: telephone lines cut, hangars and living quarters destroyed, aircraft on the ground badly damaged and the station armoury well alight. Erprobungsgruppe 210 retired without loss after completing their mission. Manston was finished. 264 Squadron, who had been operating out of Manston, retired to Hornchurch; personnel were evacuated who were not involved in station defence or the servicing of aircraft – in effect Manston became almost an emergency landing ground for the RAF.

The number of missions required to knock-out an airfield like Manston should have been used as a rider by the Luftwaffe High Command to show exactly what was needed to produce a successful conclusion in the phase against RAF airfields. Fortunately for the RAF, they appeared not to understand the depth needed to permanently disable all of the RAF's airfields in the south of England. In hindsight it may also be considered that they lacked the capability to do so.

Erprobungsgruppe 210's other mission on 24th August was against 'Kustenbefestigung' – coastal fortifications, and lasted approximately 50 minutes, from about 18:30 hours to 19:20. However the actual target has never been traced and it does not appear to have caused concern to any part of the south coast of England.

COMBAT - 26 AUGUST
FOLKESTONE

Erprobungsgruppe 210 carried out a raid on the south coast of England around lunchtime, with Balthasar Aretz taking off from Calais-Marck on his 4th Feindflug at 11:25, marking the target in the margin of his Flugbuch as 'Folkstone airfield'. Otto Hintze's Flugbuch shows him taking off five minutes later in his regular Bf 109 E-4/B, 'Yellow 1'. It has not been established that either Hawkinge or Lympne were attacked at this time on this day, and it is likely that the unit was part of a larger force which bombed Folkestone at this time. All aircraft returned to base safely, and this would appear to be the only mission carried out on this day.

Siegfried Tröppl was posted in to the unit in late August, and recorded his first flight on 28th August 1940 as a training flight with his Staffelkapitän, Oberleutnant Wilhelm-Richard Rößiger, at the controls of Bf 110 D, S9+DK. Following this flight he carried out three solo local practise flights. Tröppl was an experienced pilot, having served with 7th Staffel, Stukageschwader 77, and successively with 12th and 10th Staffeln of Lehrgeschwader 1, flying Junkers 87s with all three Staffeln. He had an impressive combat record to call upon, having flown 38 enemy missions by the time of his transfer to Erprobungsgruppe 210.

Following a visit to many units between 20th and 25th August, Erhard Milch produced a written report to Hermann Göring on 26th August. Among various matters reported by Milch on Erprobungsgruppe 210 was that the unit were short of "11 Me 110 D-0s and 1 Me 109 E-4, as well as 5 Officer-crews for Me 110, including 1 Adjutant and 1 Technical Officer, 4 NCO-crews for Me 110, and 1 officer for Me 109".

The report went on to state: "1. Staffel, which came from Zerstörers, and 3. Staffel, are in good order. 2. Staffel, which came from Stukas, has suffered heavy losses and is not on a par with the other two Staffeln". This appears to be a little harsh, as 2nd Staffel had carried out 'Jabo' missions from the outset, and had lost 2 aircraft in July due to low-level attacks on shipping, when 1st Staffel had flown pure escort missions. They had lost just over twice as many Bf 110s as 1st Staffel in training and combat, and this may have affected morale to some degree. Milch also commented that the Bf 110s and Bf 109s of the unit should be outfitted with the DB 601 'N' engines, and that 3rd Staffel had received 3 pilots without any combat experience, a matter which was not right for the special missions which the unit flew.

COMBAT - 30 AUGUST
BIGGIN HILL

On 30th August the RAF airfield whose name was to become famous as an example of the fighting spirit of the RAF during the Battle of Britain, Biggin Hill, was attacked by Erprobungsgruppe 210. Previously published accounts of the Battle of Britain have stated that the raid which took place at 18:00 hours on 30th August was carried out by a Staffel of Ju 88s. This belief has been held solely due to incorrect identification of the raiders by ground personnel at the airfield, an easy mistake to make given the circumstances of the raid.

The 'Flugbuch' of Unteroffizier Balthasar Aretz (the relevant page of which is reproduced in Appendix 4) shows that he was airborne at 17:25 British time for his 5th Feindflug, the margin entry showing the target – Flugplatz Biggin Hill. Erprobungsgruppe 210 hit Biggin Hill at 18:00 hours, the station personnel having very little warning of the impending raid. The reason for the lack of proper warning was due to a mains supply failure on eighty miles of the south coast of England which put radar stations out of action completely. Although the Germans were not to know of the problems for the British defences at the time, Erprobungsgruppe 210 took full advantage of the breakdown in the radar chain.

The unit attacked from about 1,000 feet and hit their allotted target with devastating accuracy. This was no doubt aided by the fact that there was no interference from British fighters. The airfield was left a total shambles. The death toll among station personnel was thirty-nine with another twenty-six wounded. Most of those killed were in a shelter which received a direct hit. Water mains and gas and electricity supplies were cut, and the telephone cable connecting Biggin Hill with all service operations under its control was severed. The consequences of this latter disablement was that Biggin Hill had to pass control temporarily to Hornchurch.

Elsewhere on the airfield, two aircraft were destroyed and a hangar received a direct hit. Workshops, the Guardroom and Armoury, stores, the Meteorological Office and the transport compound were also damaged, the airfield losing nearly all of its transport on charge at that time. Telephone communications were only repaired finally on the following day at mid-day, only for a further raid by Dorniers several hours later to destroy them once again.

Six Hurricanes of 79 Squadron took off from Biggin Hill during the raid and claimed to have shot down two of the raiding aircraft, but this contention is not supported by the facts. On this occasion Erprobungsgruppe 210 returned to Calais-Marck with no losses following the mission.

The undoubted success of the raid on Biggin Hill on 30th August for Erprobungsgruppe 210 was a complete vindication of the 'Jabo' technique, albeit with the assistance of the lack of radar which resulted in a clear run-in on the target. If the Luftwaffe had persisted with this type of raid and had not changed course on 7th September, the RAF may well have been crippled to a far greater extent than it was in the following weeks.

COMBAT - 31 AUGUST

On 31st August, following the successful raid on Biggin Hill the previous day, Erprobungsgruppe 210 took off just after noon to attack an airfield where, sixteen days earlier, they had suffered their heaviest loss of the Battle of Britain so far. Their mission was against the airfield at Croydon, and at this time on 31st August Erprobungsgruppe 210 was just part of a large formation heading inland for their allotted targets.

While Siegfried Tröppl continued with his Bf 110 training, carrying out 5 bombing practise flights on this day, Aretz and Schilleng were airborne with 2nd Staffel at 12:05 in what was becoming their normal mount, S9+EK. Otto Hintze, in 'Yellow 1', led his 3rd Staffel off five minutes after 2nd Staffel. It was to be Hintze's 120th Feindflug. On the ground at Croydon, pilots of 85 Squadron were in their cockpits, waiting for the order to take-off from the Kenley Controller. The Controller left it to the last possible moment before giving the 'Go-ahead' for 85 Squadron to take-off. As they cleared the ground the first bombs were falling on Croydon, the British pilots being fortunate that they evaded the bombs. Some accounts have stated that this raid was carried out by Dornier aircraft, but aircraft identification was at fault; the bombing aircraft were Bf 110s (in concert with 3rd Staffel Bf 109s) of Erprobungsgruppe 210. It would not be the last time that the unit's aircraft would be mis-identified as Dornier 17s or 215s. Squadron Leader Peter Townsend, leading 85 Squadron, ordered his pilots to pursue the Me 110 'Jaguars' which had just bombed Croydon. Although 85 Squadron set off in pursuit of Erprobungsgruppe 210, the Bf 109 E fighter cover did its job effectively in protecting the fighter-bombers. Notwithstanding that, the unit did lose one Bf 110, a D-0 variant, W. Nr. 3381, coded S9+GK, a 2nd Staffel machine crewed by Unteroffizier Ernst Glaeske, pilot, and Obergefreiter Konrad Schweda, his Bordfunker, both aged 23. Schweda was badly wounded by an attacking RAF fighter and the port engine was disabled. Glaeske landed his aircraft quickly in the hope of saving his Bordfunker's life, but was not successful. Schweda died of his wounds. Of the aircraft, the RAF crash investigators reported: 'Me 110. Shot down at Stansted, near Wrotham on 31/8/40. Markings S9+GK (G in black with white edging). Spinner coloured white. Cause of crash due to fighter action. Port engine and tail unit hit by .303 strikes. Aircraft in fair condition. Armament standard 5 machine guns and 2 20 mm cannon. No armour plate found. Aircraft fitted with DB 601 engines. Camouflage standard, green and blue'. The aircraft did not carry the unit emblem of the British Isles in a gunsight, only because there had not been time to paint the motif on the forward fuselage of the machine.

Two other Bf 110s of the unit returned to Calais-Marck after having been damaged in combat, both 2nd Staffel machines. S9+DK returned with 30% damage; S9+EK of Aretz and Schilleng, returned with 25% damage. Two photographs accompany the text showing the aircraft and crew of S9+EK after landing at Calais-Marck.

At Croydon, an account was prepared of the raid. The damage was nowhere near as extensive as on 15th August: a hangar belonging to the Redwing Aircraft company was destroyed by a direct hit by a 500 Kg. bomb and 'B' hangar suffered broken glass and damage to walls. A new 'Dennis' 30 cwt. lorry was destroyed and the Airman's cookhouse received machine gun hits. One bomb landed in the centre of Purley Way and thirteen other bombs landed on a recreation ground to the east of Purley Way. The raid lasted six minutes.

Pilots of 3rd Staffel, from left: Marx; Hintze; Drawe and Emmerich.

Below: Oberleutnant Otto Hintze taxis his Bf 109 E out of its blast pen at Denain at the start of a mission, with the help of a member of the groundcrew at the starboard wingtip. A 250 Kg. bomb hangs from the ETC 500 bomb-rack.

Messerschmitt 110 fighter-bomber freshly delivered to the unit, which has not yet had unit codes applied to it.

Unteroffizier Balthasar Aretz (left) and Gefreiter Rolf Schilleng on Bf 110, W. Nr. 3372. They flew this aircraft on two practise flights on 5th August 1940, but it is not known whether they ever flew it in combat, as the fuselage code is not known.

There is some activity in the cockpit area of this Bf 110 C-6 of 1st Staffel in bright summer conditions.

Three views of a Bf 110 C-6 of 1st Staffel. The letter 'T' is discernible under the starboard wing of the aircraft, which would mean it was the machine in which Leutnant Erich Beudel and Obergefreiter Otto Jordan were shot down and killed following the raid on Croydon on 15th August 1940. The fairing which enclosed the 30 mm. cannon can be seen on the ground below the fuselage. Leutnant Horst Marx is the officer in the peaked cap in the photographs. The multi-colored spinners, usual for 1st Staffel aircraft, are evident.

2nd Staffel 'Jabo' with bombs in place in its camouflaged pen.

Opposite
Two views of a Messerschmitt 110 of the unit being 'bombed-up', with the unit emblem showing clearly on the fuselage side. The line of the rivet holes on the lower forward fuselage conforms exactly to the shape of the 'Dackelbauch' fitted to the 'D-0' variant. In August 1940 British Intelligence intercepted a Luftwaffe memorandum which gave details of the Bf 110 D variants. It included: 'Bf 110 D-2 has 2 external containers (with choice between bombs or "basset belly" as preferred)'. This aircraft can therefore be correctly described as a 'D-2' variant, although in practise they were shown in loss tables as 'D-0' or 'D-3', as mentioned earlier.

Hauptmann Walter Rubensdörffer poses in front of a Mercedes staff car while members of his unit queue behind him at mess time.

A side view of a blast pen for a Bf 109 E-4/B of the unit, showing false trees and fencing painted on the side. Close examination shows that the unknown artist has painted the tree branches to conform exactly with the real branches visible above the pen.

Hauptmann Karl Valesi, attached to 3rd Staffel, wearing the optional white summer uniform for officers. The officer's dolch (dagger) and portepee (side-arm knot) are seen to excellent effect. Valesi was killed on a bombing practise flight on 7th August 1940 when his Bf 109 E-4/B did not pull out of its dive and crashed.

This page and opposite: Nine views of the burial ceremony for Leutnant Prokop; Unteroffizier Schultheis and Gefreiter Dust, early August 1940.

The grave of Hauptmann Karl Valesi at Denain.

Graves of Erprobungsgruppe 210 flying crew killed in flying accidents on 6th and 7th August 1940. From left: Hauptmann Valesi; Leutnant Prokop; Unteroffizier Schultheis and Gefreiter Dust.

Below: 1st Staffel Bf 110 C-6 with an unknown pilot in the cockpit and the usual distinguishing feature of 1st Staffel machines: multi-colored spinners. This C-6 carries a gun-camera in the nose, evidenced by the aperture which can be clearly seen.

Leutnant Kurt Bertram, pilot of 1st Staffel, who was shot down in combat over the Thames estuary over a convoy on 11th August 1940 while flying a Bf 110 C-6.

Flieger Christian Weiss of 1st Staffel, seen here during the early part of his military career. Weiss was shot down on the same mission as Kurt Bertram, and was also flying a Bf 110 C-6.

Obergefreiter Richard Keilhaupt, 1st Staffel Bordfunker to Christian Weiss, front row, right. Keilhaupt was posted missing with his pilot on 11th August 1940.

Christain Weiss's body was washed ashore on the coast of France and buried in a military cemetery. The inscription reads: Christian Weiss, Gefreiter, 1./Z. Gr. 210, Geb. 22.4.13 in Kulmbach, Gef. 11.8.40 über See. The adjacent grave is that of Feldwebel Herbert Aleith of 2nd Staffel, Kampfgeschwader 55, whose Heinkel 111 was shot down into the Channel on 11th July 1940.

Feldwebel Stutz in front of a 'Jabo' Bf 110 of 1st Staffel.

Flight Lieutenant Marcus Scroggie, 5th from right, and his Adjutant, with the WAAFs who were based at Pevensey radar station when Oberleutnant Martin Lutz and his 1st Staffel attacked it on 12th August 1940.

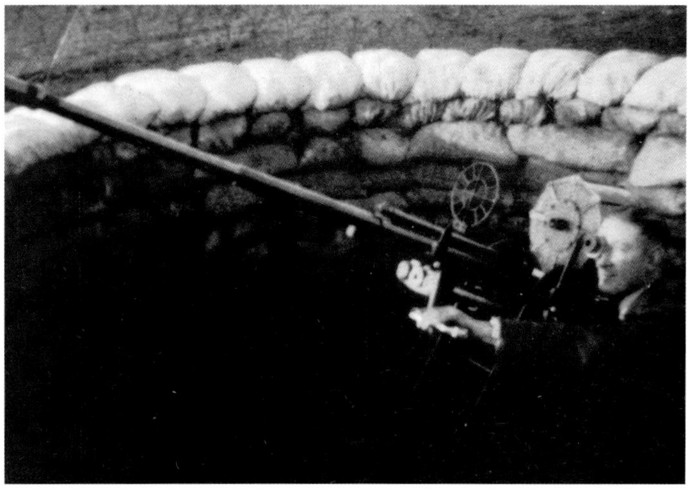

Anti-aircraft defences at Manston during the Battle of Britain, manned by Bill Brown of 600 Squadron.

Tom Beggs of 600 Squadron at a .303 post at Manston.

The remains of No. 4 Gun Post at Manston after a raid in August 1940.

600 Squadron members at No. 2 Gun Post after a raid in August 1940.

Tom Beggs of 600 Squadron holds a paddle retrieved from one of the Bf 110 Ds of Erprobungsgruppe 210 which was shot down onto Manston airfield on 14th August 1940.

Bf 110 D, S9+MK, of Steding and Schank. The tall Luftwaffe officer standing second left is Leutnant Walter Kloß

Walter Kloß is in view again in this photograph, covering the 'S' of the unit code of possibly the same aircraft as in the previous photograph.

Left: Unteroffizier Hans Steding, pilot with 2nd Staffel. Steding was shot down over Manston on 14th August 1940 and was killed when his aircraft crashed onto the airfield. Miraculously, his Bordfunker, Gefreiter Ewald Schank, baled out at low level and survived into captivity. Center: Gefreiter Ewald Schank, Bordfunker of Hans Steding, who baled out very low over Manston during the raid on 14th August 1940 and lived to tell the tale. Right: The original grave of Unteroffizier Hans Steding at the Municipal Cemetery in Minster, Kent, with the Imperial War Graves Commission marker in place.

A game of cards in progress for these men of 2nd Staffel. From left: unknown; Unteroffizier Richard Mayer, Bordfunker, and Leutnant Heinrich Brinkmann, pilot. Brinkmann and Mayer were shot down over Manston on 14th August 1940 and both were killed in the ensuing crash on the airfield.

The upside-down remains of S9+MK of Steding and Schank on Manston airfield following the raid of 14th August 1940. Behind the soldier can be seen the bomb rack and the muzzles of the two 20 mm. cannon. Also visible protruding from the leading edge of both wings are the retaining straps which held the inner wing fuel tanks in place. The censor has blanked-out buildings in the background of this photograph.

Taken at a prisoner-of-war camp in Canada during the war, this photograph shows Ewald Schank of 2nd Staffel, seated, centre, with prisoners from the other arms of the German military services.

A 500 Kg. bomb is carefully lined-up under the bomb rack of a Bf 110 of the unit. The significance of the light colored tip to the bomb is not known – the likely explanation is that it differentiates one type of bomb from another.

Another view of debris from the crash of S9+MK on Manston.

Right: The bomb in position on the starboard rack of the Bf 110. This view shows well the connection points of the bomb racks, and, immediately forward of it, the two rectangular ejection chutes for the spent cartridges of the 20 mm. cannon.

Mechanics crank the starboard engine of a Bf 110 of the unit. From the scuff marks on the bomb in this photograph, it is clear that this is the same aircraft as that shown in the two previous photographs.

Although of poor quality, this view shows a Bf 110 fighter-bomber of 1st Staffel with distinctive colored spinners and the unit emblem visible on the nose.

Army personnel pose in front of a 1st Staffel fighter-bomber with a light camouflage mottle over the upper surfaces. Again the unit emblem is visible.

An excellent photograph showing, from left to right: Walter Rubensdörffer; Otto Hintze (head bowed); Wilhelm-Richard Rößiger; Martin Lutz; Horst Marx; unknown behind Marx, and Horst Fiedler. All those identified were shot down between 15th August and 27th September 1940, only Hintze and Marx surviving into captivity.

Balthasar Aretz, left, and his Bordfunker, Rolf Schilleng, pose in front of a Bf 110 fighter-bomber with both engines running. Aretz and Schilleng flew their first combat mission on 15th August 1940 against Martlesham Heath in what was to become their regular mount, S9+EK.

Two views of SH-W of Pilot Officer Roberts of 64 Squadron. Roberts force-landed his Spitfire Mk. 1 close to Calais-Marck airfield in the afternoon of 15th August 1940. Roberts survived the crash, and Ernst Elfner recalled seeing him in the Command Room at Calais-Marck with Walter Rubensdörffer after the unit returned from the afternoon raid on Martlesham Heath.

Left: Hauptmann Walter Rubensdörffer, the Swiss-born first Commanding Officer of the unit, who was killed in action in Bf 110 D, S9+AB, W. Nr. 3338, following the Croydon raid of 15th August 1940. Center: Obergefreiter Ludwig Kretzer, Bordfunker of Walter Rubensdörffer, who was killed in action with his Gruppenkommandeur on 15th August 1940. Right: The original Imperial War Graves Commission marker on the grave of Walter Rubensdörffer and Ludwig Kretzer in Tunbridge Wells cemetery. Note the mis-spelling of Rubensdörffer. The unknown German airman buried with them is Unteroffizier Karl Geiswinkler of 6th Staffel, Jagdgeschwader 53, who crashed near Tunbridge Wells on the date shown.

Bf 109 E-4/B, 'Yellow 3' of Leutnant Horst Marx, in its blast pen at Denain.

The remains of Bf 110 D, S9+BB, W. Nr. 3374, of Oberleutnant Horst Fiedler, pilot and Adjutant of the Gruppe, and Bordfunker Unteroffizier Johann Werner, of the Staff Flight of the unit on Redhill aerodrome after being shot down on 15th August 1940. Fiedler died three days later of his wounds; Werner survived, and returned to Germany after the war following a spell of captivity. The W. Nr. 3374 can be seen on the fin, near the swastika. This is a somewhat unusual position, the normal placement of the W. Nr. being on the rear fuselage.

19 year-old Obergefreiter Otto Jordan, Bordfunker of Erich Beudel, killed in action with his pilot following the Croydon raid.

Leutnant Erich Beudel, pilot of 1st Staffel, who was killed in action following the Croydon raid in Bf 110 C-6, S9+TH. Beudel only flew a C-6 on the Croydon raid because his fighter-bomber Bf 110 was damaged on the raid against Martlesham Heath in mid-afternoon, and declared unfit for action upon return to Calais-Marck.

The wreckage of S9+TH being examined by RAF Intelligence Officers. The starboard engine has been wrenched from its mountings and the badly smashed cockpit area can also be seen.

Two further views of the wreckage of Bf 110 C-6, S9+TH. The solid green camouflage evident on the fin indicates that this C-6 carried the earlier style of camouflage, as seen in the some of the earlier photographs of the C-6 variant.

2nd Staffel Bf 110 D, S9+CK, W. Nr. 3341 of Oberleutnant Alfred Habisch, pilot, and Unteroffizier Ernst Elfner, Bordfunker. Note the single victory marking on the starboard fin.

Oberleutnant Alfred Habisch, pilot of 2nd Staffel, shot down in Bf 110 D, S9+CK, W. Nr. 3341, following the raid on Croydon on 15th August 1940. Habisch survived into captivity.

Unteroffizier Ernst Elfner, Bordfunker of Alfred Habisch, who also survived their shooting-down following the Croydon raid to spend the rest of the war in prisoner-of-war camps.

Preßluft f. Fahrw. Notbetätigung
150 atü

Opposite
Top: S9+CK of Habisch and Elfner was probably the most photographed Luftwaffe aircraft of the Battle of Britain. Here it is shown on street display with a 6d. admission charge for members of the public to examine it close-up. This view shows to good effect the top surface splinter camouflage pattern.

Below: A member of the public points to the unit emblem on S9+CK during the street display. The line giving the angle of dive is visible on the side glass panel of the cockpit, but of particular interest is what appears to be a previous emblem almost completely scraped off the aircraft beneath the Erprobungsgruppe 210 emblem. The small light colored rectangle above the man's wrist is where a manufacturer's plate had been, but was no doubt removed by a souvenir hunter when the machine came to earth in England.

Photos this page: Four views of S9+CK being prepared for display in Hendon Park, which began at 5 p.m. on Saturday 29th August 1940 and cost 6d. admission. The extended rear fuselage of the 'D' variant is clearly visible, as is the single victory marking on the fin.

When S9+CK was being prepared for display, the tail unit of the aircraft came away, revealing a collapsible boat and a set of emergency articles. These were placed on display, and, instead of displaying a German flying suit, one of the wardens decided to wear it while giving details of the aircraft to visitors. Here he is seen discussing a point with some children.

Members of the public wait patiently in line to examine the cockpit area which Habisch and Elfner had previously occupied during their incursions over southern England with the unit.

Below: S9+CK in splendid isolation in its roped-off enclosure at Hendon Park.

In the spring of 1941 S9+CK was shipped to the USA for the Vultee Corporation to examine. These five views show a close-up of the unit emblem; two views of the nose of the aircraft showing the gun-camera aperture and the machine guns to excellent effect; the fuselage being lifted off the SS Montanan at Los Angeles, and a close-up of the pilot's cockpit area, which shows that a couple of instruments had been removed.

This page and opposite: Another aircraft from the Croydon raid the subject of several photographs was the Bf 110 D, S9+CB, W. Nr. 3339, of the Technical Officer of the Gruppe, Leutnant Karl-Heinz Koch and his Bordfunker, Unteroffizier Rolf Kahl. The seven photographs show that Koch made a very good emergency landing with damaged engines. On one photograph, the censor has unsuccessfully tried to obliterate the unit code on the fuselage. The photographs also show that the starboard propeller was wrenched from the aircraft upon landing.

A 2nd Staffel 'line-shoot' with a Bf 110 forming a backdrop. Those identified are: 3rd from left – Feldwebel Bohne; 4th from right – Unteroffizier Kempenich; 3rd from right – Gefreiter Schilleng and, extreme right – Feldwebel Sommer.

Above: 1st Staffel personnel at Denain. Those marked with a '+' were killed in action against the British. Those identified are: 3rd from left – Unteroffizier Michi; 4th from left – Unteroffizier Kehren; 5th from left – Oberleutnant Martin Lutz; centre – Leutnant Ulrich Freiherr von der Horst; 5th from right – Unteroffizier Schulz; extreme right – Feldwebel Stütz.

Right: Feldwebel Martin Wohlfart, pilot, (left) pulls tongues at the camera, while Gefreiter Albert Dietrich, Bordfunker, (centre) looks quite serious. Wohlfart and Dietrich, a 2nd Staffel crew, were shot down into the sea on 20th August 1940 by 'A' Flight of 66 Squadron and posted missing.

Rolf Schilleng leans against the rear fuselage of Bf 110, S9+EK, W. Nr. 3377, after the tailwheel collapsed on landing at Calais-Marck on 21st August 1940. Aretz and Schilleng flew in this aircraft in the raid against Martlesham Heath in the afternoon of 15th August 1940, and later in the day against Croydon, when they had to abort the mission on the way to the target over the Channel.

Calais-Marck in the early afternoon of 31st August 1940. Aretz (left) and Schilleng after the second raid on Croydon by the unit. .303 hits can be seen on the fuselage and port aileron of S9+EK.

Further damage to S9+EK which was not visible in the previous photograph: a burst tyre and damage to the undercarriage. A ground mechanic also appears to be checking beneath the aircraft in the area of the port fuselage wing root.

Feldwebel Sommer and Gefreiter Schlee, a 2nd Staffel crew. Sommer was killed in action in the mid-war years; Schlee survived the war.

Hans von Boltenstern, seen here as an Oberleutnant. He was posted in as Gruppenkommandeur on 26th August 1940, succeeding Walter Rubensdörffer.

3rd Staffel officers, from left: Leutnant Heinz Schoenefeldt; Oberleutnant Otto Hintze and Leutnant Peter Emmerich. Schoenefeldt was posted to 3rd Staffel to replace Leutnant Horst Marx who was shot down into captivity on 15th August 1940.

4

September 1940

1 SEPTEMBER

On 1st September the two Messerschmitt 110 Staffeln left Denain just before 16:30 hours and landed some 45 minutes later at Amsterdam-Schipol airfield. The reason for the move was due to a reported imminent attack on the Dutch coast by British Naval units. Erprobungsgruppe 210 was the logical unit to deploy against such attacks since they had unparalleled experience of combat against naval craft. The 3rd Staffel Bf 109 'Jabos' left Denain in the early hours of the morning for their forward base of Calais-Marck but they had to wait almost 12 hours before Otto Hintze led his Staffel off at 16:00 hours for a mission over England which lasted just under an hour. In the coming weeks the practise of Erprobungsgruppe 210 not operating as a complete Gruppe would become more prevalent, ultimately resulting in the 3rd Staffel operating with the 'Jabo' Gruppe of Lehrgeschwader 2 (II./LG 2), flying as the rear formation to the other three Staffeln of that Gruppe. For the Bf 110 Staffeln at Amsterdam-Schipol nothing materialised and the aircraft returned to Denain just before 10:00 hours on the following day.

COMBAT – 4 SEPTEMBER

Soon after 06:30 hours on the morning of 4th September, the Bf 110s of Erprobungsgruppe 210 were airborne from Denain and landed at the forward base of Calais-Marck half an hour later. They had to wait until after mid-day, however, before taking off for a combat mission over southern England. Their target was the Vickers works at Weybridge. It has been previously stated that the raids on Vickers works were a waste of valuable Luftwaffe time and resulted in the needless loss of German crews since Vickers were involved at that time with the production of Wellington bombers, and the priority for the Luftwaffe was the destruction of the RAF fighter force, both in the air and in the factories. However such an argument misses an important point. On 4th September 'Operation Sealion' was still very much a viable proposition and the destruction of Great Britain's strategic bomber force must have been a high priority if an invasion fleet was to have any chance of success. That the Germans were aware of the type of aircraft being produced there is evident from the margin entry in Aretz's 'Flugbuch' which states clearly that the target was an 'airfield and works near Brooklands, Vickers Wellington'. Due to the damage to his 'E' four days previously, Aretz was in S9+BK for this mission.

Escort was provided by the Bf 110 fighters of the V./(Zerstörer) Gruppe of Lehrgeschwader 1 (V./(Z) LG 1). Based at Ligescourt, they were airborne at about 12:30 hours and met up with their charges – 14 Bf 110 fighter-bombers of Erprobungsgruppe 210. On the approach to the English coast RAF squadrons were sighted positioning for an attack on the incoming German raid. On seeing this the Gruppenkommandeur of Erprobungsgruppe 210, 34 year-old Hans von Boltenstern, tried a manoeuvre which had no chance of being successful at the height it was attempted. Putting his Bf 110 D-0, S9+AB, W. Nr. 3390, into a dive, with the intention of flattening-out at the bottom of the arc at sea level which would have left him flying towards France (a 'bunt' in RAF parlance), he quite simply did not have room to spare and crashed into the Channel without an RAF fighter having fired a shot at him. Hans von Boltenstern and his Bordfunker, Feldwebel Fritz Schneider, were killed in the crash. The rest of Erprobungsgruppe 210 reached their target but could only claim a partial success. British records show, however, that the raid of 4th September resulted in production being brought to a standstill. The damage took several days to clear and the raid resulted in the deaths of eighty-eight workers and over 600 injured. While Erprobungsgruppe 210 lost one Bf 110, V./(Z) LG 1 fared far worse, losing four Bf 110s on this raid.

Martin Lutz, who would succeed von Boltenstern as Gruppenkommandeur of Erprobungsgruppe 210, met his friend from their days in 1st Staffel, Zerstörergeschwader 1, Wolfgang Schenck, upon his return to Denain. Schenck was waiting in the crew room, and he recalled that Lutz entered the crew room and threw his flying gloves and helmet into a corner of the room in disgust at the manner of the loss of von Boltenstern. It is worthwhile at this juncture to introduce a pilot who was to become Staffelkapitän of 1st

Staffel, Erprobungsgruppe 210, would later be elevated to Gruppenkommandeur of I. Gruppe, Schnellkampfgeschwader 210 in Russia, and would eventually become Geschwaderkommodore of Schlachtgeschwader 2 and of Kampfgeschwader (J) 51, finishing the war having flown over 40 missions in the Messerschmitt 262 with the latter unit, and the unit he headed in working-up the 262 to fighter-bomber operational status, 'Kommando Schenck'. 'Bombo' Schenck had begun his war service with the I. Gruppe of ZG 1 during the Polish campaign. However all was not active service for Schenck. He had spent time at the Weapons Testing Station at Tarnowitz under the command of Oberstabsingenieur Bolan and was familiar with the 30 mm. cannon-armed Bf 110 C-6 aircraft operated by the unit in the earlier stages of the Battle of Britain. Schenck was wounded in the leg during the Battle of France in lone combat with nine Hurricanes and spent some time in hospital. Towards the end of August he heard that the Luftwaffe High Command intended to draft back into the airforce former crews who had been wounded but could take up operational flying again (an indication, perhaps, that the problem of shortage of experienced flying personnel was cutting as deeply into the Luftwaffe as it was into the RAF at that time). Schenck determined that if he were to resume combat flying again, he would do so only with his former unit and accordingly he reported to the base of Erprobungsgruppe 210, seeking out 1st Staffel. Martin Lutz advised him that there could be some problems, but that he would attend to the necessary paperwork. Schenck had his way. He was a practical man, always seeking to have implemented what he believed to be sound principles of air warfare and prepared to test operationally any idea which he believed would be successful. One example of the latter point is worth mentioning, although outside the timescale of this book: Schenck hit upon the idea of having remotely-controlled rearward-firing guns on the fuselage of the Bf 110 to pick off any enemy aircraft which might fasten on to his tail. Accordingly he contacted Bolan at Tarnowitz and Bf 110s were provided with the installation according to Schenck's instructions. However one thing was changed. Instead of a 20 mm. cannon on either side of the fuselage, the aircraft carried only rifle-calibre machine guns, much to Schenck's dismay. The major problem to be resolved was how to aim the rearward-firing armament. Schenck came up with a simple solution. He fitted a periscope to the Bf 110 which was linked to the 'Revi'. The mirrors were aligned in such a way that an aircraft which was behind his 110 would be seen by Schenck in his gunsight as though it was in front of him – port wing to his port, starboard wing to his starboard. He tested this in combat in Russia and shot down very easily a Russian aircraft which had fastened onto his tail. It was so easy too, he recalled. It only needed a couple of hits on the wing leading edge for the airflow to get inside the wing and rip it off. The Luftwaffe General Staff, whom Schenck had a low opinion of, rejected the idea at the time, but it was to be resurrected later on combat versions of the Messerschmitt 210 and 410.

Following the loss of von Boltenstern, Martin Lutz, for the second time in less than a month, penned his signature to a loss return as acting-Gruppenkommandeur. Three days later he was officially appointed Gruppenkommandeur of Erprobungsgruppe 210.

COMBAT – 6 SEPTEMBER

On 6th September Erprobungsgruppe 210 returned to the Brooklands area in an attempt to complete the job they had started two days earlier. Escort was once again provided by V./(Z) LG 1, and also by I./ZG 26. On this occasion V./(Z) LG 1 would fare better, losing no aircraft on this mission. Flying in over the English coast the unit carried out the usual jinking movements to avoid the Flak – the 'Flak waltz' as the German crews disparagingly called it. Erprobungsgruppe 210 reached the target without loss but after completing their attack several British fighters were encountered. Pilot Officer Dibnah of 1 Squadron, RAF reported that he broke away from his squadron because of trouble with the airscrew of his Hurricane but on the way back to base he sighted a large formation of 'Jaguar' aircraft bombing Brooklands aerodrome. After they had completed their work they turned for the coast and Dibnah followed, probably more in hope than expectation. He noticed a Bf 110 engaging two Hurricanes and as the Hurricanes broke away 'I did a beam attack on the e/a. He did a stall turn and I did a frontal attack on him. As I passed him he did a wavering turn and one of the crew baled out. The aircraft did a spiral dive into the ground and burst into flames. The member of the crew was captured by members of a service unit'. The only other combat report filed by an RAF pilot for combat with an enemy aircraft at that time in the area was by Pilot Officer Goodman, also of 1 Squadron. However the aircraft claimed by Goodman did not come down close to where the aircraft of Erprobungsgruppe 210 crashed, and as can be seen, the circumstances were different. Goodman claimed to have set the starboard engine of his quarry on fire, and because of accurate fire from the rear gunner of the Bf 110, Goodman had to bail out of his Hurricane.

The aircraft lost by Erprobungsgruppe 210 during the morning raid of 6th September was a Bf 110 D-0 variant coded S9+BH, W. Nr. 3373. The crew were 24 year-old Unteroffizier Gerhard Rüger, pilot, and Gefreiter Edmund Ernst, the 20 year-old Bordfunker. Nearly 44 years later Ernst vividly recalled the combat. S9+BH received hits from an enemy machine which rendered all the flying controls useless. Ernst had not been able to bring his single rearward-firing machine gun to bear on any British fighter. The engines were not hit but Rüger knew that there was no possibility of being able to return to base. Rüger instructed Ernst to bail out, which he did, and probably intended to evacuate the aircraft himself. Possibly because the Bf 110 had gone out of control, Rüger never managed to extricate himself from the aircraft and it crashed at Foyles farm, Crowhurst, near Oxted, Surrey. The RAF Intelligence Officers who visited the crash site reported that the aircraft had 'Markings S9+BH (B in Blue). Plate shows aircraft constructed by MIAG. Aircraft crashed following fighter action and lies in deep crater. Fire followed crash. 2 20 mm. cannon and 1 MG.15 have been found in crater. This aircraft is reported as having carried 2 50 Kg. bombs. No armour plate found. Crew of 2, one dead, one prisoner'. The reference to the Bf 110 only carrying 50 Kg. bombs is undoubtedly an underestimation. The more likely load would have been 2x250 Kg. or 2x500 Kg.

Ernst's recollections, considered with the combat accounts of the two British pilots, would rule out the likelihood of Goodman shooting down S9+BH. The sole candidate is Dibnah.

Ernst was taken into custody by Canadian troops stationed in the area and then passed through the usual channels before being shipped off to Canada to a Prisoner-of-War camp. While there, he became seriously ill and was repatriated in June 1944 through Spain and Italy, not the quietest of places at the time! A final twist came in 1945 when Ernst was called to military service, this time as a soldier, in that desperate attempt by Germany to halt the relentless advance by the Allied armies deep into their territory. He survived that ordeal also.

But what of Rüger? The RAF Intelligence report quoted earlier states the fate of both crewmen and would lead one to presume that Rüger would have received the normal burial given to fallen enemy aircrew in England in 1940. However a check at the Air Historical Branch of the RAF reveals that, despite the fact that burial certificates are held there for those German aircrew known to have died on British soil, no burial certificate is held for Gerhard Rüger. One individual who possibly holds the key to the solution of the ultimate fate of the body of Gerhard Rüger is Dennis Knight, author of *'Harvest of Messerschmitts'*. For many years Dennis gathered information from all over the south of England from official records and from many people who witnessed the Battle of Britain at first hand all those years ago. The account given by Dennis Knight comes from eye witnesses. It runs as follows: the aircraft of Rüger came down in a field and shortly before crashing, a body was seen to leave the aircraft. Whether Rüger had jumped, or had been sucked out of the cockpit by air pressure is not known. Apparently his body was discovered by Canadian soldiers some time later and he was buried beside a hedgerow in the field where his aircraft crashed. For many years local people used to put flowers on the simple grave on the anniversary of the crash. This is the likely solution to the mystery of where Gerhard Rüger is buried.

7-11 SEPTEMBER

Martin Lutz, who had been acting-Gruppenkommandeur following the loss of Rubensdörffer, and more recently following von Boltenstern's death, was finally appointed Gruppenkommandeur of Erprobungsgruppe 210 on 7th September. With the elevation of Martin Lutz to Gruppenkommandeur, Oberleutnant Werner Weymann became Staffelkapitän of 1st Staffel.

On 7th September the Bf 110s of the unit had no missions to fly. However 3rd Staffel flew in the huge armada of aircraft which Göring sent against London, the take-off time indicating that Erprobungsgruppe 210's Bf 109 Es were one of the last units to be airborne. As a result of this raid 3rd Staffel lost one of its 109s into the Channel on the way back to Calais-Marck. Feldwebel Otto Rückert ditched about 7 Kms. off the English coast, and aided by strong winds and an ability to keep swimming, he was rescued by the Seenotdienst close to the French coast and returned to his Staffel. Rückert was to be killed in action later in the war.

On 8th September Erprobungsgruppe 210 left Denain early in the morning and flew directly to Cherbourg-Ost airfield in order to continue their prosecution of the war against England from that base. In changing base, they also moved geographically from Kesselring's Luftflotte 2 to Hugo Sperrle's Luftflotte 3, the move bringing in its wake a different operational sphere for the unit, although loss returns to Headquarters were still recorded under Luftflotte 2. Whereas before they had operated over the south-east of England, their radius of action now took in Portsmouth, Southampton and the south-west of England. Very ominous for the Supermarine works at Southampton as events were to prove. The Flugbücher of Aretz, Tröppl and Hintze all record moving on to Dinard from Cherbourg-Ost on this day, the reason for which is unknown. They remained at Dinard overnight before returning to Cherbourg-Ost the following day.

Before commencing operations from Cherbourg-Ost, Erprobungsgruppe 210 were given a non-combat type of test to perform. The Luftwaffe High Command wanted to know whether the Channel Islands could take the two 'Jabo' types without any take-off or landing problems. Accordingly on 9th September Hintze led off his Staffel from Cherbourg-Ost at 17:25 hours and landed at Guernsey one hour and twenty five minutes later. The two Bf 110 Staffeln took off shortly after the 109s and landed at Jersey after a short flight of some fifteen minutes duration. No problems were encountered and the personnel of the unit were able to spend a day free from flying on their respective islands on 10th September before returning to Cherbourg-Ost on 11th September to take up once again the not-insignificant matter of the 'Luftschlacht gegen England'.

COMBAT – 11-26 SEPTEMBER SOUTHAMPTON

Refreshed from their spell on recently-conquered British soil, the crews of Erprobungsgruppe 210 prepared for their first mission from Cherbourg-Ost on 11th September. The target, clearly noted in Balthasar Aretz's Flugbuch was the Supermarine works at Woolston, Southampton, producing Spitfires. All three Staffeln of the unit were airborne from Cherbourg-Ost shortly after 15:30 hours and a course was set directly for the Spitfire works. Siegfried Tröppl, with his Bordfunker, Unteroffizier Otto Büttner, finally flew his first mission with the unit in S9+BK, his 39th combat mission in all. The aircraft of Erprobungsgruppe 210 approached in a shallow dive and Southampton Civil Defence records give the time of the first bombs falling as 16:13 hours. The bombs of Erprobungsgruppe 210 hit a factory and its environs, but the factory hit was the Cunliffe-Owen works which was involved in the assembly and testing of the Lockheed Hudson aircraft sent to Britain by the USA, and in the production of parts for the Stirling bomber. In the Cunliffe-Owen works, the 'Red' air raid warning sounded at 16:02 hours which was the signal for female factory workers to take shelter, the fair sex being given more time to reach the shelters than their male counterparts. Male staff remained at their workbenches until the

'Double Red' warning was given. On this occasion such was the swiftness of the incoming raid that no 'Double Red' warning was given. Casualties were 49 killed, 38 severely injured and 54 slightly injured, the majority of the deaths occurring in the factory. However there was no compensation for believing that any more lives would have been saved had the factory been evacuated in time; one of the air raid shelters which would have been full of workers received a direct hit with only two people inside. Erprobungsgruppe 210, no doubt unaware at that time that they had missed their intended target, suffered no losses and flew directly back to Denain. One eyewitness account refers to eight Stukas but this was obviously a case of mis-identifying the Jabo 109s for Ju 87s.

Reconnaissance photographs must have shown the Supermarine works to have still been intact and Erprobungsgruppe 210 was sent to Cherbourg-Ost once again on 15th September. The unit left Cherbourg-Ost at about 17:00 hours on 15th September with a force of 10 Bf 110s and 3 Bf 109s, bound once again for the Spitfire works at Southampton. Balthasar Aretz was back at Denain at this time, but Siegfried Tröppl, with Bordfunker Büttner, took part in S9+BK. The air raid warning sounded at 17:37 hours.

Erprobungsgruppe 210 had a clear run-in to the target, but failed once again to hit it. Civil Defence records state that: 'The damage to property was tremendous. It was confined almost entirely to small shops and small houses, no important buildings being affected. No damage to any military objective, though the windows in the Supermarine works were broken'. Casualties were 9 killed, 19 severely injured and 23 slightly injured. 34 properties were destroyed, 81 others were so badly damaged that they had to be demolished and 1,106 properties received damage of varying degrees which was repairable. Some damage had been done to power and water supplies but not to a critical degree. Erprobungsgruppe 210 would have to try again.

Following the raid of 15th September, 3rd Staffel did fly out to Cherbourg on 18th September and returned to Denain on the same day, and also fly out again to Cherbourg on 20th September, not returning to Denain until 22nd September, but no further combat missions were flown while at Cherbourg and they took no further part in attacks against the Supermarine works. From Denain they were sent on leave for a well-earned rest from operational duties. Otto Hintze's Flugbuch shows 135 flights of every nature in 61 days from 13th July to 11th September inclusive, of which 39 were combat missions. A heavy schedule indeed when taken with additional duties inherent in the role of a Staffelkapitän. Siegfried Tröppl's Flugbuch records no activity after returning to Denain on 18th September until 30th September. Perhaps a period of well-earned rest was taken after his 40th combat mission. However as Tröppl leaves the scene for a time, Balthasar Aretz returns for the raid of 24th September with his Bordfunker Rolf Schilleng, in his regular aircraft, S9+EK.

24th September saw Erprobungsgruppe 210 over Southampton, going flat-out for the Supermarine works once again. The works was divided into two main sections approximately half a mile apart. Both were on the eastern side of the River Itchen, the southerly site known as the Woolston works was the original site of the company from where the prototype Spitfire first saw the light of day. When the production order was placed for 310 Spitfires in 1936 a large assembly works was built to the north of the Woolston works; this was called the Itchen works.

Erprobungsgruppe 210 took off from Cherbourg-Ost at 13:00 hours and such was the suddenness of their attack that the air raid warning sirens only sounded over Southampton six minutes after the unit had released its payload. 21 year-old Woolston worker Cyril Russell kept a diary of those days at the Supermarine works and he recalls that the first the Woolston workers knew of an incoming raid on 24th September was when the Anti-Aircraft guns opened up. Running north-south adjacent to the Woolston and Itchen works is the Portsmouth-Southampton railway line on a 20-foot embankment and the shelters for the factory workers were situated on the opposite side of this embankment. Access to the shelters was by way of an archway cut through the embankment. The Woolston workers had to cover half a mile, including passage through the archway, to reach the shelters. The number of workers heading for the shelters, and the narrowness of the archway, was bound to cause problems. Cyril Russell and some of his fellow-workers decided that if a raid was imminent, they would not head for that archway.

Erprobungsgruppe 210's bombs fell at 13:30 hours very close to the Itchen works but again no damage was caused to prevent the continued operation of the Supermarine complex. Some bombs again fell in the residential area near to the factories, but the bomb which did most damage was that which scored a direct hit on the archway when it was full of workers heading for the shelters. This particular incident contributed most to the final death toll for the day of 42. Cyril Russell only managed to get between 50-60 yards away from the south end of the Woolston factory before the first bombs came hurtling down and he immediately threw himself to the ground. Regarding the archway incident, he believes that the late air raid warning actually saved lives on this occasion. 'The delay was such that there was no time for the Woolston factory staff to cover the half mile to the shelters and the bottleneck archway. It also follows that the short time available did not allow even the Itchen works staff to reach safety and they were caught in the bottleneck themselves'.

Erprobungsgruppe 210 carried out another raid over Southampton three hours later but still did not hit the Supermarine works. On this day the unit suffered the loss of one aircraft, a Bf 110 D-0, coded S9+HH, W. Nr. 3384. The crew of Leutnant Ulrich Freiherr von der Horst, the 22 year-old pilot, and 24 year-old Obergefreiter Franz Öllers, Bordfunker, crashed with their aircraft into the Channel off Southampton and were never found. Öllers would have celebrated his 25th birthday two days later. There is some discrepancy between British and German records as to the cause of the loss of S9+HH. British records state that it was shot down by Anti-Aircraft fire; German sources state that it was shot down by English fighters, although no claim can be traced. Wolfgang Schenck recalled that the pilot, Leutnant von der Horst, 'was a wonderful boy, tall, large and friendly. He always thought he was going to be killed in action. A sad loss'.

On 25th September Kampfgeschwader 55 (KG 55) carried out their attack on the Bristol Aeroplane Company at Filton, near Bristol, while Erprobungsgruppe 210 carried out what was believed to be a diversionary raid on Portland to coincide with the main attack by KG 55. Fifteen houses were destroyed by Erprobungsgruppe 210's raid, as well as damage to some oil tanks, telephone lines being disrupted and the main road to Portland being blocked. Erprobungsgruppe 210 still had some unfinished business to conduct, however; Gruppenkommandeur Martin Lutz had advised his men that the order from the Luftwaffe High Command was that Erprobungsgruppe 210 would go back to the Supermarine works again and again until it was destroyed.

On the following day at 16:30 hours a raid by two Gruppen of KG 55 and the available Bf 110s of Erprobungsgruppe 210 finally halted production at the Supermarine works. Both the Woolston and Itchen works were hit, but workers had received ample warning of the raid; Cyril Russell had cycled away at top speed and was a mile distant when the raid commenced. The raid of 26th September differed in one respect to the other raids previously carried out against Southampton. All other raids had approached from a south-easterly direction; this raid came from a southerly direction, the flight of the aircraft passing on a south-north course directly over the works. Lord Beaverbrook, on hearing of the damage caused, ordered immediate dispersal of all the work necessary to maintain Spitfire production. Cyril Russell recalled that 'by the following Monday we were back on the job in garages, laundries, car show-rooms, etc. all over Southampton. It was a magnificent achievement and I should think still unparalleled in speed'. In the final stages of the war the Germans did exactly the same thing when their aircraft production factories were in danger of being flattened; the work was simply dispersed to many small places which were well protected and the various parts were assembled at one central point. KG 55 lost one Heinkel 111 on the raid and another returned to France with two injured crew. Erprobungsgruppe 210 suffered no losses. The Flugbuch of Balthasar Aretz records: 12 Ffg (Feindflug = enemy mission) Spitfire Werke, total Kaputt.

COMBAT – 27 SEPTEMBER
YATE

Following the successful raid over Bristol by KG 55 on 25th September, Luftflotte 3 sent the 1st and 2nd Staffeln of Erprobungsgruppe 210 to attack the Parnall Aircraft Factory at Yate, near Bristol, in the late morning of 27th September. Ten Bf 110s of the unit took off took off from Cherbourg-Ost at 10:40 hours. Escort was provided by the Bf 110s of ZG 26. On the way to the target the Bf 110 of Leutnant Wolfgang Schenck developed supercharger problems and he returned to Cherbourg and played no part in the combat over England which was soon to unfold. The indefatigable Balthasar Aretz was among the raiding Erprobungsgruppe 210 pilots on this mission. He, Schilleng and S9+EK had flown a mission a day since returning to enemy missions on 24th September.

As the German formation approached the English coast 238 Squadron scrambled two Hurricanes and four minutes later twelve Hurricanes of 56 Squadron were off from Boscombe Down. The next move from the RAF in No. 10 Group was to scramble 609 squadron from Warmwell and four minutes later 152 Squadron took off from the same airfield. At this juncture part of the Bf 110 force of escort fighters from ZG 26 detached itself from the main formation and formed an 'Abwehrkreis' high above Warmwell to await the return of the raiding party. The last RAF squadron to take off, who would prove to be the first to intercept Erprobungsgruppe 210, was 504 Squadron, from Filton at 11:23 hours. The transfer of 504 Squadron suddenly from Hendon in No. 11 Group to Filton in No. 10 Group, with the move taking place in the middle of the night, suspiciously seems like foreknowledge of the Yate raid, perhaps through Enigma decrypts, rather than inspired guesswork by Fighter Command. If it is the case, and it MUST only remain speculation, then it is also possible that Fighter Command, who by this time knew a lot about Erprobungsgruppe 210 and its specialist role in the Luftwaffe's Order of Battle, wished to allow it to penetrate deep inland and hit it with several RAF squadrons. This does not sound so absurd when considered with the following passages from *British Intelligence in the Second World War, Volume 1*, published by HMSO:

> '1) In the day-to-day fighting, by giving notice of the time, the targets, and the forces committed to individual raids, the Enigma provided an increasing amount of intelligence as the GAF moved into its all-out effort.
>
> '2) During the later stages of the Battle of Britain – those marked by heavy attacks on RAF bases and on London – the GAF aircraft paid little heed to radio security. R/T intercepts in particular now increasingly supplemented the information from radar and Cheadle. Thus the HDUs could, on occasion, determine where enemy aircraft were forming up for a raid outside radar's detection range, give the altitude of the aircraft as they approached, and indicate which incoming groups were fighters and which were bombers. All this was urgently needed information. And by their frequent ability to intercept and pass on the orders given to the enemy fighter escort – orders which sometimes specified the areas for main and diversionary attack, gave information about the enemy's appreciation of RAF activity and furnished details of where the bombers would rendezvous for the return flight and the route to be taken – they were able to be useful in directions where radar could not help. In such ways, and with growing regularity and accuracy as the Battle proceeded, the organisations exploiting the GAF's low-grade signals traffic were able to give advance information about the purpose, type and scale of the enemy's attacks'.

It cannot be claimed that the above passage proves anything conclusively, but it does provide a lot of food for thought.

The German formation, Erprobungsgruppe 210 and I. Gruppe of ZG 26, pressed on towards their target and had already commenced a shallow dive towards their objective when 504 Squadron saw their quarry. The British squadron was probably sighted at the same time by the German formation. Pilot Officer Murray Frisby turned towards the German aircraft with the rest of 504 Squadron following him, and carried out a head-on attack on the leading aircraft. With the rest of 504 Squadron joining in the action, the possibility of Erprobungsgruppe 210 reaching their target was non-existent and so they jettisoned their bombs and attempted to make good their escape.

Over the Bristol area, I. Gruppe of ZG 26 lost two of their number, U8+FK of 2nd Staffel crewed by Oberfeldwebel Hans Tiepelt and his Bordfunker Unteroffizier Herbert Brosig, shot down by Flying Officer Michael Royce of 504 Squadron, and U8+GL flown by Leutnant Joachim Koepsell with Unteroffizier Joachim Schmidt as Bordfunker, shot down by Sergeant Jones of 504 Squadron. Until now something of a mystery has surrounded the Bf 110 flown by Koepsell since Ken Wakefield, author of the excellent *Luftwaffe Encore,* has a portion of the starboard fin of Koepsell's Bf 110 showing a W. Nr. 3352, yet Luftwaffe Loss Returns show the W.Nr of Koepsell's aircraft when shot down as being 3571. Furthermore the Luftwaffe Return states that Koepsell's aircraft code was U8+*C*L and therein lies the answer. Koepsell completed the entries in his Flugbuch in Sutterlin script, the old style of German handwriting, and the aircraft he flew regularly before being shot down was the 'GL'. When Koepsell was lost it is probable that back at his base it was believed that he was in 'CL' and a quick correlation of aircraft codes and Werk Nummern has resulted in his entry in the Loss Return reading U8+CL (incorrect) – W. Nr. 3571 (correct to stated aircraft). The truth is quite simple: the RAF Intelligence crash report states: 'U8+GL (G in orange)'. Koepsell was flying U8+GL whose W. Nr. was 3352 when he was shot down on 27th September. End of mystery!

But enough of ZG 26 for now, what of Erprobungsgruppe 210? Over Bristol, Flight Lieutenant Anthony Rook of 504 Squadron latched onto a Bf 110 and after firing a short burst he noted that the starboard engine was crippled. A chase then ensued with Rook getting in occasional bursts and finally 'after a terrific head-on attack this machine gradually lost height. Whereupon I was joined by another A/C US/M, but in my opinion the machine was so crippled as he was circling so low and eventually crashed into a hillside. Owing to my lack of knowledge of the county I place this machine as having crashed about 16 miles north of Poole harbour'. So ran his combat report. The aircraft coded US/M was the 56 Squadron Hurricane flown by Pilot Officer Michael Constable-Maxwell. Because of oxygen failure Constable-Maxwell had initially returned to base but took-off again at 11:25 hours and latched onto the Bf 110 which Rook had given chase to from Bristol. Constable-Maxwell later stated in his combat report that he 'saw E/A (with one engine stopped) crash after endeavouring to force land. No cine gun. Return fire from rear gun. None of the crew baled out'. After the war Alexander McKee interviewed Constable-Maxwell during his research for his book *Strike from the Sky* and Constable-Maxwell described how in the combat of 27th September 1940 the aircraft he had attacked flew low for several minutes obviously seeking out a landing place and eventually the pilot belly-landed the aircraft in a relatively intact condition. This rules out the aircraft as being that of Martin Lutz since his Bf 110 'hit trees at speed and was badly crashed' according to the crash investigation report. The only aircraft to come down as described in the combat reports of Rook and Constable-Maxwell was that of Feldwebel Friedrich Ebner, the 25 year-old pilot, and Gefreiter Werner Zwick, his 20 year-old Bordfunker. Ebner was slightly wounded, Zwick badly. Years later Zwick recalled: 'On my last mission on 27.9.40 against Bristol, our aircraft was so badly damaged on the return flight following combat with British fighters near Shaftesbury, that my pilot, Feldwebel Ebner, had no choice but to make a forced-landing. I can only recall that during the dogfight I was seriously wounded and during the ensuing air action I lost consciousness. When I came around some weeks later, I was in a British military hospital in Shaftesbury. Because of the stomach wounds and concussion which I had suffered, there were complications during my recovery and further operations had to be carried out, which resulted in my stay in hospital continuing for several months. Regarding this matter, I would like to particularly stress that I received very humane and caring treatment in this hospital, and everything possible was done to save my life. Special thanks are due to a Jewish doctor, and a nurse, Sister Hefferman. When I was fit enough to travel, I was moved to a convalescent home (I don't recall the name of this place). After a further improvement in my health I was moved from convalescent home to a Prisoner of War camp near Oldham. Following the setting-up of the International Medical Commission in 1942 to consider the repatriation of badly wounded prisoners of war on an exchange basis, I was accepted for repatriation and transferred to 'PoW Camp 13'. From there, in October 1943, I was repatriated through Sweden'.

The 'PoW Camp 13' referred to by Zwick was situated at 'The Hayes' in Swanwick, mid-way between Alfreton and Ripley in Derbyshire.

The Bf 110 of Ebner and Zwick was a D-0 variant coded S9+DK, W. Nr. 4270, of 2nd Staffel, Erprobungsgruppe 210. Confusion exists also with regard to the fuselage code of this machine. The Luftwaffe Loss Returns give the code as S9+DU and this has been accepted by other authors in their work up to present. However there are two salient points to be considered: first of all 'U' as the fourth character in the fuselage code of a 2nd Staffel aircraft is totally inconsistent with normal Luftwaffe practise on unit codes; secondly the British Intelligence A.I.(1)g report on the crash states that the code was S9+DK. It is believed that the fault lies once again with bad handwriting. A badly written 'K' when the losses were first prepared at unit level has probably led to a typewritten 'U' in the official loss list which was forwarded up the Command chain. The evidence overriding all others must be the Intelligence crash report which states: 'Crashed on 27/9/40 at Iwerne Minster, Dorset. Markings S9+DK (D black outlined white). Aircraft made by Gothaer Waggon Fabrik. Engines DB601.A1 made by Daimler Benz, Denshagen, Teltau. During fighter attack both engines were hit from astern and aircraft made good belly forced landing. A small number of hits mostly in engines. Armament: two 20 mm. cannons, four MGs in nose, one MG15 in dorsal position. Normal armour plates in nose. Pilot wounded, gunner unwounded, prisoner'. The Intelligence Officer has made a 'faux-pas' on the condition of the gunner, but by the time he arrived the crew would most likely be in custody and that part of his report would probably be based on hearsay.

What of Gruppenkommandeur Martin Lutz? From examination of the combat reports of the intercepting RAF squadrons, it would appear that the claims of 238, 152, 609 and 56 (Constable-Maxwell excepted) can be eliminated in attempting to determine who shot down the Gruppenkommandeur of Erprobungsgruppe 210, because their claims are centred exclusively on the coast and out over the Channel. This leaves only 504 Squadron, and of that squadron, Flight Lieutenant Anthony Rook can be left out since he nailed the Bf 110 of Ebner and Zwick as described earlier. Sergeant Charlton Haw's claim was for a Bf 110 into the Channel; Flying Officer Royce's claim was for the ZG 26 Bf 110 which crashed in the suburbs of Bristol; Pilot Officer Hardacre, Sergeant Haywood and Sergeant Bush did not file combat reports as they never got into a position to engage the enemy. Sergeant Jones' claim was for U8+GL of Koepsell and Schmidt and the claim made by Pilot Officer White was for a Bf 110 shot down ten miles east of Weymouth, right on the Channel coast. By this process of elimination we are left with four combat reports, those of: Flight Lieutenant Royce, Pilot Officer Stavert, Pilot Officer Rook and Pilot Officer Frisby. Frisby's claim is for one Bf 110 damaged when he led the head-on attack on the enemy formation, and if his claim for the leading aircraft is correct, then Frisby began the destruction of Martin Lutz's aircraft. Flight Lieutenant Royce attacked a Bf 110 which had turned behind a Hurricane and carried out a quarter stern attack which developed into a full stern attack. He noticed petrol flowing away from both engines which partly obscured his vision and he was unable to see the ultimate fate of the Bf 110 which he had attacked. Pilot Officer Stavert attacked a Bf 110 head-on and observed after his attack that the port engine billowed black smoke and caught fire. He was then attacked by another Bf 110 and had to break off the combat, not seeing ultimately what happened to the enemy aircraft. Finally Pilot Officer Rook chased the enemy formation fleeing from the Bristol area and 'noticed one Jaguar underneath the main formation and climbing up to join them. He was near the front of the formation. I came below the enemy formation and closed to about 300 yards. They then saw me and started to dive. I opened my throttle and got slightly beneath him. Pulling the nose of my aircraft slightly up, the E.A. came into my sights at about 200 yards, diving across my bows. I gave him a three second burst ending astern of him. Flames issued from both engines and he went down in a vertical dive enveloped in smoke. Some oil from his engine came on my windshield. I picked up my position as south of Cerne Abbas. This was after pursuing the enemy formation south'. Rook does not mention that he saw the 'Jaguar' crash, only that he noted his position as being south of Cerne Abbas after the interception. There is a very strong possibility that Pilot Officer Rook delivered the 'coup-de-grace' to Lutz's aircraft. Apart from S9+DK at Iwerne Minster, no other German aircraft came down in the inland area between Radstock (U8+GL) and Arne, east of Wareham, where 3U+IM of 4./ZG 26 crashed. It is feasible that when combat was broken off by Rook, the enemy aircraft fell away to port which would take it in the direction of Tarrant Gunville on Cranbourne Chase where Lutz's aircraft finally crashed. No one will ever know who definitely shot Lutz down, but this is likely to be the nearest estimate.

RAF Intelligence Officers who visited the site of Lutz's crashed aircraft noted that it crashed at Bussey Stool Farm, near Tarrant Gunville. The aircraft carried the fuselage marking of S9+DH (D blue outlined white). The crest was a 'red map of England in a yellow circle seen through gunsight'. The aircraft was made by Messerschmitt A.G., Augsburg and the engines were DB601.A1. 'Following fighter action in which the engines and cooler system were hit, aircraft hit trees at speed and was badly crashed. Armament: two 20 mm. cannon guns, four MG17s, one MG15. No armour plate or bullet proof wind shield fitted. Crew of two dead'. The damage inflicted upon both engines tallies well with Rook's combat report! An interesting point in the report, and in the report of S9+DK earlier, is the mention of the aircraft having DB601 A engines. Because of the increased weight caused by the fitting of a bomb-rack and the carriage of bombs, the 'Jabo' Bf 110s should have been fitted with the uprated DB 601 N engines to compensate for the increase in weight. Photographs accompanying the text clearly show some of the Bf 110 engine cowlings of the unit with the letter 'N' stencilled on, signifying that the more powerful engine was fitted. It is probable, therefore, that both Lutz and Ebner were flying underpowered aircraft when they were shot down.

When crash investigators examined the interior of Lutz's Bf 110 D-3 (W. Nr. 3378) they found a device which pointed to a new weapon, but which no doubt baffled the British scientific experts at the time. British Intelligence were aware of Martin Lutz being in Erprobungsgruppe 210 several days before his death; a document now in the Public Record Office at Kew, dated 16 September 1940, runs: 'A document addressed to Luftflotte 3, in which the chief engineer of Luftflotte 2 referred in great detail to trouble experienced with Me 110 a/c type Do. These aircraft are frequently damaged in the fuselage, near the dinghy stowage, at spar 18, due apparently to ice formation. This is stated to come not only from the dinghy stowage, but also from the tail-wheel support and loading on spar 18. A galaxy of Senior Engineer Officers from Luftflotte 2, as well as Hauptmann LUTZ of Erprobungsgruppe 210, had been confirming writing and telephoning about this trouble, and it has been agreed with Gruppe 210 that a/c so damaged would be flown back by Gruppe 210 to MESSERSCHMITT's at AUGSBURG for the necessary repairs and strengthening. LUFTZEUG 2 was requested to instruct the firm, and furthermore, it would be necessary to determine the measures for the strengthening of other Do type (Me 110) a/c'. This is one example of the type of information intercepted and decoded by British Intelligence in 1940. A further example, relevant to the device found on 27th September states: 'A new piece of equipment is being fitted into the Me 110s of KG 210 (sic). This is placed in the rear cockpit, and consists of a metal box about 10 inches high, 6 inches broad, and 3 inches deep. From the top of this are two metal-braided electric cables, and on the face an on-off switch, a switch with numbers, and three rows of rectangular glass panels, the total number being either 10 or 20. The fitting of this apparatus commenced about 2 months ago, and the first aircraft to be fitted was that of the Gruppenkommandeur, who was shot down in flames on 27/9/40. Since then, all the aircraft of the 1st Staffel, at least, have been equipped. This work is carried out in one of the hangars on Denain aerodrome, and the installation takes two to three days'. A full description of this device is given in Appendix 3 to the text, and two photographs show the device found in the cockpit.

The loss of Martin Lutz was a heavy blow to Erprobungsgruppe 210, being the third Gruppenkommandeur to be lost by the unit in 44 days. Martin Lutz and his Bordfunker, Unteroffizier Anton Schön, aged 22, were buried at Blandford cemetery, but when the British Government made a plot of land available to Germany after the war at Cannock for a central cemetery for their war dead in England, Martin Lutz and Anton Schön were re-interred there.

Nearly two months later, Generalfeldmarschall Albert Kesselring wrote a letter of sympathy to the mother of Martin Lutz. It read:

> 'I heard from Frau von Speck of your concern over your son. Nothing is worse than to suffer uncertainty. Yet for some time I have wanted to write a few words of sympathy to the mother of my dear Lutz, as I had come to know her son as a man, fighter and flyer, who to all of us was a shining example of initiative and flying spirit. Because of his ability he was, in his early years, promoted to Hauptmann under the back-dated promotion procedure and became Commander of Gruppe 210. With this Gruppe under his guidance it achieved extraordinary results. He had as his last but one predecessor, a former name surely known to you, Hptm. Rubensdörffer, whom he replaced in the truest sense of the word. And so, dear lady, the sorrow was all the greater for us for such a leader and flyer. Also he received from me, like Hauptmann Rubensdörffer, the Knights Cross of the Iron Cross. He himself gave an indication of his ability and it was acknowledged by his superiors.
>
> I believe that the hero's death itself is able to mitigate the pain of the beloved person, if such a judgment can be given as an obituary to the fallen hero. His ashes lie in England. He fell in a raid against an aircraft engine works in the Bristol area. I hope that the end of the war gives us the opportunity to return your dear departed to the homeland and so be near to you'.

With four aircraft already shot down, two from ZG 26 and two from Erprobungsgruppe 210, the German formation headed for the English coast with RAF fighters in hot pursuit. Some of the escort fighters of ZG 26 had remained further south to await the return of the Bristol raiders and another German loss occurred when the Spitfire of Pilot Officer 'Mick' Miller of 609 Squadron and the Bf 110 (3U+FT) of Gefreiter Georg Jakstadt and Gefreiter Emil Lidtke collided head-on. Jakstadt was the only survivor of the collision, parachuting into captivity. Three more German aircraft fell on land between Weymouth Bay and Poole Harbour before the formation reached the Channel. One aircraft, 3U+IM of 4./ZG 26, crashed in a wood at Arne and this ties in nicely with the claim submitted by Pilot Officer Watson of 152 Squadron who attacked a Bf 110 and 'at about 1,000 feet the E/A exploded and crashed in a wood just south-west of Poole harbour'. The other two aircraft to crash came down very close to each other near Kimmeridge. 3U+DS of 8./ZG 26 came down relatively intact; the other machine crashed into the ground with such force that Intelligence Officers were unable to offer any clues as to the unit code of the Bf 110. The only two definite claims for Bf 110s in that area were made by Pilot Officer Williams of 152 Squadron who reported after attacking a 110: 'The E/A dived steeply towards the ground and I repeatedly fired short bursts into it. I pulled out as it crashed into the ground between WEYMOUTH & POOLE HARBOUR near LULWORTH COVE'. Pilot Officer White reported making a quarter stern attack on a Jaguar and 'when I pulled out the E/A was diving hard for the ground, turning to the left. It then went vertically up, stalled, and dived straight into the ground, bursting into flames'. The place of attack was given in his combat report as 10 miles east of Weymouth.

The crew of 3U+DS are easy enough to identify, they were Unteroffizier Fritz Schupp, pilot, and Gefreiter Karl Nechwatel, his Bordfunker. The two killed in the other crash could be one of three crews who have not yet been accounted for. The only other Bf 110 crew interred by the British authorities as a result of this particular raid were Leutnant Gerhard Schmidt, pilot, and Feldwebel Gerhard Richter, Bordfunker, who were shot down on this raid flying a Bf 110 D-3, (W. Nr. 3888), coded S9+JH of 1st Staffel, Erprobungsgruppe 210. They were buried at Brookwood Military Cemetery and were not re-interred at Cannock. It is likely, therefore, that S9+JH was shot down by either Williams or White, with the balance of probabilities on the evidence available in favour of White.

The two other crews lost on this mission have never been found and it is almost certain that they crashed into the Channel. 3U+BD of the Staff Flight of III. Gruppe of ZG 26 failed to return to base, and Oberleutnant Wilhelm-Richard Rößiger, Staffelkapitän of 2nd Staffel, Erprobungsgruppe 210, flying a Bf 110 D-0 (W. Nr. 2248), coded S9+GK, and his Bordfunker, Oberfeldwebel Hans Marx, were seen to crash into the Channel. As is the case with numerous incidents in the Battle of Britain, there are more claims for aircraft into the Channel than can be matched up to German losses. Watson, who claimed the Bf 110 at Arne, claimed he had earlier shot down a Ju 88 five miles south of the Isle of Wight (no Ju 88s were lost around mid-day on this date – probable mis-identification of an enemy aircraft). Sergeant Haw of 504 Squadron claimed a Bf 110 into the Channel; Pilot Officer Noel Agazarian of 609 Squadron also claimed a Bf 110 shot down into the Channel and finally Pilot

Officer Crook and Pilot Officer Bisdee (both 609) had a joint claim for a further Bf 110 into the Channel close to the French coast.

Later that day Erprobungsgruppe 210 returned to Denain, Balthasar Aretz and Rolf Schilleng being one of five crews to survive the ordeal. Oberleutnant Werner Weymann, who had taken command of 1st Staffel when Lutz became Gruppenkommandeur, assumed temporary command of the unit. There is one final incident to record before closing on the events of 27 September. As a result of those losses, the only commanding officer of any description on duty at the time was Oberleutnant Weymann. Consequently a Bf 110 was sent to Munich on 30 September to collect Otto Hintze, but unfortunately it burst a tyre on landing which caused such damage to the machine that Hintze's own Bf 109 E was flown out and Hintze returned to Denain on 1st October. It is likely that Hintze's recall would have been due to the fact that Weymann had only been Staffelkapitän for just on three weeks and another person with experience and knowledge of administrative matters would be required.

With Weymann in temporary command, Wolfgang Schenck took over leading 1st Staffel and Oberleutnant Knappe replaced Rößiger as Staffelkapitän of 2nd Staffel. However as a result of a directive issued by the Luftwaffe High Command to the effect that the most experienced member of a unit should lead the formation, Erprobungsgruppe 210 were henceforth led in the air by Wolfgang Schenck; when Major Lessmann was posted in as the new Gruppenkommandeur on 1st November, he flew as Schenck's No. 2. Schenck believed that it was the first common-sense directive issued by the High Command since the Battle of Britain had begun!

Despite the loss of Martin Lutz and Wilhelm-Richard Rößiger on 27th September, the unit continued with missions soon after, and 2nd Staffel, at least, took part in one of the raids launched by the Luftwaffe on 30th September; Aretz and Schilleng in S9+EK and Tröppl and Büttner in S9+CK being airborne from Calais-Marck at 09:35 hours. The target was London, but Erprobungsgruppe 210 were unable to locate their exact target, and the Flugbucher of both pilots show that bombs were released over Hastings on the return flight. There were no losses suffered by the unit.

Excellent in-flight view of 2nd Staffel Bf 110s. S9+CK is behind S9+HK.

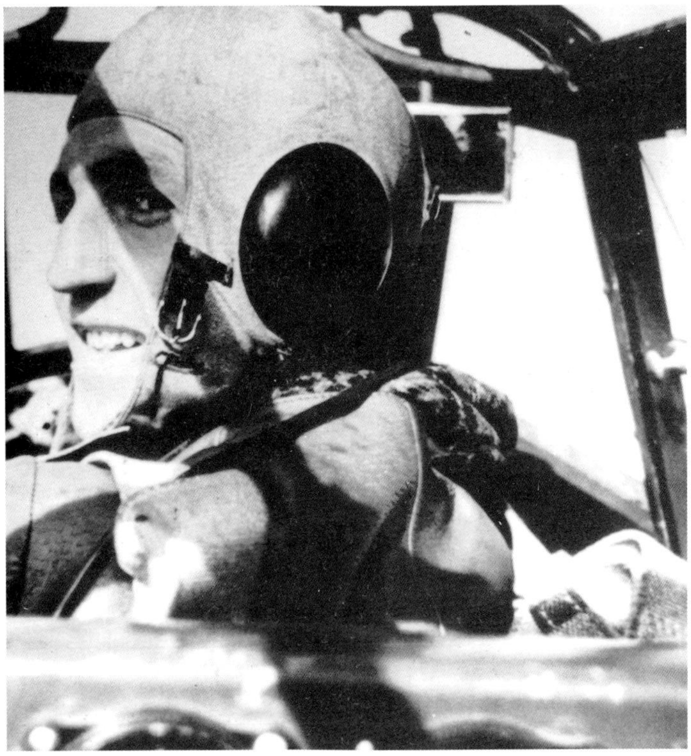

Leutnant Wolfgang Schenck in the driving seat of his Bf 110. Note the internal rear-view mirror.

Hauptmann Hans von Boltenstern, second Gruppenkommandeur of the unit, killed in action on 4th September 1940.

Flieger Gerhard Rüger, later Unteroffizier, pilot of 1st Staffel, killed in action on 6th September 1940.

2nd Staffel flying crew stroll through the centre of Denain. From left: Jachmann; Behnert, and Schilleng.

1st Staffel aircrew relaxing at Denain, summer 1940. Extreme left – Unteroffizier Gerhard Rüger; 3rd from left (in dark deckchair) – Obergefreiter Franz Öllers; 4th from left – Gefreiter Edmund Ernst; leaning forward on the right-hand side – Unteroffizier Werner Neumann.

1st Staffel in flight. On the left is S9+PH, with S9+BH in line with the photographing aircraft. On 6th September 1940 Unteroffizier Gerhard Rüger and Gefreiter Edmund Ernst were shot down in S9+BH.

Three views of a Bf 109 E-4/B of the unit. Shown to excellent effect are the netting drawn across the front of the blast pen, and how the 109 was picketed to the ground. The aircraft has a protective cover completely encompassing the engine and cockpit areas. The yellow tip to the spinner and the fuselage bomb rack are visible in all three photographs.

Excellent head-on view of a 1st Staffel Bf 110 fighter-bomber seen over the sea returning from a raid against England. The bomb rack, and multi-colored spinners associated with 1st Staffel, can clearly be seen.

A mixture of living quarters at Denain airfield.

2nd Staffel aircrew kitted out ready for the order to take off.

A very bad case of 'aeroplane hands' is displayed here by Sommer, left, and Bohne.

A back view of Balthasar Aretz, with his dog mascot, top left. From the instruments it can be established that Aretz's Bf 110 is flying at about 1,200 metres at a speed of 350 kilometres per hour. The time is four minute to five. 'EK' and 'EL' denote short and long wave radios respectively.

Another view of the inside of Aretz's cockpit, with his mascot prominently displayed. This view shows to good effect the marked difference in color tones on the upper surfaces of the port wing which would suggest a combination of dark-green (RLM 70) and gray (RLM 02).

2nd Staffel personnel head for the Casino on Jersey on 9th September 1940 after landing on part of the United Kingdom to be occupied by German forces.

A serious-looking Gerhard Schlee, Bordfunker of 2nd Staffel.

Schlee in a more light-hearted moment, with his accordion.

An unknown crewman is about to climb into a Bf 110 D of the unit.

2nd Staffel Staffelkapitän, Oberleutnant Wilhelm-Richard Rößiger, second from right, receives congratulations from groundcrew on the completion of his 100th mission.

Oberfeldwebel Hans Marx, Bordfunker of Rößiger. He was posted missing in action on 27th September 1940 together with his Staffelkapitän when their Bf 110 was shot down into the Channel on the return from the abortive raid on Yate.

Leutnant Georg Boxhammer, left, relaxes with a canine friend.

Right: Obergefreiter Franz Öllers, seen here when a Gefreiter, Bordfunker of Leutnant Ulrich Freiherr von der Horst, who were shot down on 24th September 1940 in Bf 110 D-0, S9+HH, on a raid against the Spitfire works at Southampton.

Two views of Bf 110 D, S9+AH of 1st Staffel. The letter 'A' is in blue, standard practise for 1st Staffel. The fuselage groove and extended rear fuselage are evident.

1st Staffel Bf 110s with distinctive mottle camouflage. S9+DH nearest the camera has its individual letter 'D' in blue. Using blue for the individual aircraft letters in 1st Staffel was a totally uncommon practise, perhaps unique to this Staffel within the Luftwaffe during the Battle of Britain. The standard 3rd character color for 1st Staffel aircraft was white.

S9

1st Staffel Bf 110 Ds of the unit with some activity on the aircraft in the distance.

S9+CH taxis past a Bf 110 D of the unit. Points of interest on the nearest aircraft are the wear on the port wing root, the groove down the top of the fuselage which carried the release wire for the rear fuselage section holding emergency articles, and the extended rear fuselage.

Three views of S9+HH of 1st Staffel, showing the tell-tale multi-colored spinners and third character letter in the fuselage code in blue. This aircraft has a personal emblem on the forward fuselage, which appears to be a turtle or tortoise. On the original print, the W. Nr. 3384 can be seen on the rear fuselage in the view over Cherbourg harbour, identifying it as being the Bf 110 D-0 in which Leutnant von der Horst and Obergefreiter Öllers were lost on 24th September 1940. The photographs therefore date between 8th and 24th September 1940.

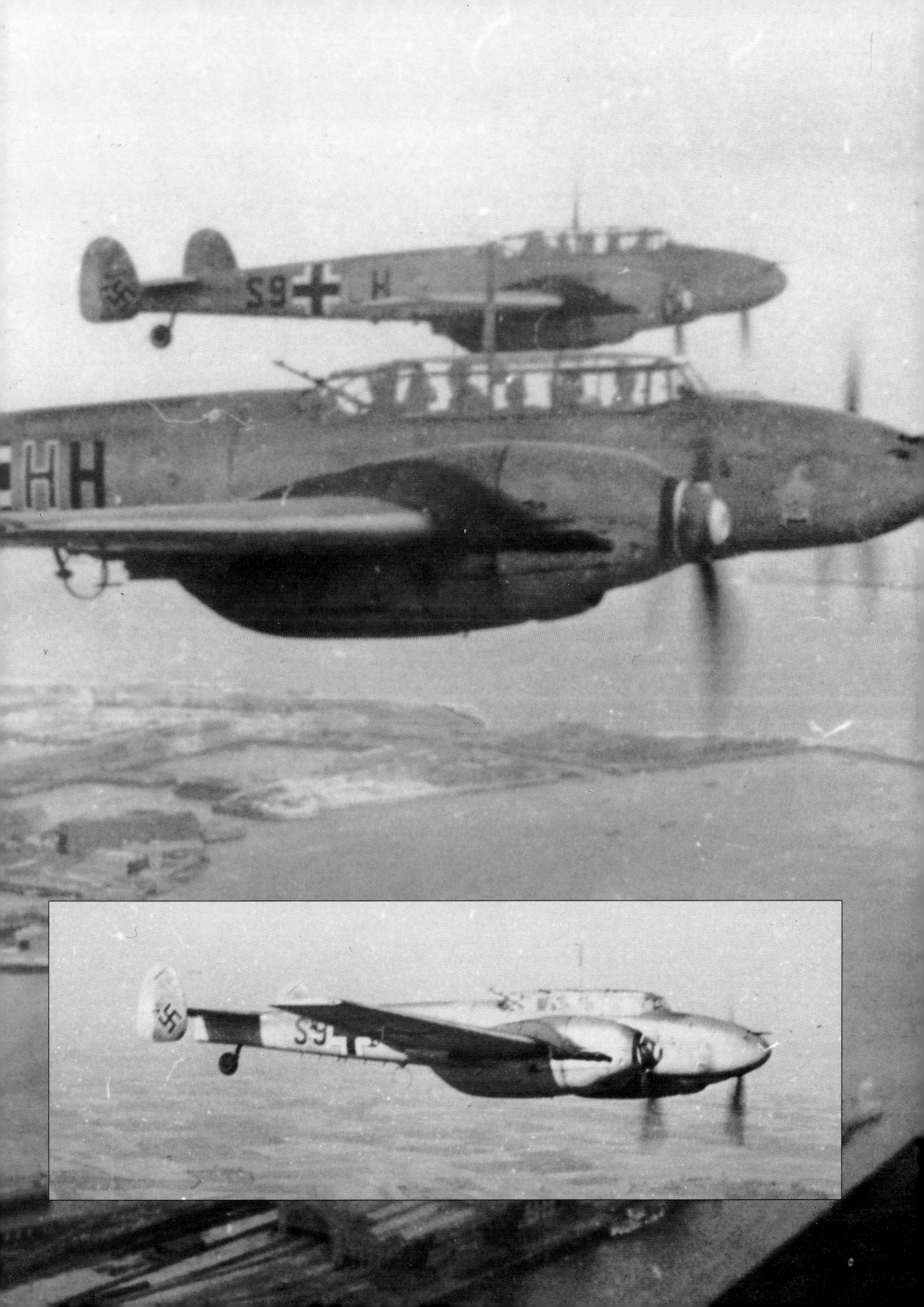

A somewhat ironic photograph of Oberleutnant Wilhelm-Richard Rößiger, undertaking dinghy practise. Rößiger was shot down into the Channel on 27th September 1940 and posted missing, together with his Bordfunker, Oberfeldwebel Hans Marx.

Taken at Cherbourg, and therefore dating between 8th and 27th September 1940, this photograph shows Oberfeldwebel Hans Marx, facing the camera, and another Bordfunker of the unit, Hans-Georg Behnert.

Far left: Leutnant Gerhard Schmidt, pilot of 1st Staffel, killed in action on 27th September 1940 together with his Bordfunker, Feldwebel Gerhard Richter, in Bf 110 D-3, S9+JH, W. Nr. 3888.

Left: Gefreiter Werner Zwick, Bordfunker of Fritz Ebner, who was badly wounded when shot down on 27th September 1940. Such was the severity of his injuries, Zwick was never sent to Canada, and was repatriated in October 1943.

Feldwebel Fritz Ebner sits casually on a bomb with S9+DK of 2nd Staffel forming a backdrop. This is almost certainly the machine in which Ebner and his Bordfunker, Gefreiter Werner Zwick, were shot down on 27th September 1940. Both survived into captivity.

2nd Staffel personnel in the sun at Denain. 2nd from left, smoking a cigarette, is Balthasar Aretz.

A 2nd Staffel Bf 110 fighter-bomber at the height of the Battle of Britain. Points to note are the lack of unit emblem, the angle of dive just visible on the side windscreen and the two-color spinners seen on most 2nd Staffel aircraft.

5

October 1940

1-2 OCTOBER

The mission over Southampton on 15th September was the last time the unit flew as a complete entity; henceforth 3rd Staffel would fly missions with the 'Jabo' Bf 109 E-4/Bs and E-7/Bs of II./LG 2, but following a period of leave, 3rd Staffel would not appear over southern England again until 15th October.

As recounted earlier, Oberleutnant Weymann took over temporary command of Erprobungsgruppe 210 but the unit was led in the air by Wolfgang Schenck. Schenck believed that the reason for some of the unit's losses in air combat was due simply to bad flying. He also believed that the RAF needed to improve its combat techniques; 'Adam and Eve' flying he dubbed the outmoded formations still used by many RAF squadrons in September and October 1940. One area where Schenck believed there could be an improvement in the unit's flying was in the matter of returning to base safely from being in the 'Abwehrkreis', the defence circle which was the standard formation of Bf 110s if attacked by RAF fighters. From what Martin Lutz had explained to him of events over Croydon on 15th August, the reason why the unit suffered such heavy losses was because the attempted 'Abwehrkreis' by Rubensdörffer was not completed and nearly all the losses came from the formation with him. The second circle, which was completed over Croydon, was able to get back to Calais-Marck with perhaps one or two shot down out of the total of seven.

The standard tactic of the German pilots in the 'Abwehrkreis' was to maintain the circle while flying lower and lower and ultimately to break for home at low level. The disadvantage for the pursuer is that he has to ensure that he sees the break for home and reacts to it instantly, and then he also has the dual problem of making effective pursuit and bringing his guns to bear on his quarry. The advantage for the pursued is that he can time the break for home and, having done so, has the single purpose of going flat-out for base.

Schenck believed there was a more effective way of breaking from the circle and in his dual role of Staffelkapitän and Officer-in-charge of training, he introduced a new method of returning home which had as an added measure a certain degree of self protection for the formation. It was basically simple and involved, in an eight aircraft formation, four aircraft breaking off to port on a given command and taking up a line abreast formation, while the other four aircraft in the manoeuvre broke to starboard and also went into line abreast. The two formations would then be on a course for base and the right-hand formation, after a given period of time, would cross behind the other formation, thus providing a complete sweep of the sky for enemy aircraft, and take up station on the port side of the other formation still flying straight ahead. The same manoeuvre would be carried out by the other formation and this criss-cross flying would continue until the entire formation was in safe territory once again. It called for very disciplined flying, but was well accepted by the pilots who operated it.

The Flugbucher of Balthasar Aretz and Siegfried Tröppl show for 1st October a combat mission lasting 60 minutes, between 14:00 and 15:00 hours, which had as its target the airfield at Lympne, but on 1st October the only entries in the Lympne Operations Record Book are for the visit to the station by Inspector-General Sir Edgar Ludlow-Hewitt, and the posting of an officer to RAF Ford. Wherever Erprobungsgruppe 210 hit on 1st October, they certainly did not hit Lympne.

However on 2nd October the two Bf 110 Staffeln took-off shortly before 11:00 hours and did attack Lympne. The Operations record Book for the station for that day recorded: 'One squadron of twin-engined enemy dive-bombers approached from south-east having been turned by Anti-Aircraft fire in the Folkestone region. Enemy aircraft approached aerodrome in a shallow dive and dropped approximately two 500 pounders per machine, about 20 bombs in all, including a few incendiary. Bombs landed along the western side of the camp, demolishing several unoccupied shelters and destroying an army lorry by fire. Four army personnel in the lorry were injured, one slightly. Little other damage. No other casualties'. The reference to 'one squadron' and the total of 'about 20 bombs in all' would tend to indicate that the serviceability state of the two Bf 110 Staffeln at this time was rather low, taking into account also the loss of four aircraft on 27 September. All the aircraft of Erprobungsgruppe 210 returned to Calais-Marck safely.

2nd October also saw new crewmen arrive for 1st Staffel: Leutnant Disper, pilot, with his Bordfunker Gefreiter Hermann; Feldwebel Kafer with Bordfunker Gefreiter Kasper; Unteroffizier Roming with Bordfunker Unteroffizier Schlund; Unteroffizier Pasiziel with Bordfunker Gefreiter Rohrschneider, and Bordfunker Gefreiter Frunzke.

COMBAT – 5 OCTOBER

The two Bf 110 Staffeln of Erprobungsgruppe 210 left Denain at about 09:15 hours on the morning of 5th October and landed at their forward base of Calais-Marck just over half an hour later. At 11:00 hours they were climbing away from Calais-Marck for a mission over England, 1st Staffel heading for Becton Gasworks on the north bank of the Thames and 2nd Staffel making for the airfield at West Malling.

1st Staffel never reached their target; on this day they had the misfortune to be intercepted by 303 (Polish) Squadron, with 501 Squadron also joining in after the initial interception. 303 Squadron were up from Northolt shortly after 11:00 hours with No. 1 (Canadian) Squadron. The Hurricanes of the Canadian Squadron became involved mainly with the Bf 109 fighter escort, although claims were made for two damaged Bf 110s after the combat. 303 Squadron attacked the Bf 110s who had formed a defensive circle near the coast at Dover. In the ensuing combat there was a degree of overclaiming by 303 Squadron, a common enough occurrence in 1940. 1st Staffel of Erprobungsgruppe 210 lost two Bf 110s in this combat, one crashed in the Channel and one on land. The acting-Gruppenkommandeur, Oberleutnant Werner Weymann and his Bordfunker, Unteroffizier Erwin Hübner, were shot down into the Channel in Bf 110 D-0 coded S9+FH, W. Nr. 3382. Flying Officer Henneberg chased a Me 110 heading for the coast and 'after firing two bursts E/A right engine burst into flames and dived straight for the sea'. Although this aircraft was not seen to crash, it was credited as destroyed on his combat report. Flying Officer Pisarck reported that he 'attacked a Me 110 from the rear and above. Firing several short bursts I saw e/a begin to smoke, one engine stopped and E/A fell into the sea'. Finally Pilot Officer Feric 'noticed an Me 110 break away from the circle, and dive towards the sea, smoking slightly, but maintaining a very high speed. I chased E/A and catching up with him about seven miles from the coast fired a burst from a distance of about 20 yards into his cockpit. E/A immediately dived into the sea'. There is a distinct possibility that Henneberg's 110 returned to France damaged, but the other two reports claim unequivocally that a Bf 110 was shot down into the Channel. Although there is no reference in either report to sharing the victory with another aircraft, it is possible that attacks were made on the same aircraft at different times and the pilots saw the aircraft they attacked crash into the Channel and made their claims accordingly. After Rubensdörffer, von Boltenstern and Lutz, Oberleutnant Weymann was the fourth Gruppenkommandeur to be killed in action in the 42 day period between 15th August and this day.

Another 1st Staffel machine was lost during this action, S9+GH, a Bf 110 D-3, W. Nr. 3383, crewed by Feldwebel Fritz Duensing, the pilot, and his Bordfunker, Feldwebel Helmut Krappatsch. This aircraft crashed on land at Willowbrook Farm, Kingsnorth, near Ashford. The RAF Intelligence Officers who visited the site reported: 'Markings not decipherable. Following fighter action during which pilot appears to have been killed, aircraft dived with engine on and exploded on impact, scattering wreckage over large area. Traces of 2 20 mm. cannon found and also parts of MG 17. A portion of external bomb-rack fitted beneath one wing also found. Armour plate as usually fitted behind MGs found. Crew, 2, dead. Owing to the condition of crash no further details possible.' Duensing and Krappatsch were interred at Hawkinge cemetery; they remain there to this day, not having been re-interred at Cannock. There are two possible claimants to the victory over this Bf 110. Sergeant Belc of 303 Squadron claimed in his combat report: 'Flying south we met a formation of Me 110s flying over Dover from the sea. I attacked from the front and below. Me 110 dived. I followed and firing a burst from about 50 yds. saw one of the crew jump. E/A crashed to earth near Lympne'. This is the only claim made by a 303 Squadron pilot for a Bf 110 which was alleged to have crashed on land.

501 Squadron became involved in the combat over the south coast, having taken off from Kenley at 11:18 hours with the order to join up with 253 Squadron and patrol base. It became evident that there was combat to the south so 501 Squadron headed in the general direction to become involved. The squadron was split up through being attacked by Bf 109s, but Squadron Leader Hogan 'was able to attack an Me 110 with two short bursts. The Me 110 attempted to evade by diving and turning but I followed and as he went into a steep diving turn, I gave him one long burst and he rolled onto his back and went in, crashing two miles south of Ashford'. Kingsnorth is two miles south of Ashford and the claim made by Squadron Leader Hogan can only be that of the Bf 110 of Duensing and Krappatsch.

One aircraft of 1st Staffel returned to Calais-Marck with a wounded crew member. S9+EH, a Bf 110 D-0, W. Nr. 3598, returned with 15% damage to the aircraft and with 28 year-old Bordfunker Oberfeldwebel Robert Schulze seriously wounded. It is probable that this aircraft was subjected to attack from one or more of the 303 Squadron pilots mentioned above.

What of 2nd Staffel? They apparently reached their target and dropped some bombs on West Malling airfield but the damage was not great. 2nd Staffel did not lose any aircraft on this mission but one returned to base with 40% damage and a wounded pilot on board. Unteroffizier Balthasar Aretz recalled that shortly before they reached the target, British fighters were seen and the order was given for an 'Abwehrkreis' to be formed immediately. Before this was done, his Bf 110, S9+EK, was attacked from below and behind by a Spitfire. The starboard engine was damaged and Aretz was wounded in a delicate part of his rear anatomy. He almost passed out, and momentarily pressed all his weapons buttons. The result was that he released his 2x250 Kg. bombs, and loosed off a burst from his two 20 mm. cannon and four MGs. Hearing other crews over the intercom, he followed their instructions and went into a dive from 4,500 metres levelling out only a few hundred metres above the ground. 'When I was level again, the right engine emitted smoke – engine on fire. I switched everything off, feathered the engine and trimmed the aircraft. My Bordfunker had already released the canopy roof. During this time, I realised that I would have to make a belly-landing. I flew low over the English coast in the direction of Calais. My rear gunner stooped down directly behind me, as far as that was possible. Later, head armour was installed for the pilot. No one could have helped me if that had been the case. After sighting the French coast, I brought the 'E' into Calais-Marck airfield at a height of 500 metres'. Emergency services had been alerted at Calais-Marck by Aretz's Bordfunker, Gefreiter Rolf Schilleng, and when the Bf 110 came to a halt, Schilleng quickly vacated his position in order to help his pilot, if necessary. 'When the Me 110 stopped, I very carefully climbed out of the cockpit and slid on my belly down the left wing, where my gunner was waiting. The medical vehicle with a doctor and ground personnel was already speeding towards us'. A photograph accompanying the text shows the first examination of Aretz by the doctor at Calais-Marck. Although slightly amusing to him in later years, at the time he was transferred to hospital in Calais and was taken by Junkers 52/3m on 16 October to a hospital in Hannover. He was hospitalised for nearly three months, being discharged on 10th February 1941.

Gefreiter Rolf Schilleng continued on operations with the unit, and was eventually killed in action on 12 May 1941 in a Bf 110 coded S9+CK (W. Nr. 3459) on a nocturnal mission against Martlesham Heath. By this time the unit had been redesignated Schnellkampfgeschwader 210. 'Bubi' Engels, the pilot and a former member of Erprobungsgruppe 210 was also killed when the aircraft was lost.

The Spitfire which attacked Aretz's Bf 110 was almost certainly that of Pilot Officer J. Lund of 92 Squadron. Flying as 'Red 3', his squadron saw Bf 109s but the Spitfires were too low to intercept. Seeing anti-aircraft fire, they flew north towards it and saw enemy aircraft circling round. Lund later reported: 'I approached them and attacked a Me 110 from 30° astern firing a long burst from 250-80 yards. I saw the hood fly off as the enemy aircraft turned in an attempt to escape. I broke away and attacked again from underneath. Clouds of white smoke and flashes were visible from both engines. When last seen the enemy aircraft was losing height. The combat took place over Maidstone about 11:30 hours'.

Aretz's account was given without any knowledge of the existence of Lund's combat report and the two accounts, one written at the time and the other nearly forty-four years later, are remarkably similar. There are no other accounts remotely similar in the records of 92, 303 and 501 squadrons for combat at the time on this particular day.

Whereas Balthasar Aretz was to return to operational flying and see service on the Russian front, in the Mediterranean theatre (Africa, Sicily and Italy) and finally on 'defence of the Reich' duties before enjoying a long post-war life, Pilot Officer Lund was killed in action later in the war.

Intermittent missions were carried out during the rest of October by the Bf 110 Staffeln; on 17th October, for example, Tröppl records a mission in his Flugbuch for mid-afternoon with Büttner in S9+LK. The target is given as 'English coast'. Again, on 27th October he records an attack on London in S9+CK with Büttner.

COMBAT – 29 OCTOBER

3rd Staffel, after their respite at the end of September/early October, returned to combat missions on 15th October. The Staffel had ceased to operate with the two Bf 110 Staffeln of the unit and, although still based at Denain, they now flew missions with the 'Jabo' Bf 109 Es of II./LG 2, as stated earlier. The earlier policy of using fighter-bombers to attack selected targets had now been abandoned and the bomb-carrying Bf 109 Es were used as nuisance raiders flying in high over the English coast and dropping their bombs in a random manner and then heading back to base. Whilst this form of aerial warfare continued to draw the British fighters up into combat, its value was worthless in the overall strategy of the Battle of Britain period. That the 'Jabo' had proved its worth there is no doubt. However it was a criminal waste of resources, in both manpower and machines, to apply them in this haphazard way. By doing so, the Luftwaffe was to lose pilots of considerable experience who would have proved to have been an asset in the following campaigns of 1941 onwards.

In this vein, 3rd Staffel flew 13 missions in the period 15th October to 29th October. One aircraft was lost in combat, but the pilot concerned was a valuable 'catch' for the British.

On 29th October Otto Hintze, on his 53rd mission in the Battle of Britain, led off his 3rd Staffel from Calais-Marck at 12:40 hours in concert with a Gruppe of 'Jabo' Bf 109 Es from LG 2. The next time he would see Calais would be during a holiday in France in the 1960s. The raid managed to get through to London and unload their bombs, but on the return journey Spitfires of 222 and 602 Squadron were waiting to intercept. Hintze witnessed the shooting down of one Bf 109 E before he became the target of a Spitfire himself. Flying Officer Thomas, leading 222 Squadron, fastened onto Hintze's 109, coded 'Yellow 6' and his burst of fire hit the 109, causing damage to the cooling system and the radio. Hintze knew 'Yellow 6' was in trouble and quickly realised that he would have little chance of making the French coast. After flying 41 missions in the Bf 109 E which he selected when he joined Erprobungsgruppe 210 (coded 'Yellow 1'), he was to be shot down, after flying several other aircraft, on his 6th mission in 'Yellow 6'. Unknown to Hintze at the time, events were unfolding behind him which would cause him to evacuate his Bf 109 far quicker than he would have wished. Another pilot of 222 Squadron, Sergeant Burgess, had taken up the chase, and Flying Officer Thomas, deciding that it was not prudent to wait to discover whether the aircraft behind him was friend or foe, broke off combat. The combat report of Sergeant Burgess sets down the details as he saw them at the time: 'I sighted an aircraft diving and leaving a white smoke trail, being closely pursued by another aircraft. After a little while the second aircraft broke away, whereupon the first aircraft flattened out and the emission of white smoke ceased. I pursued this aircraft which was flying just above the clouds and after 2-3 minutes I caught up and saw it was a 109. I gave it one 7-second burst from slight deflection round to dead astern closing from 300 to 50 yards. As I broke away to the side I saw his hood go up and the pilot baled out. The machine crashed just to the south of Pluckley Station (West of Ashford). I force-landed (wheels down) at Lanham as I was shot at myself and was hit in the glycol system.

Hintze was contemplating bailing out when there was a great flash from the engine (the seven-second attack by Burgess) which caused him to jettison the hood immediately and bail out. The recommended aircraft speed for bailing out of the Bf 109 was 155 mph (250 Km./Hr.) or less; Hintze left the aircraft when it was travelling at over 248 mph (400 Km./Hr.). Hintze hit the tailplane on bailing out, dislocating his left shoulder, but he was able to deploy his parachute fully and made a safe landing. His aircraft, W. Nr. 2024, crashed at Sheerlands Farm, Pluckley, Kent. The injuries to Hintze's left shoulder caused him to be hospitalised for two days but on release from hospital he was taken to London to where all Luftwaffe survivors ended up in 1940 – the interrogation centre known as the 'Cage'. He was eventually moved to a prison camp near Sheffield and ultimately shipped to Canada, where he was to spend the rest of the war. The award of the Ritterkreuz – the Knights Cross of the Iron Cross – was promulgated on 24th November 1940. His tally of 53 combat missions in the Battle of Britain was probably exceeded by few pilots.

The Bf 110 Staffeln had a combat mission on this day also, in the late afternoon. In a raid against London, the Bf 110s were intercepted by Spitfires of 92 Squadron, and several claims were lodged by the RAF pilots. The Bf 110 D (W. Nr. 3655) of Siegfried Tröppl, pilot, and Otto Büttner received damage to the port engine, which stopped, causing the aircraft to lose power and drop out of formation. Upon landing, Tröppl's 2nd Staffel reported his aircraft as crash-landing in England.

Of the 92 Squadron pilots who filed claims, Flight Lieutenant Villa claimed a Bf 110 into the sea 15 miles SSE of Rye; Pilot Officer Saunders claimed damage to the port engine of a Bf 110; Pilot Officer Sherrington claimed to have hit the port engine of a Bf 110 which went into a vertical dive; Pilot Officer Wade claimed a Bf 110 probable with a smoking starboard engine, and Sergeant Bowen-Morris claimed a probable with one engine stopped. Saunders, Sherrington and Bowen-Morris appear to have the strongest claims, but it is possible that all attacked the same aircraft.

During the night, 2nd Staffel received a message that Tröppl's Bf 110 had crashed into a hillside near St. Ingelvert airfield. Apparently the aircraft had reached the French coast shortly before nightfall flying on one engine, and attempted to reach St. Ingelvert. However the second engine stopped, the aircraft lost height rapidly and crashed. German soldiers who arrived at the scene of the crash found Büttner dead in the aircraft, and Tröppl badly injured. Siegfried Tröppl was taken to hospital, but he died from his injuries in the early hours of 30th October. Tröppl and Büttner were buried on 31st October in Pihon cemetery near St. Ingelvert.

9th October 1940. 3rd Staffel enjoy a celebration meal at Denain on the occasion of Staffelkapitän Otto Hintze's 27th birthday.

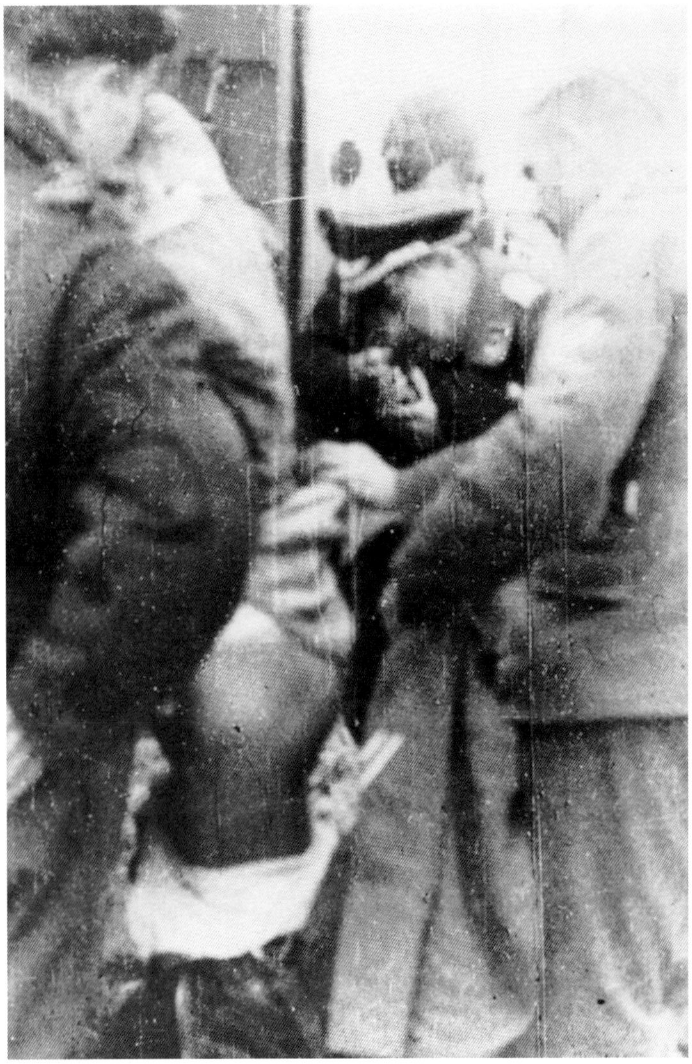

Calais-Marck, 5th October 1940. Balthasar Aretz having the wounds in a delicate part of his anatomy examined by the Medical Officer and other interested onlookers after being attacked from behind and below by a Spitfire over England in his Bf 110.

Left: From left: Tillheim;. Kloß and Roth. Leutnant Walter Kloß wears his pilot's badge and the Iron Cross, First Class, on the left side of his tunic, and the Iron Cross, Second Class, ribbon attached to his top button. In the background, a Bf 110 of the unit is well protected against the elements.

Siegfried Tröppl, seen here early in his Luftwaffe career when a Gefreiter. Feldwebel Tröppl died on 30th October 1940 of his injuries following the crash-landing of his Bf 110 near St. Inglevert airfield on 29th October after a combat mission. His Bordfunker, Unteroffizier Otto Büttner, was killed in the crash.

A view not usually seen of the Bordfunker's position in the Bf 110. Crew member is Rolf Schilleng.

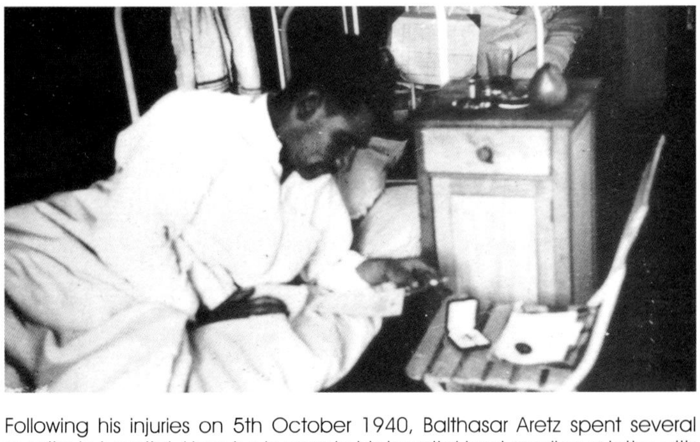

Following his injuries on 5th October 1940, Balthasar Aretz spent several months in hospital. Here he is seen in his hospital bed reading a letter with an award of some kind on the chair alongside.

2nd Staffel Bf 110 D, S9+HK, in a classic 'Kopfstand'. The usual cause of such incidents was soft ground and too-heavy braking.

Feldwebel Sommer of 2nd Staffel in front of a Bf 110 about to receive some attention from ground mechanics.

Seven views of another Bf 110 which has nosed-over in soft ground. The underwing bomb racks can be clearly seen on this Bf 110 E in one of the photographs.

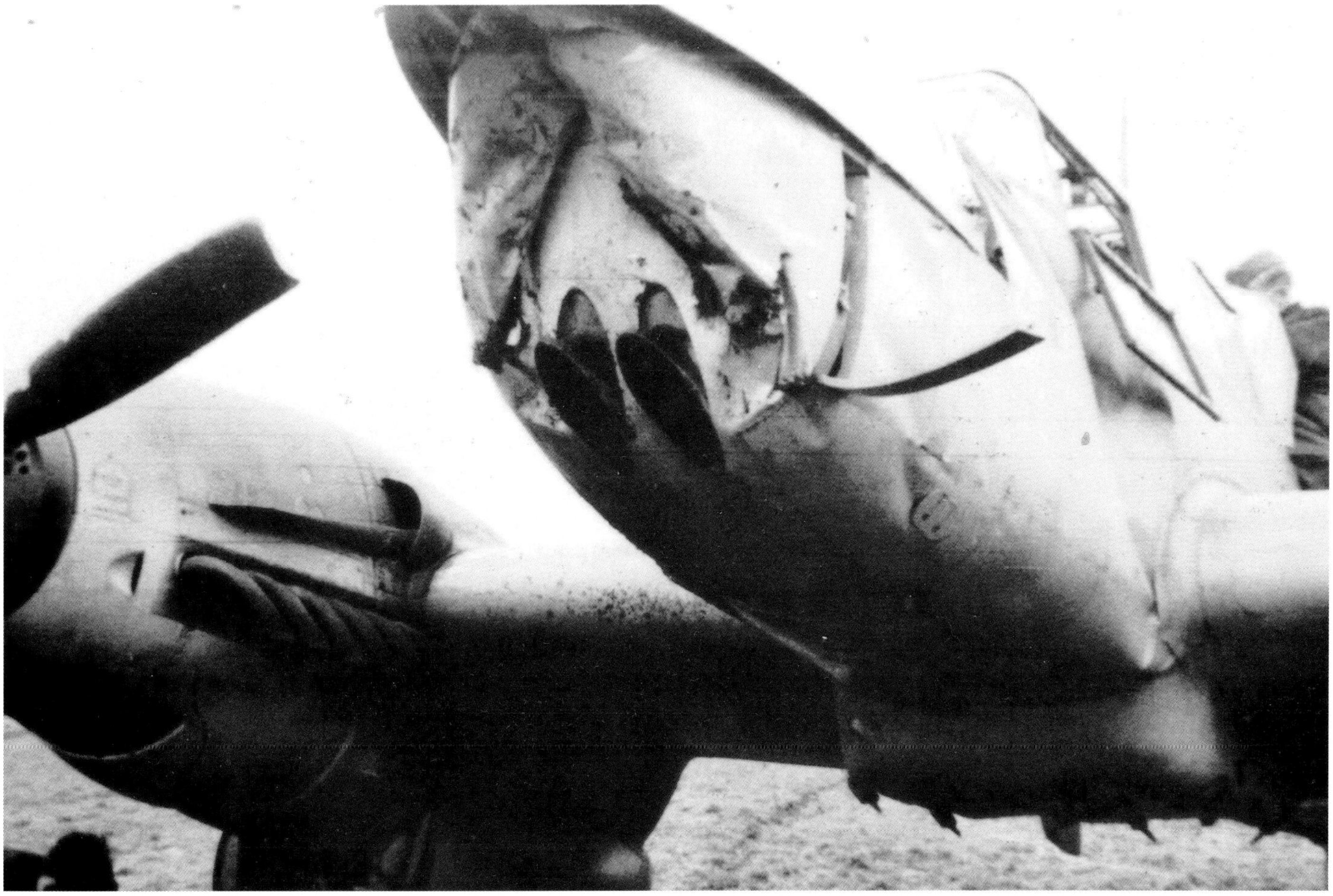

This Bf 110 E, S9+OH, of 1st Staffel, is bombed-up, and the unit emblem and multi-colored spinners are in evidence.

6

November 1940 to April 1941

The period from November 1940 up to 24th April 1941, when the unit was incorporated into the newly-formed Schnellkampfgeschwader 210, was marked by two major changes. First of all, the move to equip all three Staffeln with the Messerschmitt 110, and secondly, the change from attacks in Gruppe strength to raids carried out by smaller units of aircraft, with the consequent reduction in striking power. The winter period also contributed to a slackening-off of combat missions and the night offensive carried out by the standard Luftwaffe bombers over many British cities did not lend itself particularly to Erprobungsgruppe 210's style of work.

This period then is one of transition, and perhaps also one of preparation for events which would start the following June on the eastern front. The great days of the unit had gone: for those who had been killed during the Battle of Britain, it can be said that they only knew Germany triumphant; those captured endured the long years of Prisoner-of-War camps with the gradual realisation that the country they had fought for had been defeated; for those who had come through the Battle of Britain, there were the many future campaigns to fight, again with the gradual realisation that the tide had turned and that defeat was all they had to look forward to.

This chapter 'rounds-off' the history of the unit, although the amount of information contained in it is, in view of the changed circumstances, necessarily less.

By the beginning of November, all of the original 'Command' officers had changed. Rubensdörffer, Fiedler, Koch, Lutz, Rößiger and Hintze had all been shot down, only Koch and Hintze surviving into captivity. The end of the unit's era.

COMBAT – NOVEMBER 1940

November opened with the posting-in of a new Gruppenkommandeur, Major Karl-Heinz Lessmann, formerly Gruppenkommandeur of II./ZG 2. November also saw a return to attacks on shipping targets in the Thames estuary and along the south-east coast of England. Wolfgang Schenck requested permission to use the Bf 110 C-6s still on charge with 1st Staffel to destroy the buoys in the Thames estuary which marked the safe (unmined) lanes for shipping, arguing that if the buoys were destroyed, shipping losses would rise dramatically as British ships drifted onto uncharted mines. The request was refused. Perhaps the reason was that, in leaving the marked shipping lanes alone, the ships in them would be able to take very little avoiding action when attacks were carried out by German aircraft. The first alternative was surely the better; it was probably the vainglorious belief of the Luftwaffe High Command that as many, if not more, ships could be sunk in the marked shipping lanes as in the open waters of the Thames estuary with a combined aircraft/mines threat.

While Major Lessmann was no doubt a useful pilot of Bf 110s, the problem for the unit was that he was not well versed in the 'Jabo' technique and plans sometimes went awry: on one occasion, on 12th November, the unit were unable to find their targets and instead dropped their bombs on Ramsgate harbour without much success. The unit suffered no losses in combat in November against shipping, but things changed on 17th November when Bf 110s of the unit set out to attack the airfield at Wattisham.

1st and 2nd Staffeln of the unit, accompanied by the Bf 109 Es of Jagdgeschwader 26 led by Major Adolf Galland, were sighted by 17 Squadron who had taken off from Martlesham Heath, 6 Hurricanes at 08:55 hours and another 5 at 09:05 hours. 17 Squadron's task was to provide top cover for 257 Squadron who were also airborne on convoy patrol. 257 Squadron became involved with the Bf 109 escort fighters. and Flying Officer Czernin led one Flight of 17 Squadron Hurricanes onto the bombers, which he identified as Italian Fiat BR 20 bombers. This was clearly a case of mis-identification as no Italian bombers were involved in this raid. Czernin claimed to have damaged one of the aircraft which he attacked, but was forced to bail out of his Hurricane following an attack by one of the Bf 109 E escort fighters. The other Hurricanes of 17 Squadron attacked a formation of German aircraft which they correctly identified as Bf 110s. Flight Lieutenant Bayne, Flying Officer Niemiec, Pilot Officer Kordula and Sergeant Cameron all claimed to have damaged Bf 110s, but none of the four pilots saw them crash. However following the attack, two Bf 110s were seen by the searchlight post at Butley flying out over the coast in flames at less than 2,000 feet and back at Martlesham Heath, the Intelligence Officer totalled the claims as being '3 Me 110 destroyed, 2 Me 109 damaged and 1 Fiat BR 20 damaged (sic!)'. Erprobungsgruppe 210 lost 3 Bf 110s on this raid, one of them being the 1st Staffel machine of Unteroffizier Werner Neumann, pilot, and Obergefreiter Karl Stoff, Bordfunker, both by now seasoned combat veterans having flown missions during the height of the Battle of Britain in August and September. Their aircraft was coded S9+MH, W. Nr. 3659, a Bf 110 D-3 variant. Karl Stoff recalled the mission on which he was shot down: 'We were on a flight to Wattisham near Ipswich – it was Sunday 17th November – around the area of Harwich, when the last two Me's of our formation became separated, with the result that we were weakened. Suddenly there was a fighter about 400 m. directly behind us. Was it a 109 of our escort? Too late I recognised the English cockades! In the same instant that I loosed off the first burst from my machine gun, we received a full salvo from the eight MGs of the Hurricane. As a result of this deadly burst the left engine caught fire and my gun jammed. Furthermore I suffered a forehead wound from shrapnel. My pilot released the two bombs and at about 4,000 m. we went into a steep glide towards the coast, hoping to land in the sea. We feared the aircraft might explode and so my pilot told me to bail out immediately, as he knew we would be unable to reach Calais. With great difficulty I succeeded in bailing out and landed heavily in the dunes near Ufford, to the south of Great Yarmouth. After about an hour the Home Guard came and took me prisoner. My pilot bailed out 3 Kms. from the coast and landed in the sea. He was rescued 2-3 hours later by a British coastal ship'.

Karl Stoff landed badly and injured his left shoulder. When British soldiers finally arrived, they told him to put his hands up as they approached. Matters were not improved when one of the soldiers hit Stoff's left arm with his rifle butt. Slowly Stoff raised his good right arm into the air. On seeing this, and getting the wrong impression, one soldier shouted: 'Put that ******* arm down, you're not in Germany now!'

Werner Neumann had also managed to bail out of the stricken Bf 110 and landed in the sea, coming down to the south-east of Aldeburgh. At about 09:30 hours the motor lifeboat *Abdy Beauclerk* was launched. There was a doctor on board, Major R. Acheson, and Werner Neumann was rescued alive and brought ashore. For their pains the lifeboat crew were paid £22 14s 6d.

2nd Staffel lost two aircraft on this raid. S9+JK, W. Nr. 3648, a Bf 110 C-4/B, was crewed by Unteroffizier Johannes Kowatsch, pilot, and Unteroffizier Hans-Georg Bade, Bordfunker. This aircraft was stated to have been shot down into the North Sea and tallies, together with the Bf 110 of Neumann and Stoff, with the two seen to be flying low on fire by the Searchlight post mentioned earlier. The other aircraft was a Bf 110 E-2, S9+LK, W. Nr. 3465, flown by Unteroffizier Hermann Strobel, pilot, and Unteroffizier Willy Radermacher as Bordfunker. This aircraft crashed into the Channel off Dunkirk and both crew were killed.

Strobel's Staffelkapitän, Hauptmann Knappe, wrote to Strobel's widow on 19th November: "It is with the greatest regret that today I have to convey to you the sad news that your husband Hermann Strobel gave his life on 17th November 1940 for Führer, People and Fatherland.

"On a mission against an English airfield, on the grounds of confidentiality I cannot be more specific, the Staffel was attacked by fighters, and your husband's aircraft was badly damaged. Flying on one engine, he succeeded in reaching within 15 kms. of Dunkirk. As a result of losing coolant, the second engine suddenly stopped, and the aircraft had to set down on the water. The aircraft slithered 50 m. on the water, when it suddenly tipped onto its nose and sank in the waves. Neither the pilot nor the Bordfunker were seen to have got clear of the aircraft.

"Rest assured that I and the whole Staffel regret very deeply the loss of your husband, and that it will be our duty to preserve always the memory of the dead."

The reference to Italian aircraft has always been something of a mystery for this raid. One thing is certain: the aircraft seen by Czernin were definitely Bf 110s. Why then, did he mis-identify them as Fiat BR 20 bombers? Six days earlier the Italian Air Force carried out a raid on the south-east coast of England and were intercepted by 257 Squadron, in company with 17 and 46 Squadrons. The sighting of Italian aircraft on 17 November was a corollary of the earlier action and is not entirely unpredictable – don't forget RAF pilots saw many He 113s and Luftwaffe pilots were seeing, and claiming, Curtiss Hawks and single engined radial fighters! The answer may lie in a very simple explanation given by Wolfgang Schenck, which at the time was entirely unconnected with the raid of 17th November. Schenck stated that when he became Staffelkapitän of 1st Staffel he introduced, as an additional aid to quick identification in the air, the painting of the part of each rudder with the colour blue, which was already being used on the aircraft of 1st Staffel for the third character letter in the fuselage code, the individual aircraft letter within the Staffel. Czernin reported that he attacked twin-engined twin-tailed aircraft and it is likely that in the high speed combat he was involved in, he confused the swastika and blue colour on the fin/rudder of the enemy aircraft for the Italian insignia and reported accordingly.

The three losses on 17th November were the last to be suffered in combat by the unit in 1940. Before the unit was redesignated Schnellkampfgeschwader 210 in April 1941, however, there were to be others.

As November wore on, so the raids of Erprobungsgruppe 210 diminished with the onset of winter. Plans were now set in motion to equip the unit solely with Bf 110s and personnel had begun to arrive by the end of the month to form a Bf 110 3rd Staffel. The original 3rd Staffel with their Bf 109s would ultimately be transferred to Jagdgeschwader 51.

DECEMBER 1940 to APRIL 1941

With the coming of December 1940, and the onset of winter, combat missions almost ceased, and because the weather made airfields at Denain and Calais-Marck quite unserviceable for Gruppe operations, the unit was dispersed to Merville (Belgium), Berck-sur-Mer and Abbeville.

December 1940 also saw the formation of the Bf 110 3rd Staffel get into full swing with many of the new personnel for that Staffel coming from Seeflieger units. Karl-Fritz Schröder, a Bordfunker who joined 3rd Staffel in December 1940, recalled that it was very strange for him at first as most of the commands were given in naval language! In January 1941, the Bf 110 3rd Staffel returned to Germany to a Blind-Flying school. January 1941 also seemed bereft of any great combat activity for the other two Staffeln. However in February, things were to change.

February 1941 brought a return to combat missions for the unit and, inevitably, the commencement of losses in combat again. The missions carried out by the unit in 1941 differed from those of 1940 in that they were conducted mainly from dusk onwards, targets being military or industrial sites on or around the coastline of the south-east coast of England. The unit was also actively engaged in weather-reconnaissance and armed-reconnaissance missions, but gone were the heady days of 1940 when incursions over the south of England were in Gruppe strength, many times in concert with other large Luftwaffe formations. Now twilight missions were flown, more often than not in pairs, sometimes the 'Schwarme' would be used.

A typical night mission of the time is described by Heinz Natzinger of 2nd Staffel: "In the evening I was told to report to my Staffelkapitän at 22:00 hours. He informed me that at midnight I had to fly a mission against Chatham dockyards. Although I had experience of 'blind flying', I had never flown a Me 110 at night before, so I had to do 3 practise take-offs and landings, which were completed without difficulty.

"Now the preparations commenced. The machine was bombed-up with two 500 Kg. and four 50 Kg. bombs, The two 500 Kg. under the fuselage and two 50 Kg. bombs under each wing. The map was checked. Complete radio silence was required.

"Promptly at midnight a green flare gave me clearance; I could take off. The combat height, and the manner in which the mission is carried out, is decided solely by the pilot, as he alone has to depend on his own judgment. From Merville to the coast, I reached a flying height of about 4,000 metres. The view in the moonlight was unique; one could discern almost everything below. Over the Thames estuary I had reached about 6,000 metres, and it was time to concentrate on the target. To the north-east everything was clear in the moonlight, but my target was in darkness. Then suddenly I had no time. In the same moment my Bordfunker Rudi (Grossmann) shouted "Nightfighter!", and bullets zipped over my wings. Now it was time to act. I came half off the gas, so that the nightfighter was faster than me, and I dived in a steep turn to starboard. My feint worked, and I was rid of my attacker. It could so easily have gone wrong. The enemy fighter was lost, but because of shortage of fuel and time I could no longer reach my target. I therefore dropped my 'eggs' on Manston airfield and set course for home. I had now to continually change my flying height in case of nightfighters, besides having to fly on one motor in order to preserve fuel, until I could see 'Beacon Paula' in the distance, when I could be certain of reaching the airfield on two engines. I had received no hits".

The first combat loss of the new year occurred on 3rd February when a 1st Staffel Bf 110 E, S9+EH, W. Nr. 3852, was lost with the pilot, Unteroffizier Josef Roming, and Bordfunker Gefreiter Robert Schlund, posted as missing following an armed-reconnaissance mission in the Thames estuary area. The following day it was the turn of 2nd Staffel to lose a Bf 110. S9+PK, W. Nr. 3849, an 'E-1/N' version, was shot down by Flak while attacking a convoy off Margate. The crew of Unteroffizier Gustav Drews, pilot, and Unteroffizier Rudolf Steindl, Bordfunker, were presumably drowned.

The next loss suffered by Erprobungsgruppe 210 is interesting in that the aircraft is ostensibly a 2nd Staffel machine, yet the crew are given as 3rd Staffel in the Luftwaffe loss returns. On 20th February S9+PK, W. Nr. 3474, a Bf 110 E-1, was shot down into the Channel with the loss of Leutnant Fritz Heunisch, pilot, and Gefreiter Rudolf Gärtner. The reason for this apparent anomaly was simple. When 3rd Staffel crews were sent to Germany for blind flying training, crews which had already undergone that training were allowed to stay behind and had the opportunity to continue combat missions with the Staffeln on the western front. Heunisch and Gärtner remained in Merville, and subsequently lost their lives flying a 2nd Staffel machine. So, the machine was recorded correctly as a 2nd Staffel loss, while the crew were entered correctly for the 'Namentliche Verlustmeldung' return as 3rd Staffel.

The losses in the new year were notable for one thing: with the actions against convoys, the chances of survival if shot down were very slim indeed. Unless rescue occurred immediately, death by drowning or from exposure to the icy waters was certain. What is interesting at this time is that raids conducted against inland targets carried a far higher safety margin than against shipping. Anti-aircraft fire from ships had by now become uncomfortably accurate, and with night-fighting still in its relative infancy compared to what was achieved in the later war years, inland raids were definitely the lesser of two evils.

The above point was particularly relevant in the case of the loss of a 2nd Staffel Bf 110 E, S9+IK, W. Nr. 3827, on 7th March. The aircraft was shot down near Harwich during an attack on a ship and the crew of Feldwebel Konrad Fleischmann, pilot, and Feldwebel Gustav Helling, Bordfunker, were seen by the crew of another Bf 110 of the unit to have successfully evacuated the aircraft and to be waving to the other Bf 110. A dinghy was thrown to the men in the water but agonisingly, it landed too far away from them and eventually sank. It was later found that the call to the Seenotdienst had not been received, and although the two men were listed as missing in the official records at first, when no word had been received through the Red Cross of their survival from the British side, the records were changed from 'two missing' to 'two dead'.

By this time the unit was using Ursel and Wevelgem as bases as well as Merville, which would be used by 3rd Staffel when they returned to the Channel front. For the first time in 1941 an aircraft of the unit which was badly damaged in combat managed to get back to friendly soil. On 19th March a 1st Staffel Bf 110 E-1 crash-landed at Hazebrouck after receiving damage inland of the south-east coast of England. The pilot, Unteroffizier Hermann Hilden, was seriously wounded and later died of his injuries in hospital. His Bordfunker, Gefreiter Wolfgang Henneberger, was killed in the crash.

On 21st March, our friend from Battle of Britain days, Balthasar Aretz, appeared on the scene again, but not in a way he would have wished. After being discharged from hospital in February, he returned to his old Staffel and commenced flying again on 9th March. His first combat mission following return to duty was on 21st March, his 18th mission in all to that date. In a combat mission which lasted three hours, Aretz, with Feldwebel Jachmann as Bordfunker, in S9+LK, recorded in his Flugbuch: '2 500 kg – 1 Treffen, Pott gesunken!'. However he also recorded 'Notlandung (bauch)'. For the second time in his Erprobungsgruppe 210 career in a Bf 110 he had to make a belly-landing, this time near Dieppe. He landed at 21:35 hours, and when he returned to the machine the following morning he was horrified to see how close he had been to bringing down power cables onto his aircraft, as one of the photographs accompanying the text shows.

Returning to missions against land targets for the moment, the unit did attack some industrial targets, but also seemed to have their fair share of airfields to attack. Manston, Martlesham Heath, Rochford and Wattisham, all came in for attention from the unit. They also had the occasional aerial success. Leutnant Georg Boxhammer on one occasion claimed a victory over a British nightfighter.

On 9th April, 3rd Staffel lost a Bf 110 E-1/N over Lowestoft in an attack on a convoy, an all too familiar occurrence since the turn of the year. S9+OL, W. Nr. 3841, carried Leutnant Anton Henscheid, pilot, and Gefreiter Josef Schubert, his Bordfunker, to their deaths. This would prove to be the final loss due to enemy action for Erprobungsgruppe 210.

The final loss to the unit happened on the evening of 16th April when, at Abbeville, a Bf 110 E-2/N, S9+OK, W. Nr. 4407, crashed shortly after take-off, diving straight into the ground. The crew of Oberfeldwebel Franz Deuerling, pilot, and Feldwebel Horst Schramke, Bordfunker, were killed instantly.

Eight days later, on 24 April, Schnellkampfgeschwader 210 came into existence, the three Staffeln of Erprobungsgruppe 210 forming the I. Gruppe of the new unit. Major Lessmann, the unit's final, and longest serving, Gruppenkommandeur, moved back to standard Bf 110 fighters, taking command of III./ZG 76, his place being taken by Hauptmann Karl-Heinz Stricker. The new unit would continue missions against the south coast of England, but would shortly transfer to Poland in preparation for the all-out assault on the Soviet Union. But that is another story altogether.

Unteroffizier Werner Neumann, left, pilot of 1st Staffel, seen here with his brother. Werner Neumann was shot down off the south-east coast of England on 17th November 1940 in Bf 110 D-3, S9+MH, W. Nr. 3659. Both he and his Bordfunker, Obergefreiter Karl Stoff, survived into captivity.

Obergefreiter Karl Stoff, Bordfunker of Werner Neumann, seen here at Calais-Marck on 5th October 1940.

Unteroffizier Hermann Strobel, pilot of 2nd Staffel, whose Bf 110 E-2, S9+LK, W. Nr. 3465, crashed into the Channel on 17th November 1940 just short of the French coast. Strobel and his Bordfunker, Obergefreiter Willy Radermacher, were killed.

Two good friends of 2nd Staffel: Unteroffiziere Schlee (left) and Jachmann.

Göttliches Herz Jesu, bekehre die Sünder, errette die Sterbenden, tröste die armen Seelen im Fegfeuer!

Zur frommen Erinnerung
im Gebete
an unsern lieben Sohn und Bruder
Obergefreiter
Willy Radermacher
Bordfunker einer Fliegerstaffel

geboren am 18. August 1919
gefallen am 17. November 1940
im Kampf gegen England.

Er hat mit seinem Flugzeugführer sein Grab im Kanal gefunden.

Gebet.

Gerechter und barmherziger Gott. Wir bitten Dich, erbarme Dich Deines treuen und standhaften Dieners Willy, den Du würdig befunden hast, ihn durch seinen frühen Opfertod uns zu entreißen und schenke ihm dafür die Krone des ewigen Lebens. Möge er Wegbereiter sein für uns alle auch, daß wir einstens mit ihm vereinigt werden. Uns gib Trost und Kraft in unserem großen Schmerz.

O Maria, Mutter der Liebe, der Schmerzen, der Barmherzigkeit, bitte für uns.

Milder Herr Jesu, gib ihnen die ewige-Ruhe!

Obituary notice for Obergefreiter Willy Radermacher.

Unteroffizier Heinz Natzinger in the cockpit of a Bf 110 of the unit. The helmet and harness strap would indicate an imminent take-off. Note the line on the pilot's starboard windscreen, used to line up the correct angle of dive.

Herr, gib ihm die ewige Ruhe!

Und das ewige Licht leuchte ihm!

ZUR FROMMEN ERINNERUNG
im Gebet an unseren lb. Sohn und Bruder

JOSEF KOPF

Feldwebel, Äpfingen
geb. am 30. Januar 1914
gefallen den Fliegertod für Führer und Volk am 19. November 1940
begraben auf dem Soldatenfriedhof in Charleroi (Belgien)

Above and right: On 19th November 1940, on an overland flight to Liegenitz in a Focke-Wulf 58, four members of the unit lost their lives when their aircraft crashed 3 kilometres north of Charleroi. These three photographs show the obituary notice for Feldwebel Josef Kopf, and views of his grave in the Military Cemetery in Charleroi in Belgium.

Below: From left: unknown; Feldwebel Büttner; Oberfeldwebel Vögel; Feldwebel Michi; Leutnant Heunisch and Unteroffizier Eckleben, all 3rd Staffel pilots.

Bf 110 Es of 2nd Staffel, S9+GK and S9+EK. Fin/rudder locks are evident on S9+GK, as is the letter 'N' on the port engine cowling of the same machine, denoting the presence of the uprated DB 601 N engine in the aircraft.

S9 GK

Two views of a crash-landed Bf 110 E of 1st Staffel, S9+CH. Points to note are the multi-colored spinners, the letter 'N' on the port engine cowling, and the pilot's armour protection.

The three flying crew seen in this photograph are: 2nd from left – Unteroffizier Heinz Natzinger; 4th from left – Unteroffizier Jachmann; extreme right – Leutnant Walter Kloß.

Christmas 1940, and the dining room at Denain appears well-stocked for the Christmas festivities to follow.

Leutnant Georg Boxhammer holds a framed record of "Erprobungs=Gruppe 210, Die Erfolge der Gruppe im Jahre 1940", the success of the Gruppe in 1940, with Major Karl-Heinz Lessmann looking on.

2nd Staffel aircrew and groundcrew pose for the camera. The aircrew in 'Mae Wests' are, from left: Natzinger; Grossmann; Engels; Patzer and Joos.

Leutnant Friedrich Heunisch, pilot of 3rd Staffel, killed in action off Harwich on 20th February 1941 together with his Bordfunker, Gefreiter Rudolf Gärtner, in Bf 110 E-1, S9+PK, W. Nr. 3474.

Unteroffizier Heinz Natzinger, pilot of 2nd Staffel, with his aircraft at Merville.

An aircraft of the unit takes off on a dusk mission, silhouetted against a cloudy skyline. Two bombs are visible under the fuselage.

S9+GL of 3rd Staffel. Note that the Bf 110-equipped 3rd Staffel adopted the multi-colored spinners previously the exclusive preserve of 1st Staffel.

2nd Staffel aircrew with the tools of their trade. Standing, left to right: Knef; Natzinger; Jachmann. On the ground, left to right: Tillheim; Wiese and Schilleng.

Right: Groundcrew re-arm a Bf 110 of 2nd Staffel. Note the pilot's armour plate in the cockpit.

2nd Staffel personnel pose in front of S9+CK of the unit receiving attention to its starboard engine. The two seated on the bombs are unknown. Standing are Hans Tillheim (left) and Rolf Schilleng. This aircraft, W. Nr. 3459, was lost on a combat mission on 12th May 1941 taking to their deaths Engels, Knöckel and Schilleng. Erprobungsgruppe 210 had by then been re-designated Schnellkampfgeschwader 210.

Four 2nd Staffel Unteroffiziere who appear to have had a riotous time with a guitar. From left: Knef; unknown; Natzinger and Schlee.

The square in Merville. From left: Tillheim; Schlömer; Wiese; Schlee; Natzinger and Grossmann.

In-flight view of S9+AL of 3rd Staffel, ostensibly the aircraft of the Staffelkapitän, Oberleutnant Heinz Forgatsch.

Right: Personnel of 2nd Staffel relaxing on Bf 110 E, S9+GK. Photographs of 2nd Staffel aircraft towards the end of the Battle of Britain show the appearance of the individual identity letter on the nose of the machine, as shown here.

21st March 1941, near Dieppe. Three views of S9+LK which crash-landed at 21:35 hours after an eventful mission. Balthasar Aretz, with Bordfunker Unteroffizier Jachmann, sank a steamer, then had to make a 'Bauchlandung' in the dark on his first mission with the unit since being wounded in combat on 5th October 1940.

Pilot Aretz, left, and Bordfunker Jachmann, centre, crew of S9+LK on 21st March 1941.

Leutnant Anton Henscheid, pilot of 3rd Staffel, killed in action on 9th April 1941 off the English coast near Lowestoft in Bf 110, S9+OL, W. Nr. 3841.

In-flight view of S9+OL.

16th April 1941. Transfer flight from Abbeville to Wevelgem for 3rd Staffel Bf 110 E, S9+EL with Unteroffizier Ernst and Gefreiter Schröder on board.

Unteroffizier Albert Ernst, pilot, left, and Gefreiter Karl-Fritz Schröder, Bordfunker, both of 3rd Staffel, pose with Staffel pets. Ernst was lost in action in a mission against Ipswich on 12th May 1941. Schröder survived the war.

Oberleutnant Heinz Forgatsch, Staffelkapitän of 3rd Staffel, strides away as Oberleutnant Brunzel closes the car door, Merville, April 1941.

Leutnant Paul Drawe poses in front of S9+BL of 3rd Staffel. The multi-colored spinner, 'N' on the port engine cowling and pilot's armour plate can all be seen. This aircraft, W. Nr. 3483, was lost on 19th May 1941 on a mission up the south-east coast of England.

Two views of Bf 110 E, S9+AL, W. Nr. 3484 with Leutnant Paul Drawe in attendance. Drawe was killed on a training flight on 1st May 1941 when his Bf 110 crashed. S9+AL did not return from a mission on 12th May 1941 with Unteroffizier Albert Ernst on board.

Aircrew of the unit in the final stages of preparation for a mission in front of S9+OK of 2nd Staffel. The back pack parachute of the man in the centre identifies him as a Bordfunker. The tall officer striding to the right in front of the port engine could only be Leutnant Walter Kloß – no one else in the unit was so tall!

The same aircraft, S9+EK, forms a backdrop to these two photographs. Balthasar Aretz sits on the edge of the deckchair while a game of table tennis goes on to the left. The table tennis game is between Feldwebel Horst Schramke (left) and his pilot, Oberfeldwebel Franz Deuerling. Both were killed when their Bf 110 E-2, S9+OK, crashed at Abbeville on take-off for an evening mission on 16th April 1941. Standing, right, is Unteroffizier Herbert Wiese.

Dawn on 17th April 1941 revealed the full horror of the nocturnal crash on the previous evening of Bf 110 E-2/N, S9+OK, W. Nr. 4407, as seen in these two photographs of the crash site and remains of the aircraft. The 2nd Staffel machine crashed shortly after take-off, the crew of Oberfeldwebel Franz Deuerling, pilot, and Feldwebel Horst Schramke, Bordfunker, having no chance of survival.

Prisoner-of-war line-up taken in Canada shows Leutnant Horst Marx of 3rd Staffel on the extreme left of this photograph.

Another prisoner-of-war line-up from 1943 shows Werner Neumann of 1st Staffel, 5th from right, with his Bordfunker, Karl Stoff, 6th from right.

7

The Final Verdict

How can the record of Erprobungsgruppe 210 be evaluated to arrive at an objective assessment of their performance, bearing in mind that they have previously been described as a crack unit, and also as a unit which did not quite live up to expectations? Perhaps the truth lies somewhere between the two.

The success or otherwise of the unit can be judged from two major standpoints. First of all, how does its record stand up to close scrutiny in the period July 1940 to April 1941, and secondly, what effect on the future conduct of warfare did its missions have. It is accepted that with the latter point, regard must also be had of the performance of the Bf 109 'Jabos' of II./LG 2.

First of all, let us consider their record with particular reference to the period July to the end of October 1940, the most intense period of combat undertaken by the unit. The first point which becomes clear is that hitherto the Luftwaffe had primarily been active in a ground-support role: air superiority over the immediate vicinity of the battlefield as a prerequisite for success on the ground. The use of fighter-bombers in 1940 would have suited that role perfectly. However the English Channel militated against the immediate use of Erprobungsgruppe 210 in such a role. The unit was therefore not employed in the role to which it was best suited. It was first of all used against shipping during the first phase of the Battle of Britain, a role at which they became particularly useful, but even at that early stage in the battle, one must question to a degree the reasoning behind attacking merchant shipping if an invasion of the south-east coast was imminent. Would it not have been more logical to husband such aerial forces for the all-out land attack? With hindsight it is apparent that if the Luftwaffe had not indulged in a phase of attacking shipping and had plumped instead for immediate attacks on RAF airfields in England, the crisis Fighter Command found itself in at the end of August 1940 would have been greatly exacerbated. That is not to say, however, that the shipping phase was unsuccessful, taken in isolation. The text clearly shows the concern shown by the Royal Navy over the attacks on shipping, and Erprobungsgruppe 210 played their part to the full in the prosecution of that particular aspect of the war against Britain.

In the second phase of the Battle of Britain, commencing with Erprobungsgruppe 210's attack on the radar stations on 12th August and developing into the raids against RAF airfields, in the second half of August and the first week of September, the unit was in the thick of the action. Understandably, previous authors have not given the unit the credit it deserves (in strictly military terms) with regard to the effectiveness of their raids in the second phase. They have been hindered by the fact that certain raids were not ascribed to Erprobungsgruppe 210, partly due to incorrect aircraft identification on the ground which subsequently entered official records, and partly due to the depth of their own research. On this particular point are offered the raids against Manston on 24th August; Biggin Hill on 30th August; Croydon on 31st August; Cunliffe-Owen on 11th September and the Supermarine works on 26th September as particular examples. It also has to be conceded that with the passage of time, there may have been other raids successfully carried out by the unit which will never be discovered. Equally, there were times when raids by the unit were not successful; Yate on 27 September and Becton Gasworks/West Malling airfield on 5th October spring immediately to mind. Another matter sometimes not brought into play in an objective assessment of the events of the summer of 1940 is the performance of those other units on which the bombers and fighter-bombers of the Luftwaffe relied for protection over England. It is conceded that in the early pages of this work reference was made to the fact that Erprobungsgruppe 210 operated as a complete offensive/defensive entity, but it was equally true that on many occasions they were provided with fighter escort on their combat missions. The success or otherwise of the escort fighters sometimes had a direct influence on the casualties suffered by Erprobungsgruppe 210: witness the Croydon debacle on 15th August when the unit lost its escort from JG 52; also the losses on the Yate raid of 27th September when escorted solely by the slower Bf 110s of ZG 26. That latter point is not intended as a criticism of the ZG 26 crews, merely a factual statement of the inability of the Bf 110 to provide effective protection in the face of the then modern RAF fighters.

Another factor which had a bearing on the success of, indeed even the ability to carry out, raids on targets on the English mainland was the unpredictable weather over southern England. 13th August 1940 was a day when 'Adlerangriff' should have gone off at full steam but after a bungled opening the day proceeded in fits and starts. At that time one would have expected that Erprobungsgruppe 210 would have been in the thick of the action but all that happened was an abortive morning and a mission in the afternoon which became a fiasco because of the prevailing weather conditions over southern England.

In the third phase, the move away from attacks on RAF airfields and the commencement of the assault on London, the unit very quickly found itself transferred to Cherbourg from where it carried out the raids on Southampton and the ill-fated raid against Yate on 27th September. Honest assessment of the 'Luftflotte 3' period for the Gruppe shows that it was a rather indifferent time. Apart from demolishing Cunliffe-Owen on 11th September, and being involved in the successful attack on the Supermarine works on 26th September, there was a singular lack of success in the missions flown.

Upon return to Denain and the continuing of operations into October, it must be said that Erprobungsgruppe 210, like all other Luftwaffe units, took part in missions which appeared to be lacking in any cohesive planning. The unit had to follow the orders passed down to it, and with British leaders knowing as early as 17th September that the planned invasion had been cancelled, it is clearly evident that a large proportion of the effort in the second half of September and all of October was of little consequence and a waste of aircraft and personnel. The only value was in perhaps the gaining of combat experience for many crews but this point must be considered against the fact that in the same period the Luftwaffe lost many experienced aircrew also, Erprobungsgruppe 210 included, in an exercise which amounted to little more than face-saving in daylight missions. November's return to attacks on shipping showed events turning full circle from the heady days of July and early August when the threat to the British Isles was very real indeed. This time round however, both the RAF and the Royal Navy were far more experienced in defending the shipping around the British coastline.

In summing up this first point, it can be stated that the opening phase against shipping was an encouraging start, and the second phase consolidated that start. What little Intelligence information is available shows that RAF Intelligence was particularly interested in finding out as much as possible about Erprobungsgruppe 210 in view of the 'specialist' nature of its role at the time. The third phase shows a diminishing effectiveness in the operations carried out, in line with what was happening to the Luftwaffe in general. Overall, however, the unit acquitted itself well in the Battle of Britain and could look back on the months July to October with a great degree of satisfaction.

With hindsight, the second standpoint in assessing the success of the unit can be stated more clearly. In a nutshell, the 'Jabo' operations of Erprobungsgruppe 210 and Lehrgeschwader 2 had a profound effect on *all* future military air operations, both in the Second World War and in all air operations following the war. It would be plainly incorrect to say that without the above two units there would not have been fighter-bombers, but what is certain is that they gave a lead, set a standard, for units following on to achieve or emulate. Every fighter variant reaching combat status post-1940 was developed into a fighter-bomber; indeed there was a belief in Luftwaffe circles that the earlier success of fighter-bomber aircraft in the Luftwaffe was one of the reasons why Hitler was so insistent on the Messerschmitt 262 programme being almost entirely devoted to the 'Jabo' version when entering production for combat service. On the Allied side, as the war progressed, the inventories of the many airforces showed an ever-increasing number of fighter-bomber aircraft and they played a very important part in the preparation for, and the subsequent action in, the Allied invasion of Europe in June 1944. The 'Jabo' wind sown by Erprobungsgruppe 210 and Lehrgeschwader 2 in 1940 truly became the whirlwind in 1944.

The final confirmation in the appraisal of the 'Jabo' is found in the verdict of all the major air forces of the world. The fighter-bomber is the primary strike aircraft; the straightforward strategic bomber was ultimately relegated to a secondary role, in spite of what we are led to believe of the potency of the Vulcan attacks on Port Stanley airfield in the Falklands war. The truth was much different to the propaganda put out at the time, but then truth is still the first casualty of war. With space-age warfare upon us, the fighter-bomber is the only viable strike aircraft in a conventional war. The techniques pioneered by Erprobungsgruppe 210 in 1940 are as valid now as they were then. The unit can have no greater epitaph than that.

Appendices

Appendix 1
ERPROBUNGSGRUPPE 210 LOSS/DAMAGE LIST

Date	Name of crew and rank	Staffel	Status	Fate	Aircraft code & W. Nr.	Damage state	Reason for casualty	Place
08-07-40	Uffz. Volz	3	P	K	Bf 109 E-4/B	100%	Crashed on bombing training flight.	Near Köln.
13-07-40					Bf 110	45%	Force-landed with supercharger trouble following attack on shipping.	Near Gent.
13-07-40	Lt. Erich Beudel	1	P		Bf 108 KE+NU		Force-landed on flight from St.-Omer/ Arques to Denain.	Douai.
18-07-40	Gefr. Ludwig Spreitzer	3	P	K	Bf 110	100%	Right wing broke off during flight.	Antwerp.
21-07-40	Oblt. Alfred Habisch Uffz. Ernst Elfner	2 2	P Bf		Bf 110 S9+CK		Damaged on combat mission.	Channel.
24-07-40	Uffz. Paul Hermann Uffz. Heinz Meinhardt	2 2	P Bf	K K	Bf 110	100%	Shot down by A-A fire.	30 Kms. east of Harwich.
27-07-40	Oblt. Franz Fallenbacher Fw. Friedrich Oberland	2 2	P Bf	K K	Bf 110	100%	Shot down by A-A fire.	55 Kms. north-east of Harwich.
29-07-40	Lt. Erich Beudel Ogefr. Heinrich Diemer	1 1	P Bf	 W	Bf 110 C-6 2N+RH		Damaged over convoy by 151 Sqdn. Hurricanes.	Off Orfordness.
30-07-40	Lt. Hans Herold Ogefr. Lotar Lilienthal	1 1	P Bf	K K	Bf 110 C-6	100%	Shot down by Allard and Hamilton of 85 Sqdn..	40 Kms. east of Harwich.
06-08-40	Lt. Kurt Prokop Gefr. Herbert Dust	2 2	P Bf	K K	Bf 110	100%	Crashed on training flight.	Near Denain.
06-08-40	Uffz. Heinrich Schultheis	2	P	K	Bf 110	100%	Killed whilst bailing out of aircraft on test flight.	Near Denain.
07-08-40	Hptm. Karl Valesi	3	P	K	Bf 109 E-4/B	100%	Crashed on training flight.	Near Denain.
11-08-40	Lt. Kurt Bertram Ogefr. Gerhard Mertins	1 1	P Bf	K K	Bf 110 C-6	100%	Shot down by RAF fighters over convoy.	Near Harwich.
11-08-40	Gefr. Christian Weiss Ogefr. Richard Keilhaupt	1 1	P Bf	K K	Bf 110 C-6	100%	Shot down by RAF fighters over convoy.	Near Harwich.
12-08-40	Lt. Erich Beudel Ogefr. Otto Jordan	1 1	P Bf		Bf 110 D S9+EH	100%	Starboard engine seized on landing.	Calais-Marck airfield.
14-08-40	Lt. Heinrich Brinkmann Uffz. Richard Mayer	2 2	P Bf	K K	Bf 110 D S9+NK	100%	Shot down by A-A fire over Manston.	Manston airfield.
14-08-40	Uffz. Hans Steding Gefr. Ewald Schank	2 2	P Bf	K PoW	Bf 110 D S9+MK	100%	Shot down by A-A fire over Manston.	Manston airfield.
14-08-40	Oblt. Werner Weymann	1	P		Bf 110 D		Returned to Calais-Marck on one engine.	Manston/Channel.
14-08-40		1			Bf 110		Attack on Manston aborted due to engine trouble.	Channel.
14-08-40		1			Bf 110		Attack on Manston aborted due to engine trouble.	Channel.
15-08-40	Lt. Erich Beudel Ogefr. Otto Jordan	1 1	P Bf		Bf 110 D		Damaged in combat following raid on Martlesham Heath airfield.	Martlesham/south-east coast of England.
15-08-40	Hptm. Walter Rubensdörffer (Gruppenkommandeur) Ogefr. Ludwig Kretzer	Stab Stab	P Bf	K K	Bf 110 D S9+AB 3338	100%	Shot down by Duckenfield of 501 Sqdn. following raid on Croydon airfield.	Rotherfield, Sussex.
15-08-40	Oblt. Horst Fiedler (Gruppenadjutant) Uffz. Johann Werner	Stab Stab	P Bf	K PoW	Bf 110 D S9+BB 3374	100%	Shot down by Dymond of 111 Sqdn. and Pearce of 32 Sqdn..	Redhill aerodrome.
15-08-40	Lt. Karl-Heinz Koch (Gruppe Technical Officer) Uffz. Rolf Kahl	Stab Stab	P Bf	W (PoW) W (PoW)	Bf 110 D S9+CB 3339	100%	Shot down by Russell of Biggin Hill Training Flight after initial damage over Croydon.	Hooe.
15-08-40	Lt. Willi Benedens Uffz. Maas	Stab Stab	P Bf	W	Bf 110		Damaged in combat over Croydon.	
15-08-40	Lt. Erich Beudel Ogefr. Otto Jordan	1 1	P Bf	K K	Bf 110 C-6 S9+TH	100%	Shot down by Connors and 'Green 2' of 111 Sqdn..	Crawley.

Date	Name of crew and rank	Staffel	Status	Fate	Aircraft code & W. Nr.	Damage state	Reason for casualty	Place
15-08-40	Uffz. Werner Neumann Ogefr. Karl Stoff	1 1	P Bf		Bf 110		Damaged in combat over Croydon. Returned to Calais-Marck with 57 .303 hits.	
15-08-40	Oblt. Alfred Habisch Uffz. Ernst Elfner	2 2	P Bf	PoW PoW	Bf 110 D S9+CK 3341	100%	Damaged in combat over Croydon. Force-landed as unable to get back to France.	Hawkhurst.
15-08-40	Lt. Helmut Ortner Ogefr. Bernhard Lohmann	2 2	P Bf	PoW K	Bf 110 D	100%	Shot down by Crossley, Worrall and 'Red 3' of 32 Sqdn..	Ightham.
15-08-40	Lt. Horst Marx	3	P	PoW	Bf 109 E-4/B Yellow 3	100%	Shot down following raid on Croydon.	Frant.
20-08-40	Fw. Martin Wohlfart Gefr. Albert Dietrich	2 2	P Bf	K K	Bf 110 D	100%	Shot down by 'A' Flight, 66 Sqdn. over convoy.	15 Kms. south-east of Aldeburgh.
21-08-40	Uffz. Balthasar Aretz Gefr. Rolf Schilleng	2 2	P Bf		Bf 110 D S9+EK 3377	10%	Tailwheel collapsed on landing.	Calais-Marck.
22-08-40	Uffz. Ernst Glaeske Ogefr. Konrad Schweda	2 2	P Bf		Bf 110 D		Starboard engine hit following attack on convoy.	Over the Channel.
28-08-40		3			Bf 109 E-4/B 1208	60%	Airframe damage following combat.	
31-08-40	Uffz. Ernst Glaeske Ogefr. Konrad Schweda	2 2	P Bf	PoW K	Bf 110 D-0 S9+GK 3381	100%	Shot down by RAF fighters after raid on Croydon.	Wrotham Hill.
31-08-40		2			Bf 110 D-0 S9+DK 3370	30%	Damaged by RAF fighters after raid on Croydon.	
31-08-40	Uffz. Balthasar Aretz Gefr. Rolf Schilleng	2 2	P Bf		Bf 110 D-0 S9+EK 3568	25%	Damaged by RAF fighters after raid on Croydon.	
04-09-40	Hptm. Hans von Boltenstern (Gruppenkommandeur) Fw. Fritz Schneider	Stab Stab	P Bf	K K	Bf 110 D-0 S9+AB 3390	100%	Crashed into the Channel on combat mission. No RAF fighters involved.	Off Littlehampton.
06-09-40	Uffz. Gerhard Rüger Gefr. Edmund Ernst	1 1	P Bf	K PoW	Bf 110 D-0 S9+BH 3373	100%	Shot down by Dibnah of 1 Sqdn..	Crowhurst.
07-09-40	Fw. Otto Rückert	3	P		Bf 109 E-4/B 2021	100%	Aircraft damaged in combat. Rückert baled out into the Channel and rescued by Seenotdienst	Channel.
08-09-40		3			Bf 109 E-4/B	30%	Take-off accident.	Denain
24-09-40	Lt. Ulrich Freiherr von der Horst Ogefr. Franz Öllers	1 1	P Bf	K K	Bf 110 D-0 S9+HH 3384	100%	Shot down by A-A fire over Southampton.	Channel coast.
27-09-40	Hptm. Martin Lutz (Gruppenkommandeur) Uffz. Anton Schön	Stab 1	P Bf	K K	Bf 110 D-3 S9+DH 3378	100%	Shot down by Hurricane(s) of 504 Sqdn..	Tarrant Gunville.
27-09-40	Lt. Gerhard Schmidt Fw. Gerhard Richter	1 1	P Bf	K K	Bf 110 D-3 S9+JH 3888	100%	Shot down by either White of 504 Sqdn. or Williams of 152 Sqdn..	Kimmeridge.
27-09-40	Oblt. Wilhelm-Richard Rößiger (Staffelkapitän) Ofw. Hans Marx	2 2	P Bf	K K	Bf 110 D-0 S9+GK 2248	100%	Shot down into the Channel by RAF fighters.	Channel.
27-09-40	Fw. Fritz Ebner Gefr. Werner Zwick	2 2	P Bf	W W (PoW)	Bf 110 D-0 S9+DK 4270	100%	Shot down by A. Rook of 504 Sqdn. and Constable-Maxwell of 56 Sqdn..	Iwerne Minster.
05-10-40	Oblt. Werner Weymann (Acting-Gruppenkommandeur) Uffz. Erwin Hübner	1 1	P Bf	K K	Bf 110 D-0 S9+FH 3382	100%	Shot down into the Channel by RAF fighters.	Channel.
05-10-40	Fw. Fritz Duensing Fw. Helmut Krappatsch	1 1	P Bf	K K	Bf 110 D-3 S9+GH 3383	100%	Shot down by S/Ldr. Hogan of 501 Sqdn..	Kingsnorth.
05-10-40	Ofw. Robert Schulze	1	P	W	Bf 110 D S9+EH 3598	15%	Damaged by RAF fighters. Crash-landed at Calais-Marck.	Channel.

Date	Name of crew and rank	Staffel	Status	Fate	Aircraft code & W. Nr.	Damage state	Reason for casualty	Place
05-10-40	Uffz. Balthasar Aretz Gefr. Rolf Schilleng	2 2	P Bf	W	Bf 110 E S9+EK 4209	40%	Damaged in combat with Lund of 92 Sqdn..	South of London.
21-10-40	Uffz. Werner Hesse Uffz. Stephan Stadler	2 2	P Bf	W W	Bf 110 D-0 3367	80%	Crashed on local flight.	St. Leger.
25-10-40		3			Bf 109 E-4/B 3765	20%	Damaged on landing.	Calais-Marck.
29-10-40	Fw. Siegfried Tröppl Uffz. Otto Büttner	2 2	P Bf	K K	Bf 110 D 3655	100%	Crashed in France following combat with 92 Sqdn. over England.	St. Ingelvert.
29-10-40	Oblt. Otto Hintze (Staffelkapitän)	3	P	W (PoW)	Bf 109 E-4/B Yellow 6 2024	100%	Shot down by Burgess of 222 Sqdn..	Pluckley.
16-11-40					Bf 110 3462	30%	Damaged while taxi-ing.	Merville.
17-11-40	Uffz. Werner Neumann Ogefr. Karl Stoff	1 1	P Bf	PoW PoW	Bf 110 D-3 S9+MH 3659	100%	Shot down by Hurricane of 17 Sqdn. into the North Sea.	Off Orfordness.
17-11-40	Uffz. Johannes Kowatsch Uffz. Hans-Georg Bade	2 2	P Bf	K K	Bf 110 C-4/B S9+JK 3648	100%	Shot down by Hurricanes of 17 Sqdn. into the North Sea.	Not known.
17-11-40	Uffz. Hermann Strobel Ogefr. Willy Radermacher	2 2	P Bf	K K	Bf 110 E-2 S9+LK 3465	100%	Crashed into the Channel after combat with 17 Sqdn. Hurricanes.	15 Kms. from Dunkirk.
19-11-40	Lt. Johannes Göhlich Uffz. Kurt Rehkugler Fw. Josef Kopf Flgr. Hermann Schicker	2 2 2 Stab	P Passenger Passenger Passenger	K K K K	Focke Wulf 58 3594	100%	Crashed on local flight to Liegnitz.	3 Kms. north of Charleroi.
11-12-40					Bf 110 3435	5%	Light damage following enemy strikes.	Over the North Sea.
23-01-41	Lt. Erich Disper Gefr. Ulrich Herrmann	3 3	P Bf		Bf 110 3831	25%	Crash-landed after enemy action.	Zuydcoote.
03-02-41	Uffz. Josef Roming Gefr. Robert Schlund	1 1	P Bf	K K	Bf 110 E S9+EH 3852	100%	Did not return from combat mission.	Thames estuary.
04-02-41	Uffz. Gustav Drews Uffz. Rudolf Steindl	2 2	P Bf	K K	Bf 110 E-1/N S9+PK 3849	100%	Shot down by A-A fire.	Near Margate.
06-02-41		3			Bf 110 E-1 3824	20%	Damaged while taxi-ing.	Vechta.
20-02-41	Lt. Friedrich Heunisch Gefr. Rudolf Gärtner	3 3	P Bf	K K	Bf 110 E-1 S9+PK 3474	100%	Shot down by A-A fire.	Near Harwich.
03-03-41		2			Bf 110 E-1 3824	15%	Crash landing.	Ursel.
07-03-41	Fw. Konrad Fleischmann Fw. Gustav Helling	2 2	P Bf	K K	Bf 110 E S9+IK 3827	100%	Shot down by A-A fire.	Near Harwich.
08-03-41		1			Bf 110 E 3475	10%	Damaged while taxi-ing.	Ursel.
11-03-41	Lt. Erich Disper	3	P	W	Bf 110 E-1 3859	45%	Belly-landing due to bad weather.	Merville.
15-03-41		2			Bf 110 E-1 3455	10%	Crash landing.	Merville.
19-03-41	Uffz. Hermann Hilden Gefr. Wolfgang Henneberger	1 1	P Bf	K K	Bf 110 E 3825	100%	Crashed after combat mission.	Hazebrouck.
19-03-41	Ogefr. Ernst Bieber			W	Bf 110 E-1 3843	35%	Emergency landing due to running short of fuel.	Niederbardenberg.
19-03-41	Gefr. Hermann Leckner		Bf	W	Bf 110 E-2 3463		Crashed following combat mission.	Roanne.

Date	Name of crew and rank	Staffel	Status	Fate	Aircraft code & W. Nr.	Damage state	Reason for casualty	Place
21-03-41	Uffz. Balthasar Aretz Uffz. Jachmann	2 2	P Bf		Bf 110 E S9+LK 3485	10%	Crash-landed after combat mission.	South-east of Dieppe.
21-03-41					Bf 110 E-1/N 3438	20%	Emergency landing due to engine damage.	Moosele.
02-04-41					Bf 110 E-2 3830	10%	Crash landing.	Wevelgem.
03-04-41		1			Bf 110 E-2/N 3467	25%	Engine failure following enemy hits.	Wevelgem.
04-04-41	Oblt. Waldemar Krause Fl. Stabs. Ing. Hans Puls	Stab Stab	P Passenger	K K	Bf 110 E-1 3435	100%	Aircraft overturned on landing.	Near Abbeville.
09-04-41	Lt. Anton Henscheid Gefr. Josef Schubert	3 3	P Bf	K K	Bf 110 E-1/N S9+OL 3841	100%	Shot down on combat mission.	Near Lowestoft.
09-04-41					Bf 110 E-1 3450	20%	Damaged while taxi-ing.	Abbeville.
10-04-41					Bf 110 E-2/N 4405	50%	Damaged while taxi-ing.	Wevelgem.
16-04-41	Ofw. Franz Deuerling Fw. Horst Schramke	2 2	P Bf	K K	Bf 110 E-2/N S9+OK 4407	100%	Crashed on take-off.	Abbeville.
17-04-41					Bf 110 E-1 3847	15%	Crash landing.	Abbeville.

Appendix 2
The 30 mm. cannon-armed Messerschmitt 110 C-6

Towards the end of the first phase of the war in the West, in early June 1940, a variant of the Messerschmitt 110 appeared in the skies of France which was breaking fresh military ground at the time. In place of the standard two 20 mm. cannon in the lower nose of the 110, the Bf 110 C-6 carried a single 30 mm. cannon. Two such aircraft were delivered to I. Gruppe, Zerstörergeschwader 1, and they were tested by two of the most experienced pilots of the unit, Oberleutnant Martin Lutz and Oberleutnant Victor Mölders. Both flew with 1st Staffel, and Victor Mölders recalled his experiences of flying the Bf 110 C-6 in early June 1940 as follows: 'My Gruppe of ZG 1 received 2 Me 110 with 'Dackelbauch', as we jokingly called it. Oberleutnant Lutz and I received the commissioned machines and weapons to test on the direct orders of Göring. We were then considered to be among the most experienced pilots on the Me 110. Our orders were to test the effectiveness of "tank-busting" operations, particularly in low level attacks. However the machines were not to fall into enemy hands under any circumstances. After our usual escort missions with the Staffel, Lutz and I would climb into our new machines, and were free to choose out targets.

'One mission of this special type was as follows: German troops were advancing on Paris. Not only the French, but also particularly the English, flew the roads and highways in the direction of Le Havre, laden with equipment. I made an attack on locomotive engines, and established that they were harder to hit side-on than head-on, but were easier to destroy in that manner. The billowing steam told me that I had scored hits. I received a few hits from the accompanying Flak, but I fired back as best as I could.

'Suddenly 1,000 metres above me – a transport aircraft. I settled myself behind it, gave a short burst with the 3 cm. Kanone, and the crate caught fire. I closed in and saw it crash soon after. Then I saw a Gasometer 30-40 metres high, attacked and fired at it, but could not see the results. As this thing could have exploded at any time, I did not carry out any further attacks on it.

'Then I saw a goods train with military equipment – tanks and transport vehicles. After I had brought the train to a halt, I destroyed many tanks and vehicles until I ran out of Kanone ammunition. The ground fire was quite considerable, resulting in my machine receiving numerous small-arms and cannon strikes. I then set off on the return flight to Norrent-Fontes, from where I had taken off. I pulled my damaged machine high into the clouds, in order to avoid any further combat with the enemy.

'Suddenly, through a gap in the clouds, I came across 6 English Blenheims. Although I no longer had Kanone ammunition, I sought to position myself behind the complete English formation. Those lads flew really well, and tried to get me into a position where the whole formation could fire at me. However I came behind them. When the fire from the six rear gunners came towards me, I felt like a man standing under a shower. I fired what my 4 machine guns had to offer. I had already emptied two machine guns, when the aircraft on the outside right-flank of the formation tipped over. I dived behind it and watched it crash after it spiralled down in flames.

'I had to set off once again for my airfield, but I no longer knew where I was. My faithful Bordfunker passed me the bearings to follow to regain our base. Suddenly, he cried out: "Fighter behind us!" I pulled up higher, but my machine was hit once again. There were several Me 109s behind me, who had mistaken my aircraft for an enemy machine, because of the 'Dackelbauch'. Fortunately, I was able to make it to the clouds. My Bordfunker sat in the aircraft bleeding, but I could see that he was still at his radio.

'Exhausted and relieved, I then landed smoothly on the airfield, although one tyre was shot through. I carried out each and every test on the Me 110, whether as a night fighter, with the 3 cm. Kanone, or as a fighter-bomber'.

RAF Intelligence Section had to wait over two months before gaining concrete evidence that this variant of the Bf 110 was in service with the Luftwaffe, but eventually, one fell into their hands, albeit in a badly smashed state after being shot out of the sky following the raid on Croydon on 15th August 1940.

On 16th August 1940 at 19:55 hours the Air Ministry issued a 'Telegram en clair' to all Home Commands. The telegram read: 'Me 110 crashed 15/8 near Crawley Kent found to carry one large gun 30 mm bore instead of two 20 mm cannon. Four magazines of 10 rounds each discovered and gun still being excavated. This gun is mounted under fuselage and faired off by metal cowling about 9 feet long, 3_ feet broad and 20 inches deep.' Thus British Air Intelligence recorded their first meeting with the 30 mm. cannon-armed Bf 110 C-6. Four days later, a further telegram gave the following further details: 'Me 110. Crashed 15.8.40 at Copthorne, Sussex, Nr. East Grinstead. The 30mm shell gun referred to was type MG101 made by Rheinmetall Works, and was fitted under the fuselage in a large fairing approximately 9' long, 43" wide, 24" deep. Eight magazines each containing 10 rounds were found, a complete shell being 11_" in length. Two types of shell found, one projectile painted yellow marked with black band and white band above driving band, and the second painted black with yellow band and white band above driving band. The yellow shell is high explosive tracer. The black shell is high explosive armour-piercing tracer. This ammunition is being investigated and a further report will follow shortly.'

As stated earlier in the text, the aircraft found to have carried the 30 mm. cannon was the Bf 110 C-6, S9+TH, crewed by Leutnant Erich Beudel and Obergefreiter Otto Jordan, shot down following the early evening raid on Croydon on 15 August 1940. This aircraft was not the first Bf 110 C-6 to be lost by the unit, but it was to be the only example to crash on the British mainland during the war.

British Intelligence showed an obvious interest in the 30 mm. cannon. The very scant information available in the Public Record Office in Kew on the interrogation of prisoners-of-war gives no indication of the individuals concerned, and rightly so. However there is reference to the 30 mm. cannon in a file containing general information on the Messerschmitt 110: 'P/W said that only one aircraft in the whole Gruppe – possibly in the whole G.A.F. – was fitted with this gun, which was entirely experimental. This is probably incorrect, and this Gruppe probably had at least three aircraft so armed. A note in the above-mentioned diary is to the effect that it is very troublesome and always going wrong.' This small snippet of information, obviously extracted from a complete report, highlights some interesting points. The phrase: 'This is probably incorrect' shows that British Air Intelligence were uncertain at that time of the number of C-6s on charge with Erprobungsgruppe 210. Also, the phrase: 'this Gruppe probably had at least three aircraft so armed' is interesting for two reasons. First of all, 'this Gruppe' clearly shows that British Air Intelligence acknowledged a connection between the 30 mm. cannon-armed aircraft and Erprobungsgruppe 210, and secondly, taking into account the fact that German signals were being intercepted and decoded in Britain, and German 'Verluste' were transmitted to higher authority in such a manner, the reference to three aircraft is uncannily accurate, in view of the fact that as well as Beudel's aircraft, the two Bf 110 lost on 11 August 1940 were shown as 'C-6's in the 'Verluste' returns. (It should also be pointed out here that the Bf 110 of Helmut Ortner, also lost on 15 August 1940, was given as a 'C-6' in the 'Verluste' returns, but there is no intelligence evidence to show that it was, and Ortner's 2nd Staffel did not operate the C-6, that being the exclusive preserve of 1st Staffel. Furthermore, in an interview with Helmut Ortner, he quite clearly stated that he never flew a Bf 110 with a 30 mm. Kanone under the fuselage on a combat mission.)

The diary referred to is that of Eric Beudel, and it is perhaps worth quoting here an extract from a British Intelligence document prepared at the end of the war: 'During the Battle of Britain the quantities of prisoners documents requiring examination were considerable. At that time German aircrew had not been trained to any extent in security, and their pockets and aircraft contained such things as maps, code tables, diaries, private letters and lecture notebooks, the latter particularly valuable in supplying information on tactics and equipment.' The diary of Erich Beudel is not available to the public but it is likely that British Air Intelligence obtained much useful information from it concerning the 30 mm. cannon.

The 30 mm. MG 101 cannon used in the Bf 110 C-6 during the Battle of Britain was a development of the Solothurn S-18-1000 20 mm. anti-tank rifle; Rheinmetall 'scaled-up' that weapon with the necessary modifications for installation in an aircraft. In order to accommodate the 30 mm. cannon in a Bf 110, the two 20 mm. cannon were removed (as mentioned earlier) and the MG 101 was sited centrally under the fuselage housed in a large ventral fairing. The four MG 17s remained in place in the nose of the aircraft, their servicing and operation not being affected by the 30 mm. installation.

The initial test-bed was a Bf 110 B-1, coded D-AAPY, and air trials were a complete success. In flight the pilot did not suffer unduly from any additional noise, nor vibration, during the firing of the gun. Firing was no different from that of the MG 17 or MG.FF. As a result of these tests in 1938, conducted with four test pilots, the weapon was incorporated into production aircraft in 1940 as the 'C-6' variant. The 30 mm. cannon installation was factory-fitted, not in the field.

Although the S-18-1000 and the MG 101 were designed principally for the anti-tank role, Erprobungsgruppe 210 used the Bf 110 C-6 in combat against shipping and land-based targets during the Battle of Britain. Its continued use after 15th August 1940 by 1st Staffel cannot, however, be confirmed: the next 1st Staffel machine to be lost after 15th August was a Bf 110 D-0 on 6th September. It would appear, therefore, that the use of the 'C-6' was discontinued sometime between 15th August and 6th September 1940.

There is no record in the Luftwaffe Loss Tables of any other Zerstörer unit having lost a Bf 110 C-6 during the Battle of Britain and, considering the heavy losses suffered by all operational Zerstörer units during the Battle, and the experimental nature of such an aircraft, it is relatively safe to assume that Erprobungsgruppe 210 were the only unit in the Battle of Britain operating the unique Bf 110 C-6. Furthermore Wolfgang Schenck recalled that Erprobungsgruppe 210 were the only unit to use the C-6 and because of reports submitted by the unit concerning the problems they had experienced with the cannon, no further C-6s were issued from the factories; those already constructed in the factories were converted back to the standard-armed version with two 20 mm. cannon.

There is an interesting postscript to the story of the Bf 110 C-6. Although the use of the C-6 was discontinued over England, the remaining aircraft of the Gruppe were not struck off charge. In June 1941 when Germany invaded the Soviet Union, the two Gruppen of Schnellkampfgeschwader 210 (Erprobungsgruppe 210 had formed the 1st Gruppe of this unit) were operational on that front. It appears that the C-6s taken to the eastern front were distributed among the other Staffeln of the unit, as on 18th October 1941, 4th Staffel of Schnellkampfgeschwader 210 reported the loss of a Bf 110 C-6 coded S9+AM, W. Nr. 2254, 25 Kilometres west-south-west of Moscow; on 16th December 1941 5th Staffel lost a Bf 110 C-6 coded S9+MN, W. Nr. 2152, 5 Kilometres south-west of Chomntowo – of interest is that there was a crew of three in this aircraft, one being a 'Waffenwart' (armament mechanic), almost certainly observing the working of the cannon; on 27th February 1942 6th Staffel of Zerstörergeschwader 1 (SKG 210 had formed the nucleus of this reconstituted unit in early 1942) lost a Bf 110 C-6, S9+SP, W. Nr. 2249, 30 Kilometres west of Moszalsk.

Later in the war, the Germans brought into combat use a Bf 110 G-2 variant which had a 37 mm. cannon slung under the fuselage in the same manner of the earlier C-6 with the intention of it being used against Russian armour. An acknowledgement, perhaps, of the sound principle of the under-fuselage cannon, in which Erprobungsgruppe 210 were at the forefront of combat testing in 1940.

Appendix 3
Seilbomben

Towards the end of November 1940 British Air Intelligence reported that: 'A new piece of equipment is being fitted into the Me 110's of KG210 (sic). This is placed in the rear cockpit and consists of a metal box about 10 inches high, 6 inches broad and 3 inches deep. From the top of this are two metal-braided electric cables, and on the face an on-off switch, a switch with numbers and three rows of rectangular glass panels, the total number being either 10 or 20.

'The fitting of this apparatus commenced about 2 months ago, and the first aircraft to be fitted was that of the Gruppenkommandeur, who was shot down in flames on 27/9/40. Since then, all the aircraft of 1st Staffel, at least, have been equipped. This work is being carried out in one of the hangars on Denain aerodrome and the installation takes two to three days.' A further report in early December 1940 stated: 'Further interrogation has been carried out on the subject of the box near the W/T Operator's seat in the Me 110's belonging to Gruppe 210. It has now been established that this is definitely connected with "Seilbomben". As previously reported, the first of these boxes appeared about 7 or 8 weeks ago, which was shortly after a visit to Denain aerodrome, made by a party of engineers of senior rank (Major), which arrived by Ju 52 from Rechlin.

'In addition to the previous description, in the bottom right-hand corner, underneath the on/off switch, there is a push button, and on the box is a metal tab bearing the words "Siemans Gerät", and probably also 'SB'.

'According to this prisoner of war's belief, the "Seilbombe" consists of a line let down, like a trailing aerial, for about 220 feet, with a simple weight at the end. By means of this wire high-tension cables are short-circuited, and at the aircraft end there is a weak link which will break if there is any strain. It is possible that the weight has a small exploding charge.'

From the foregoing it is apparent that the information on 'Seilbomben' acquired by RAF Intelligence was quite substantial but incomplete. It would appear that although the control box for the device had been found, the 'Seilbomben' had not been discovered in the wreckage of any aircraft; if they had, reference would certainly have been made to them in a precise manner in the reports.

The 'box' was subjected to detailed examination by the Royal Aircraft Establishment at Farnborough and the findings were the subject of Report No. E.A.30/2, Dept. 1. No. E&I.1252. The report, which should be of interest to the general reader and the technically-minded alike, is reproduced below in its entirety.

ENEMY AIRCRAFT: MESSERSCHMITT Bf 110
NUMBER AND DATE UNKNOWN

Control unit for release of 'S.Bo'

R.A.E. Ref: E&I/G.1943

SUMMARY.

'D'

The report describes a control box for releasing missiles named S.Bo., the nature of which is at present unknown. There is provision for 20 release units, of which 10 only are used on the Messerschmitt installation. A rotary stud switch makes contact with each circuit in turn, a press button inching the switch round one stud each time it is pressed and released. Judging by the crude and simple nature of the mechanism, it is experimental.

REPORT

1. Description of apparatus.

The complete unit is shown in Fig. 1. The twenty Siemans indicators show, when the main switch is on, which carriers are loaded. The winding knob (marked Aufzug) for the spring driving the rotary switch has 21 positions, the initial one being marked 0, when all circuits are open. Positions 1 to 20 correspond to the numbers of the indicators and release circuits. Each time the push button (Abwurf) is pressed and released, the switch inches round and makes the next release circuit (when button is released).

Figure 2 shows the mechanism removed from the case, and illustrates the spring loaded catch, which, actuated by the release button, operates the escapement which allows the wheel carrying the rotary brush to inch round one tooth at a time.

Two 12 way jack type plugs, with silver plated contact surfaces, make contact with corresponding sockets in the case. Fig. 3 gives the circuit diagram for the 10 way installation. The twenty way installation uses three external plugs and sockets. The 10 way diagram was stuck over the 20 way diagram in the base.

2. Dimensions.

The case is 20.0 cm. wide, 19.6 cm. high and 7.5 cm. deep, not including knobs. The weight is 4.5 lb.

3. Comments on the design.

The case is built up of light alloy sheet, welded at the corners, with a strip riveted round the top edge to form a channel for a rubber sealing strip. The apparatus as a whole bears no maker's mark, and there is no reference or type number. Components are made by at least two manufacturers: the indicators by Siemans-Halske, and the main switch is type KSII/30, by List of Teltow (see report EA.M/

25, E&I.1236). These facts, coupled with the unusually simple design, suggest that this device may be experimental.

4. Purpose for which apparatus is used

There is a notice on the front panel as follows: 'Achtung. Bei Beladung mit Sbo Notzug blockieren. Keine andere Abwurfmunition laden.'

i.e. Warning. On loading with Sbo, block jettison release. Do not load with any other 'stores'.

It is not known what 'Sbo' are, but since release by this device cannot be very accurately timed, it is unlikely that they are ordinary bombs.

The expression 'Dosensockel' on the circuit diagram Fig. 3 means literally 'Box-pedestal' and may perhaps be translated 'container bracket'.

ADDENDUM TO REPORT No. 453, FEBRUARY 1941

Control unit for release of 'SBO'

The control box described is for releasing 'Sbo' i.e. Seilbomben. Translated – wire rope bombs.

The existence of bombs has been reported from various sources and they are said to be for dropping so as to trail across high-tension cables. The actual missile has however never been found but is thought to be a small bomb at the end of a long wire, it may even be only a weight at the end of a wire to short-circuit the H.T. cables.

It is said that one 'geschwader' of Me 110s was fitted with the device some months ago but no report has been received of the use of these bombs in this country.

• • • • • •

Wolfgang Schenck remembered the Seilbomben as being a very effective device. The leading edges of the wire were razor-sharp and would have been able to cut through high-tension cables easily. The device was not used over England for one simple reason according to Schenck: it was held back deliberately from combat use until the invasion of England had commenced, when it would be used to telling effect to disrupt entirely the supply of electricity in the invasion area in particular, and a large area of southern England in general. The invasion never happened, therefore the Seilbomben were never used. There is no evidence to show that they were used by the Germans when they invaded the Soviet Union.

The available evidence therefore shows that aircraft of Erprobungsgruppe 210 were fitted with the control box for Seilbomben. There is no evidence to show how they were released. Karl Stoff recalled that: 'It consisted of a rectangular steel frame with two pulleys which carried a thin steel wire made from a special alloy about 150 m. in length, with small bombs shapes on the end made from lead weights. This frame was supposed to hold the hanging bombs in place. The intention was that important high-tension cables in southern England could be cut through in low flight and thereby the provision of electric current be cut off. Corresponding maps were also prepared showing the route of important H-T cables.

Until now the matter of Seilbomben has never been mentioned in publication, let alone explained. The foregoing information resolves the enigma of Seilbomben. It must remain one of the more curious experimental devices considered by the Luftwaffe in 1940.

Appendix 4
Flugbücher of four pilots of Erprobungsgruppe 210 in 1940

The 'Flugbuch' of a Luftwaffe pilot is a source of great information for the researcher and general reader alike. Copies of the Flugbücher of four Erprobungsgruppe 210 pilots are reproduced, and it is useful that they cover all three Staffeln. Given that all entries are manual, there are occasional errors, and sometimes entries are not in exact sequence: note Hintze's last flight of the day on 11th August and first flight on 12th August are entered out of sequence. The Flugbuch entries sometimes pose a query which can probably never be answered. Why the unit flew to Dinard from Cherbourg-Ost on 8th September and returned on the 9th will probably never be known.

Flugbuch of Leutnant Erich Beudel, 1st Staffel

The entries reproduced start with Erich Beudel's first flight with Erprobungsgruppe 210. It should be noted that the unit code carried on Bf 110s of 1st Staffel during July, prior to receiving the fighter-bomber variant of the Bf 110, was 2N. Note that no correction has been made to the entries to correspond with British Summer Time.

Flight No.	Pilot	Crew	Type	Code	Type of Flight	Take-off place	Take-off day	Take-off time	Landing place	Landing day	Landing time	Flight time	Kms.	Remarks
893	Lt. Beudel	Obgefr. Diemer	Bf 110	G	Solo flight	Köln-Ostheim	7.7	1245	Köln-Ostheim	7.7	1307	22'		
894	"	"	"	P	Practise Flight	"	9.7	1507	"	9.7	1540	33'		
895	"	"	"	R	Solo Flight	Denain	11.7	1725	Denain	1805	40'			
896	"	"	"	"	Practise Flight	"	12.7	1740	"	12.7	1830	50'		
897	"	3 M.	Bf 108	KE+NU	Overland Flight	"	13.7	707	St. Omer-Arques	13.7	743	36'		
898	"	"	"	"	"	St. Omer-Arques	"	2150	Douai	"	2255	65'		Emergency landing.
899	"	1 M.	"	"	"	Douai	14.7	1335	Denain	14.7	1345	10'	30	
900	"	1 M.	Bf 110	O	Solo Flight	Denain	"	1745	"	"	1825	40'		
901	"	Diemer	"	R	Overland Flight	"	15.7	610	St. Omer-A	15.7	632	22'		
902	"	"	"	O	"	St. Omer-A	"	1453	Denain	"	1533	40'		
903	"	Ogefr. Öllers	"	P	"	Denain	18.7	1020	St. Omer-A	18.7	1045	25'		
904	"	"	"	"	Front Mission	St. Omer-A	"	1120	"	"	1305	105'		1. Enemy mission. Channel near Lowestoft
905	Lt. Beudel	Ogefr. Öllers	Bf 110	O	Overland Flight	St. Omer-A	18.7	1723	Denain	18.7	1748	25'		
906	"	2 Uffz.	Bf 108	KE+NU	"	Denain	20.7	1100	Köln-Ostheim	20.7	1207	67'		
907	"	1 Uffz.	"	"	"	Köln-Ostheim	"	1342	Antwerp	"	1442	60'		
908	"	"	"	"	"	Antwerp	"	1915	Denain	"	1953	38'		
909	"	Diemer	Bf 110	N	Practise Flight	Denain	22.7	1640	"	22.7	1750	70'		
910	"	"	"	T	"	"	24.7	1100	"	24.7	1200	60'		
911	"	"	"	N	Air Firing	"	26.7	1505	"	26.7	1535	30'		27.7 Oblt Fallenbacher shot down
912	"	"	"	R	Overland Flight	"	29.7	625	St. Omer-A	29.7	645	20'		
913	"	"	"	"	Front Mission	St. Omer-A	"	1735	"	"	1905	90'		Channel, near Orfordness
914	Oblt. Lutz		"	T	Overland Flight	"	30.7	1850	Denain	30.7	1908	18'		Lt. Herold shot down
915	Oblt. Lutz		"	S	Practise Flight	Denain	31.7	1515	"	31.7	1545	30'		
916	Uffz. Bernhard	Lt. v. Steinhart	Ju 52	1Z+FP	Overland Flight	Denain	1.8	1505	Erfurt	1.8	1755	170'		
917	Uffz. Wiebert	Lt. v. Steinhart	Ju 52	1Z+HP	Overland Flight	Erfurt	1.8	1818	Erfurt-Biudessl.	1.8	1823	5'		
918	"	"	"	"	"	Erfurt-Buidessl.	"	1850	Liegnitz	"	2033	103'		
919	Lt. Beudel	Fw. Schulze	Bf 110	CG+OT	Overland Flight	Liegnitz	2.8	1105	Gorlitz	2.8	1135	30'		
920	"	"	"	"	"	Gorlitz	2.8	1358	Karlsbad	"	1434	36'		
921	"	"	"	"	"	Karlsbad	"	1810	Juterbog-W	"	1855	45'		
922	"	—	"	"	"	Juterbog-W	"	1944	Neuruppin	"	2010	26'		
923	"	—	"	"	"	Neuruppin	3.8	1605	Köln-O	3.8	1747	102'		
924	"	—	"	"	"	Köln-O	"	1845	Denain	"	2000	75'		
925	"	Obgfr. Jordan	"	NF+BA	Diving Practise	Denain	4.8	1130	"	4.8	1200	30'		
926	"	"	"	CG+OM	Bombing Practise	Denain	"	1240	"	"	1252	12'		
927	"	"	"	"	"	"	"	1306	"	"	1319	13'		
928	"	"	"	"	"	"	5.8	1230	"	5.8	1250	20'		
929	Lt. Beudel	Obgfr. Jordan	Bf 110	CG+OM	Bombing practise	Denain	5.8	1556	Denain	5.8	1617	21'		
930	"	"	"	"	Practise Flight	"	6.8	1431	"	6.8	1527	56'		Lt. Prokop + (Bf110)
931	"	"	"	T	Firing Test	"	7.8	1600	"	7.8	1715	75'		Hptm. Valesi + (Bf109)
932	"	Oblt. Opkamp	"	"	Work Test Flight	Denain	8.8	1245	St. Omer-A	8.8	1310	25'		
933	"	Jordan	"	"	"	St. Omer-A	"	1440	Denain	"	1505	25'		
934	"	"	"	D	Bombing Practise	Denain	9.8	1510	"	9.8	1530	20'		
935	"	"	"	"	"	"	"	1835	"	"	1900	25'		
936	"	—	"	P	Work Test Flight	"	10.8	1500	"	10.8	1530	30'		
937	"	Jordan	"	D	Overland Flight	"	11.8	720	Marck	11.8	750	30'		
938	"	"	"	"	Front Mission	Marck	"	1220	"	"	1340	80'		Lt. Bertram shot down. Channel near Felixstowe
939	"	"	"	"	Overland Flight	"	"	2010	Denain	"	2035	25'		
940	"	"	"	E	"	Denain	12.8	900	Marck	12.8	925	25'		
941	Lt. Beudel	Jordan	Bf 110	E	Front Mission	Marck	12.8	1015	Marck	12.8	1100	45'		Rye
942	"	"	"	"	"	"	"	1315	"	"	1405	50'		Manston
943	Oblt. Lutz		Bf 110	C	Overland Flight	"	"	1937	Denain	"	2002	30'(sic)		
944	Lt. Beudel	Jordan	"	J	"	Denain	13.8	630	Marck	13.8	700	30'		
945	"	"	"	"	Front Mission	Marck	"	1615	"	"	1730	75'		Canterbury
946	"	"	"	"	Overland Flight	"	"	1835	Denain	"	1910	35'		
947	"	"	"	"	"	Denain	14.8	740	Marck	14.8	810	30'		
948	"	"	"	C	Front Mission	Marck	"	1230	"	"	1345	75'		Lt. Brinkmann shot down. Manston airfield
949	"	"	"	"	Overland Flight	"	"	1840	Denain	"	1910	30'		

No flight entries were made in Erich Beudel's Flugbuch for 15th August 1940. The only entries were: '15.8' in the day column, and '+' in the remarks column.

Flugbuch of Unteroffizier Balthasar Aretz, 2nd Staffel

The entries reproduced start with Balthasar Aretz's first flight with Erprobungsgruppe 210. Note that no correction has been made to the entries to correspond with British Summer Time.

The timings in Flight number 653 do not link correctly with the times in the previous flight on the same day.

Flights 662 and 663 are in the wrong order.

Flights 676 and 677 are in the wrong order.

On occasions, the calculations of flight minutes are wrong, but have been left in their original form for authenticity.

Flight 684 showed no take-off or landing times.

On missions against England, Aretz shows the location of the target in the 'Landing Place' column of his Flugbuch, which is unusual, incorrect, but nevertheless is priceless in providing the exact location of targets!

Flight No.	Pilot	Crew	Type	Code	Type of Flight	Take-off place	Take-off day	Take-off time	Landing place	Landing day	Landing time	Flight time	Kms.	Remarks
643	Aretz	Oblt. Fallenbacher	Me 110	3336 KE+US	Training Flight	Köln-Ostheim	6.7	1045	Köln	6.7	1125	40'		
644	Aretz	Oblt. Fallenbacher	Me 110	3334 DE+CX	"	"	6.7	1133	"	6.7	1208	35'		
645	Aretz	—	"	"	"	"	6.7	1228	"	6.7	1250	22'		
646	"	"	"	"	"	"	6.7	1253	"	6.7	1312	19'		
647	Aretz	Schilleng	"	3337 DE+CY	"	"	8.7	1428	"	8.7	1431	3'		
648	"	"	"	"	"	"	8.7	1433	"	8.7	1441	8'		
649	"	"	"	"	Diving Practise	"	8.7	1444	"	8.7	1517	33'		
650	"	"	"	"	Airfield Flight	"	9.7	1325	"	9.7	1338	13'		
651	"	"	"	"	"	"	9.7	1345	"	9.7	1359	14'		
652	Aretz	Schilleng	Bf 110	DE+CY	Diving Practise	Köln-Ostheim	9.7	1402	Köln-Osth.	9.7	1423	21'		
653	"	"	"	"	"	"		1422	"	9.7	1442	20'		
654	"	"	"	"	"	"	9.7	1444	"	9.7	1505	21'		
655	"	"	"	3321	Transfer Flight	"	10.7	857	Denain	10.7	943	46'		
656	"	"	"	K	Airfield Flight	Denain	17.7	1145	"	17.7	1150	5'		
657	"	"	"	"	"	"	17.7	1152	"	17.7	1155	3'		
658	"	"	"	"	Diving Practise	"	17.7	1158	"	17.7	1214	16'		
659	"	"	"	"	"	"	17.7	1216	"	17.7	1234	18'		
660	"	"	"	"	"	"	17.7	1236	"	17.7	1254	18'		
661	"	"	"	L	"	"	18.7	1340	"	18.7	1515	35'		
662	Aretz	Reichelsdörfer	"	S9+BK	Work Test Flight	St. Omer	21.7	1927	Köln-Ostheim	21.7	2027	60'		1. crash in Bf 110
663	"	"	"	"	Work Test Flight	St. Omer	21.7	1830	St. Omer	21.7	1850	20'		
664	Aretz	Schilleng	Bf 110	3377	Bombing Practise	Denain	4.8.40	1012	Denain	4.8	1040	28'		
665	"	"	"	"	"	"	4.8	1119	"	4.8	1134	15'		
666	"	"	"	"	"	"	4.8	1142	"	4.8	1205	23'		
667	"	"	"	"	"	"	4.8	1226	"	4.8	1247	21'		
668	"	"	"	3372	"	"	5.8	1720	"	5.8	1755	35'		
669	"	"	"	3372	"	"	5.8	1915	"	5.8	1950	35'		
670	"	"	"	3377	High Flight	"	7.8	1345	"	7.8	1415	35'		
671	"	"	"	"	Formation Flight	"	9.8	1130	"	9.8	1215	45'		
672	"	"	"	"	"	"	10.8	1325	"	10.8	1445	83'		
673	"	"	"	E	Transfer Flight	"	13.8	905	Mark (sic)	13.8	945	40'		Codeword 'Adlertag' 13 August. Start of the Luftschlacht um England
674	"	"	"	E	Enemy Flight	Mark	15.8	1517	S.E. England	15.8	1640	83'		1. enemy mission. Ipswich airfield.
675	"	"	"	"	Enemy Flight	"	15.8	1901	Mark	15.8	1951	51'		2. enemy mission aborted due to airframe damage. Bombs released into the Channel. Counts as enemy mission.
676	Aretz	Schilleng Gefr.	Bf 110	3377 E	Transfer Flight	Mark	16.8	1350	Denain	16.8	1420	30'		
677	Aretz	—	"	"	Work Test Flight	"	15.8	2005	Marck	15.8	2020	15'		
678	"	Schilleng	"	"	Formation Flight	Denain	19.8	1522	Denain	19.8	1607	45'		
679	"	"	"	"	Transfer Flight	"	20.8	830	Mark	20.8	900	30'		
680	Aretz	—	"	B	Work Test Flight	Mark	20.8	1050	"	20.8	1110	20'		
681	Aretz	Prüfer	"	1. Staffel	"	"	20.8	1130	"	20.8	1200	30'		
682	"	Schilleng	"	E	Transfer Flight	"	20.8	1400	Denain	20.8	1450	50'		
683	"	"	"	E	"	Denain	21.8	1030	Mark	21.8	1100	30'		Crashed.
684	Aretz	—	"	3370 D	Transfer Flight	St. Omer	31.8		Denain	21.8		20'		
685	"	Schilleng	"	E	Transfer Flight	Denain	24.8	830	Mark	24.8	900	30'		
686	"	"	"	D	Enemy Flight	Mark	24.8	1515	S.E. England	24.8	1600	45'		2. enemy mission, Manston airfield.
687	"	"	"	"	"	"	24.8	1930	"	24.8	2020	50'		3. enemy mission, coastal fortifications.
688	Aretz	Schilleng	Bf 110	D	Transfer Flight	Mark	24.8	2045	Denain	24.8	2105	20'		

Flight No.	Pilot	Crew	Type	Code	Type of Flight	Take-off place	Take-off day	Take-off time	Landing place	Landing day	Landing time	Flight time	Kms.	Remarks
689	"	"	"	"	"	Denain	25.8	840	Mark	25.8	910	30'		
690	"	"	"	"	"	Mark	25.8	1915	Denain	25.8	1945	30'		
691	"	"	"	E	"	Denain	26.8	900	Mark	26.8	930	30'		
692	"	"	"	"	Enemy Flight	Mark	26.8	1225	E. England	26.8	1307	42'		4. enemy mission. Folkstone airfield.
693	"	"	"	"	Transfer Flight	"	26.8	1935	Denain	26.8	2005	30'		
694	"	"	"	E	"	Denain	27.8	800	Mark	27.8	825	25'		
695	"	"	"	"	"	Mark	27.8	1925	Denain	27.8	1950	25'		
696	"	"	"	"	"	Denain	30.8	1640	Mark	1710	30'			
697	"	"	"	"	Enemy Flight	Mark	30.8	1825	S. England	30.8	1955	90'		5. enemy mission, Biggin Hill airfield.
698	"	"	"	"	Transfer Flight	Mark	30.8	2025	Denain	30.8	2055	30'		
699	"	"	"	"	"	Denain	31.8	715	Mark	31.8	745	30'		
700	Aretz	Schilleng	Bf 110	E	Enemy Flight	Mark	31.8	1305	S.W. London	31.8	1445	100'		6. enemy mission. Croydon airfield, 40 hits in the 'E'.
701	"	"	"	H	Transfer Flight	Denain	1.9	745	Mark	1.9	815	30'		
702	"	"	"	"	"	Mark	1.9	1415	Denain	1.9	1440	25'		
703	"	"	"	F	"	Denain	1.9	1725	Schipol, Amsterdam	1.9	1810	45'		
704	"	"	"	"	"	Schipol	2.9	945	Mark	2.9	1035	50'		
705	"	"	"	"	"	Mark	2.9	1120	Denain	2.9	1145	25'		
706	"	"	"	B	"	Denain	4.9	745	Mark	4.9	815	30'		
707	"	"	"	"	Enemy Flight	Mark	4.9	1325	S.W. London	4.9	1525	120'		7. enemy mission - airfield and works near Brookland, Vickers Wellington
708	"	"	"	"	Transfer Flight	Mark	6.9	1745	Denain	6.9	1825	40'		
709	"	"	"	H	"	Denain	8.9	835	Cherbourg-Ost	8.9	945	70'		
710	"	"	"	"	"	Cherbourg-Ost	8.9	1805	Dinard	8.9	1835	30'		
711	"	"	"	"	"	Dinard	9.9	1005	Cherbourg-Ost	9.9	1045	40'		
712	Aretz	Schilleng	Bf 110	H	Transfer Flight	Cherbourg-Ost	9.9	1840	Jersey	9.9	1855	15'		
713	"	"	"	"	"	Jersey	11.9	1325	Cherbourg-O	11.9	1345	20'		
714	"	"	"	"	Enemy Flight	Cherbourg-O	11.9	1630	S. Küste England	11.9	1740	70'		8. enemy mission, Spitfire works and airfield.
715	"	"	"	"	Transfer Flight	"	11.9	1855	Denain	11.9	2005	70'		
716	"	—	"	H	Ferry Flight	Denain	16.9	1145	Köln-Ostheim	16.9	1236	51'		
717	"	"	"	"	"	Köln	16.9	1714	Augsburg	16.9	1823	69'		
718	"	"	"	"	"	Augsburg	18.9	1705	Denain	18.9	1850	105'		On landing, right tyre flat.
719	"	Schilleng	"	K	Transfer Flight	Denain	22.9	1410	Cherbourg	22.9	1520	70'		
720	"	"	"	"	"	Cherbourg	22.9	1735	Denain	22.9	1850	75'		
721	"	"	"	B	Formation and Test Flight	Denain	23.9	1210	Denain	23.9	1235	25'		
722	"	"	"	E	Transfer Flight	Denain	24.9	835	Cherbourg-O	24.9	945	70'		
723	"	"	"	"	Enemy Flight	Cherbourg	24.9	1400	Southampton	24.9	1500	60'		9. enemy mission, very heavy Flak. Spitfire works and airfield.
724	Aretz	Schilleng	Bf 110	E	Enemy Flight	Cherbourg-O	24.9	1655	Southampton	24.9	1755	60'		10. enemy mission. Enemy fighters. Spitfire works
725	"	"	"	"	Transfer Flight	"	24.9	1855	Denain	24.9	1955	60'		
726	"	"	"	"	"	Denain	25.9	830	Cherbourg, O	25.9	940	70'		
727	"	"	"	"	Enemy Flight	Cherbourg-O	25.9	1130	Portland	25.9	1245	75'		11. enemy mission, without fighter escort. Oil installations. Flak.
728	"	"	"	"	"	"	26.9	1630	Southampton	26.9	1755	85'		12. enemy mission. Spitfire work totally destroyed.
729	"	"	"	"	"	"	27.9	1140	Bristol	27.9	1325	105'		13. enemy mission. Airfield. Strong fighter forces Kom-Hptm. Lutz, Chef-Oltn. Rößiger u. Fw. Ebner did not return from enemy mission.
730	"	"	"	"	Transfer Flight	"	27.9	1550	Denain	27.9	1656	65'		
731	"	"	"	"	"	Denain	30.9	845	Mark	30.9	910	25'		
732	"	"	"	"	Enemy Flight	Mark	30.9	1035	London and Hastings	30.9	1155	80'		14. enemy mission to London - bombs on Hastings.
733	"	"	"	"	Transfer Flight	"	30.9	1745	Denain	30.9	1820	35'		
734	"	"	"	"	"	Denain	1.10	1250	Mark	1.10	1325	35'		
735	"	"	"	"	Enemy Flight	Mark	1.10	1500	Folkstone	1.10	1600	60'		15. enemy mission. Lympden (sic) airfield.
736	Aretz	Schilleng	Bf 110	E	Transfer Flight	Mark	1.10	1650	Denain	1.10	1730	40'		
737	"	"	"	"	"	Denain	2.10	820	Mark	2.10	850	30'		
738	"	"	"	"	Enemy Flight	Mark	2.10	1145	Lympden (sic)	2.10	1245	60'		16. enemy mission - enormous 1000m. Hall
739	"	"	"	"	Transfer Flight	Mark	2.10	1715	Denain	2.10	1745	30'		
740	"	"	"	"	"	Denain	5.10	1020	Mark	5.10	1100	40'		
741	"	"	"	"	Enemy Flight	Marck	5.10	1200	London	5.10	1300	60'		17. enemy mission (London) Maidstone(wounded, hospital). Rolf shot 1 fighter down.

Flugbuch of Feldwebel Siegfried Tröppl, 2nd Staffel

The entries reproduced start with Siegfried Tröppl's first flight with Erprobungsgruppe 210. Note that no correction has been made to the entries to correspond with British Summer Time.

Flight No.	Pilot	Crew	Type	Code	Type of Flight	Take-off place	Take-off day	Take-off time	Landing place	Landing day	Landing time	Flight time	Kms.	Remarks
852	Rößiger	Tröppl	Me 110	S9+DK	Training Flight	Denain	28.8.40	1741	Denain	28.8.40	1749	8		Me 110 400 Km/h
853	Tröppl	—	"	"	Airfield Flight	"	"	1755	"	"	1801	6	40	
854	"	"	"	"	"	"	"	1805	"	"	1812	7	47	
855	"	"	"	"	"	"	"	1815	"	"	1821	6	40	
856	"	Büttner	"	"	"	"	29.8	925	"	29.8	935	10	67	
857	"	"	"	"	Practise Flight	"	"	945	"	"	1015	30	200	
858	"	"	"	"	Formation Flight	"	"	1315	"	"	1345	30	200	
859	"	"	"	EK	Diving Practise	"	"	1415	"	"	1440	25	166	
860	"	"	"	S9+DK	Bombing Practise	"	30.8	907	"	30.8	931	24	160	
861	"	"	"	S9+BK	"	"	"	1106	"	"	1115	9	60	
862	"	"	"	S9+BK	"	"	"	1128	"	"	1140	12	80	
863	"	"	"	S9+HK	"	"	31.8	1029	"	31.8	1044	15	100	
864	Tröppl	Büttner	Me 110	S9+HK	Bombing Practise	Denain	31.8.40	1052	Denain	31.8.40	1108	16	107	
865	"	"	"	"	"	"	"	1315	"	"	1327	12	80	
866	"	Stadler	"	"	"	"	"	1341	"	"	1354	13	87	
867	"	"	"	"	"	"	"	1529	"	"	1544	15	100	
868	"	Büttner	"	"	"	"	2.9	1100	"	2.9	1113	13	87	
869	"	"	"	"	"	"	"	1122	"	"	1138	16	107	
870	"	4 Mann	W34	SA+VR	Transport Flight	"	"	1240	Marck b. Calais	"	1325	45	142	W34 190 km/h.
871	"	3 Mann	"	"	"	Marck b. Calais	"	1406	Reims	"	1516	70	222	W34 190 km/h.
872	"	"	"	"	"	Reims	"	1815	Denain	"	1857	42	135	W34 190 km/h.
873	"	Büttner	Me 110	S9+BK	Bombing Practise	Denain	3.9	1042	"	3.9	1058	16	107	
874	"	"	"	"	"	"	"	1114	"	"	1148	34	226	
875	"		"	"	Air Firing	"	"	1429	"	"	1455	26	174	
876	Tröppl	2 Mann	W34	SA+VR	Transport Flight	Denain	6.9.40	1639	Marck/Calais	6.9.40	1715	36	115	
877	"	"	"	"	"	Marck/Calais	"	1800	Denain	"	1841	41	130	
878	"	Büttner	Me 110	S9+HK	Formation Flight	Denain	7.9	1035	"	7.9	1133	58	387	
879	"	"	"	"	"	"	"	1320	"	"	1400	40	265	
880	"	Büttner/Rhode	"	S9+BK	Transport Flight	"	8.9	835	Cherbourg-Ost	8.9	945	70	467	
881	"	"	"	"	"	Cherbourg-Ost	"	1805	Dinard	"	1835	30	200	
882	"	"	"	"	"	Dinard	9.9	1005	Cherbourg-Ost	9.9	1045	40	265	
883	"	"	"	"	"	Cherbourg-Ost	"	1845	Jersey	"	1905	20	134	
884	"	"	"	"	"	Jersey	11.9	1330	Cherbourg-Ost	11.9	1350	20	134	
885	"	Büttner	"	"	39. Enemy Flight	Cherbourg-Ost	"	1630	"	"	1740	70	467	Attack: Aircraft works in Eastleigh north of Southampton; (heavy Flak, fighters and barrage balloons)
886	"	"/Rhode	"	"	Transport Flight	"	"	1900	Denain	"	2010	70	467	
887	"	Büttner	"	"	"	Denain	15.9	1345	Cherbourg-Ost	15.9	1500	75	500	
888	Tröppl	Büttner	Me 110	S9+BK	40. Enemy Flight	Cherbourg-Ost	15.9.40	1815	Cherbourg-Ost	15.9.40	1930	75	500	Attack: Electricity works in Southampton. Barrage balloons, Flak, Fighters.
889	"	"/Rhode	"	"	Transport Flight	"	18.9	1630	Denain	18.9	1730	60	400	
890	"	"/Reichelsdörfer	"	S9+FK	"	Denain	30.9	845	Calais/Marck	30.9	910	25	166	
891	"	Büttner	"	"	41. Enemy Flight	Calais/Marck	"	1035	"	"	1150	75	500	Attack: 6000m. over London. Bombs dropped over Hastings (no Flak).
892	"	"/Reichelsdörfer	"	"	Transfer Flight	"	"	1745	Denain	"	1820	35	235	
893	"	"/Hämler	"	S9+CK	"	Denain	1.10	1250	Calais/Marck	1.10	1325	35	235	
894	"	Büttner	"	"	42. Enemy Flight	Calais/Marck	"	1500	"	"	1600	60	400	Attack: Lympne airfield. No defensive fire.
895	"	"/Hämler	"	"	Transfer Flight	"	"	1650	Denain	"	1730	40	265	
896	"	"/Nolan	"	"	"	Denain	2.10	820	Calais/Marck	2.10	850	30	200	
897	"	Büttner	"	"	43 Enemy Flight	Calais/Marck	"	1145	"	"	1245	60	400	Attack: Lympne airfield. Heavy defensive fire.
898	"	Godatke	"	S9+MK	Work Test Flight	"	5.10	915	"	5.10	930	15	100	
899	"	Büttner/"	"	"	Transfer Flight	"	"	1345	Denain	"	1415	30	200	
900	Tröppl	Büttner/ Reichelsdörfer	Me 110	S9+LK	Transfer Flight	Denain	15.10.40	1110	Marck	1510	1140	30	200	
901	"	"/ "	"	"	"	Marck	"	1550	Denain	"	1645	55	365	
902	"	Büttner	"	"	Test Flight	Denain	16.10	1430	"	16.10	1510	40	265	
903	"	"/Reichelsdörfer	"	"	Transfer Flight	"	17.10	905	Calais/Marck	17.10	930	25	166	
904	"	Büttner	"	"	44. Enemy Flight	Calais/Marck	"	1545	"	17.10	1625	40	265	Attack: English coast. No defensive fire.
905	"	"/R	"	"	Transfer Flight	"	"	1725	Denain	"		25	166	

Flight No.	Pilot	Crew	Type	Code	Type of Flight	Take-off place	Take-off day	Take-off time	Landing place	Landing day	Landing time	Flight time	Kms.	Remarks
906	"	Büttner	"	S9+BK	Test Flight	Denain	19.10	1417	"	19.10	1539	82	546	
907	"	"	"	S9+LK	Transfer Flight	"	20.10	1315	Calais/Marck	20.10	1345	30	200	
908	"	"	"	"	"	Marck/Calais	"	1515	Denain	"	1545	30	200	
909	"	"	"	S9+CK	"	Denain	27.10	1435	Calais/Marck	27.10	1510	35	235	
910	"	"	"	"	45. Enemy Flight	Calais/Marck	"	1725	"	"	1840	75	500	Attack: London
911	"	"	"	"	Transfer Flight	"	28.10	1550	Denain	28.10	1615	25	166	

There were no entries made in Siegfried Tröppl's Flugbuch for 29th October 1940

Flugbuch of Oberleutnant Otto Hintze, Staffelkapitän of 3rd Staffel

The entries reproduced start with Otto Hintze's first flight with Erprobungsgruppe 210. Note that no correction has been made to the entries to correspond with British Summer Time. Hintze entered the overall total of missions in the 'Kms.' column of his Flugbuch, with the number of fighter-bomber missions against England in brackets. From flight 875, however, the totals were entered in the 'Remarks' column. From flight 934 he no longer recorded totals at all in his Flugbuch until flight 959.

Take-off airfield ('Absprungshafen') from 9th August is Calais-Marck
The flight details and times in entry 798 should precede those of 797.
The flight details of flights 854 and 855 should precede those of 852.

Flight No.	Pilot	Crew	Type	Code	Type of Flight	Take-off place	Take-off day	Take-off time	Landing place	Landing day	Landing time	Flight time	Kms.	Remarks
773	Hintze	—	Bf 109	6286	Bombing Practise	Köln-Ostheim	1.7.40	1312	Köln-Ostheim	1.7.40	1355	0,43		
774	"	—	"	6286	"	"	2.7.40	1345	"	2.7.40	1420	0,35		
775	Hintze	—	Bf 109	6299	Bombing Practise	Köln-Ostheim	2.7.40	1515	Köln-Ostheim	2.7.40	1550	0,35		
776	"	—	"	6299	"	"	2.7.40	1608	"	2.7.40	1638	0,30		
777	"	—	"	6299	"	"	3.7.40	1004	"	3.7.40	1127	1,23		
778	"	—	"	6299	"	"	"	1142	"	"	1207	0,25		
779	"	—	"	6286	"	"	"	1242	"	"	1306	0,24		
780	"	—	"	1997	"	"	6.7.40	0945	"	6.7.40	1025	0,40		
781	"	—	"	1997	"	"	"	1102	"	"	1148	0,46		
782	"	—	"	+1	Test Flight	"	8.7.40	0953	"	8.7.40	1106	1,13		
783	"	—	"	+1	Bombing Practise	"	"	1444	"	"	1456	0,12		
784	"	—	"	+1	"	"	"	1500	"	"	1512	0,12		
785	"	—	"	+1	"	"	"	1515	"	"	1530	0,15		
786	"	"	"	+1	Transfer Flight	"	10.7.40	0910	Denain	10.7.40	1000	0,50		
787	Hintze	—	Bf 109	+1	Transfer Flight	Denain	13.7.40	0710	St. Omer	13.7.40	0727	0,17		
788	"	—	"	+1	Mission	St. Omer	"	1250	"	"	1415	1,25	84.	89.06 (1)
789	"	—	"	+1	Transfer Flight	"	"	2011	Denain	"	2030	0,19		
790	"	—	"	+1	"	Denain	14.7.40	0610	Douai-Süd	14.7.40	0708	0,58		
791	"	—	"	+1	"	Douai-Süd	"	0900	"-West	"	0905	0,05		
792	"	—	"	+1	"	"-West	"	1110	St. Omer	"	1129	0,19		
793	"	—	"	+1	"	St. Omer	"	1845	Denain	"	1903	0,18		
794	"	—	"	+1	"	Denain	15.7.40	0535	St. Omer	15.7.40	0555	0,20		
795	"	—	"	+1	"	St. Omer	"	1506	Denain	"	1524	0,18		
796	"	—	"	+1	"	Denain	18.7.40	1054	St. Omer	18.7.40	1113	0,19		
797	"	—	"	+1	"	St. Omer	"	1853	Denain	"	1912	0,19		
798	"	—	"	+1	Fighter Escort	"	"	1615	St. Omer	"	1650	0,35	85.	
799	Hintze	—	Bf 109	+1	Transfer Flight	Denain	19.7.40	0614	St. Omer	19.7.40	0632	0,18		
800	"	—	"	+1	Mission	St. Omer	"	1304	"	"	1350	0,46	86. (2)	Attack on ships in Dover harbour.
801	"	—	"	+1	"	"	"	1607	"	"	1702	0,55	87. (3)	Attack on ships in Dover harbour.
802	"	—	"	+1	Transfer Flight	"	"	1803	Denain	"	1823	0,20		
803	"	—	"	+1	"	Denain	20.7.40	0728	St. Omer	20.7.40	0749	0,21		
804	"	—	"	+1	Mission	St. Omer	"	0945	Vlissingen	"	1145	2,00	88. (4)	Emergency release of bombs.
805	"	—	"	+1	Transfer Flight	Vlissingen	"	1210	St. Omer	"	1245	0,35		

Flight No.	Pilot	Crew	Type	Code	Type of Flight	Take-off place	Take-off day	Take-off time	Landing place	Landing day	Landing time	Flight time	Kms.	Remarks
806	"	—	"	+1	Mission	St. Omer	"	1850	"	"	1935	0,45	89. (5)	Shipping in the Channel (Deal).
807	"	—	"	+1	Transfer Flight	"	"	2033	Denain	"	2052	0,19		
808	"	—	"	+1	"	Denain	22.7.40	0830	St. Omer	22.7.40	0851	0,21		
809	"	—	"	+1	Fighter Escort	St. Omer	"	1712	"	"	1728	0,16	90.	
810	"	—	"	+1	Transfer Flight	"	"	1859	Denain	"	1918	0,19		
811	Hintze	—	Bf 109	+1	Transfer Flight	Denain	23.7.40	0650	St. Omer	23.7.40	0710	0,20		
812	"	—	"	+1	Mission	St. Omer	"	1215	"	"	1258	0,43	91. (6)	
813	"	—	"	+1	"	"	"	1558	"	"	1652	0,54	92. (7)	
814	"	—	"	+1	Transfer Flight	"	"	1802	Denain	"	1823	0,21		
815	"	—	"	+1	"	Denain	24.7.40	1004	St. Omer	24.7.40	1025	0,21		
816	"	—	"	+1	Mission	St. Omer	"	1200	"	"	1238	0,38	93. (8)	
817	"	—	"	+1	"	"	"	1345	"	"	1418	0,33	94. (9)	
818	"	—	"	+1	"	"	"	1852	"	"	1943	0,51	95. (10)	
819	"	—	"	+1	Transfer Flight	"	"	1950	Denain	"	2013	0,23		
820	"	—	"	+1	"	Denain	25.7.40	1004	St. Omer	25.7.40	1027	0,23		
821	"	—	"	+1	Mission	St. Omer	"	1150	"	"	1237	0,47	96. (11)	
822	"	—	"	+1	"	"	"	1703	"	"	1742	0,39	97. (12)	
823	Hintze	—	Bf 109	+1	Mission	St. Omer	25.7.40	1902	St. Omer	25.7.40	1932	0,30	98. (13)	
824	"	—	"	+1	Transfer Flight	"	"	1958	Denain	"	2020	0,22		
825	"	—	"	+1	"	Denain	27.7.40	1305	St. Omer	27.7.40	1323	0,18		
826	"	-	"	+1	Mission	St. Omer	"	1514	"	"	1548	0,34	99. (14)	
827	"	—	"	+1	"	"	"	1714	"	"	1752	0,38	100. (15)	
828	"	—	"	+1	"	"	"	1816	"	"	1907	0,51	101. (16)	
829	"	—	"	+1	Transfer Flight	"	"	2017	Denain	"	2035	0,18		
830	"	—	"	+1	"	Denain	29.7.40	0630	St. Omer	29.7.40	0648	0,18		
831	"	—	"	+1	"	St. Omer	"	2007	Denain	"	2025	0,18		
832	"	—	"	+1	"	Denain	30.7.40	1325	St. Omer	30.7.40	1345	0,20		
833	"	—	"	+1	"	St. Omer	"	1854	Denain	"	1911	0,17		
834	"	—	"	+1	"	Denain	31.7.40	1418	St. Omer	31.7.40	1440	0,22		
835	Hintze	—	Bf 109	+1	Transfer Flight	St. Omer	31.7.40	2038	Denain	31.7.40	2055	0,17		
836	"	—	"	+1	"	Denain	1.8 40	1303	St. Omer	1.8.40	1320	0,17		
837	"	—	"	+1	"	St. Omer	"	2026	Denain	"	2044	0,18		
838	"	—	"	+1	"	Denain	2.8 40	1520	St. Omer	2.8.40	1536	0,16		
839	"	—	"	+1	Mission	St. Omer	"	1710	"	"	1805	0,55	102. (17)	
840	"	—	"	+1	"	"	"	1930	"	"	2025	0,55	103. (18)	
841	"	—	"	+1	Transfer Flight	"	"	2105	Denain	"	2122	0,17		
842	"	—	"	+1	"	Denain	3.8.40	1700	St. Omer	3.8.40	1716	0,16		
843	"	—	"	+1	"	St. Omer	"	1929	Denain	"	1946	0,17		
844	"	—	"	+1	"	Denain	5.8.40	0933	St. Omer	5.8.40	0950	0,17		
845	"	—	"	+1	Mission	St. Omer	"	1655	"	"	1735	0,40	104. (19)	
846	"	—	"	+1	Transfer Flight	"	"	1942	Denain	"	2000	0,18		
847	Hintze	—	Bf 109	+1	High Level Flight	Denain	8.8.40	1152	Denain	8.8.40	1245	-,53		
848	"	—	"	+5	Transfer Flight	"	9.8.40	1312	Take-off airfield	9.8.40	1335	-,23		
849	"	—	"	+5	"	Take-off airfield	"	1614	Denain	"	1642	-,28		
850	"	—	"	+1	"	Denain	11.8.40	0706	Take-off airfield	11.8.40	0730	-,24		
851	"	—	"	+1	Mission	Take-off airfield	"	1220	"	"	1324	1,04	105. (20)	
852	"	—	"	+1	"	"	12 8.40	1030	"	12.8.40	1125	0,55	106. (21)	
853	"	—	"	+1	"	"	"	1315	"	"	1405	0,50	107. (22)	
854	"	—	"	+1	Transfer Flight	"	11 8.40	1955	Denain	11.8.40	2020	-,25		
855	"	—	"	+1	"	Denain	12 8.40	0835	Take-off airfield	12.8.40	0900	-,25		
856	"	—	"	+1	Mission	Take-off airfield	"	1755	"	"	1855	1,—	108. (23)	
857	"	—	"	+1	Transfer Flight	"	"	1954	Denain	"	2018	-,24		
858	"	—	"	+1	"	Denain	13 8.40	0626	Take-off airfield	13.8.40	0652	-,26		
859	Hintze	—	Bf 109	+1	Mission	Take-off airfield	13 8.40	0715	Take-off airfield	13.8.40	0850	1,35	109. (24)	
860	"	—	"	+1	"	"	"	1615	"	"	1739	1,24	110. (25)	
861	"	—	"	+1	Transfer Flight	"	"	1820	Denain	"	1850	0,30		
862	"	—	"	+1	"	Denain	14.8.40	0720	Take-off airfield	14.8.40	0745	0,25		
863	"	—	"	+1	"	Marck	"	1820	Denain	"	1845	0,25		
864	"	—	"	+1	"	Denain	15.8.40	0815	Marck	15.8.40	0840	0,25		
865	"	—	"	+1	Mission	Marck	"	1520	"	"	1635	1,15	111. (26)	
866	"	—	"	+1	"	"	"	1915	"	"	2042	1,27	112. (27)	
867	"	—	"	+1	Transfer Flight	"	16.8.40	1405	Denain	16.8.40	1431	0,25		
868	"	—	"	+1	Practise Flight	Denain	17,8.40	1619	"	17.8.40	1755	1,36		
869	"	—	"	+1	"	"	18.8.40	1041	"	18.8.40	1118	-,37		
870	"	—	"	+1	Transfer Flight	"	20.8.40	0807	Marck	20.8.40	0832	-,25		

Flight No.	Pilot	Crew	Type	Code	Type of Flight	Take-off place	Take-off day	Take-off time	Landing place	Landing day	Landing time	Flight time	Kms.	Remarks
871	Hintze	—	Bf 109	+1	Transfer Flight	Marck	20.8.40	1805	Denain	20.8.40	1830	-,25		
872	"	—	"	+1	"	Denain	21.8.40	1032	Marck	21.8.40	1058	-,26		
873	"	—	"	+13	"	Marck	"	1816	Denain	"	1842	-,26		
874	"	—	"	+13	"	Denain	22.8.40	0931	Marck	22.8.40	1001	-,30		
875	"	—	"	+1	Mission	Marck	"	1332	"	"	1405	-,33		113. (28)
876	"	—	"	+1	"	"	"	1930	"	"	2012	-,42		114. (29)
877	"	—	"	+1	Transfer Flight	"	"	2045	Denain	"	2113	-,28		
878	"	—	"	+1	"	Denain	23.8.40	0835	Marck	23.8.40	0904	-,29		
879	"	—	"	+1	"	Marck	"	1849	Denain	"	1918	-,29		
880	"	—	"	+1	"	Denain	24.8.40	0831	Marck	24.8.40	0900	-,29		
881	"	—	"	+14	Mission	Marck	"	1515	"	"	1555	-,40		115. (30)
882	"	—	"	+1	"	"	"	1930	"	"	2015	-,45		116. (31)
883	Hintze	—	Bf 109	+1	Transfer Flight	Marck	24.8.40	2048	Denain	24.8.40	2118	-,30		
884	"	—	"	+1	"	Denain	25.8.40	0945	Marck	25.8.40	1014	-,29		
885	"	—	"	+1	"	Marck	"	1920	Denain	"	1948	-,28		
886	"	—	"	+1	"	Denain	26.8.40	0905	Marck	26.8.40	0933	-,38		
887	"	—	"	+1	Mission	Marck	"	1230	"	"	1305	-,35		117. (32)
888	"	—	"	+1	Transfer Flight	"	"	1940	Denain	"	2009	-,29		
889	"	—	"	+1	"	Denain	27.8.40	0813	Marck	27.8.40	0841	-,28		
890	"	—	"	+1	"	Marck	"	1923	Denain	"	1953	-,30		
891	"	—	"	+1	"	Denain	28.8.40	0904	Marck	28.8.40	0934	-,30		
892	"	—	"	+1	"	Marck	"	1648	Denain	"	1718	-,30		
893	"	—	"	+1	"	Denain	29.8.40	0900	Marck	29.8.40	0927	-,27		
894	"	—	"	+1	"	Marck	"	1309	Denain	"	1343	-,34		
895	Hintze	—	Bf 109	+1	Transfer Flight	Denain	30.8.40	0716	Marck	30.8.40	0745	-,29		
896	"	—	"	+1	Mission	Marck	"	1533	"	"	1617	-,44		118. (33)
897	"	—	"	+1	"	"	"	1825	"	"	1945	1,20		119. (34)
898	"	—	"	+1	Transfer Flight	"	"	2038	Denain	"	2107	-,29		
899	"	—	"	+1	"	Denain	31.8.40	0719	Marck	31.8.40	0749	-,30		
900	"	—	"	+1	Mission	Marck	"	1310	"	"	1425	1,15		120. (35)
901	"	—	"	+1	Transfer Flight	"	"	1607	Denain	"	1633	-,26		
902	"	—	"	+1	"	Denain	1.9.40	0704	Marck	1.9.40	0733	-,29		
903	"	—	"	+1	Mission	Marck	"	1700	"	"	1758	-,58		121. (36)
904	"	—	"	+1	Transfer Flight	"	"	1840	Denain	"	1911	-,31		
905	"	—	"	+1	"	Denain	2.9.40	0728	Marck	2.9.40	0758	-,30		
906	"	—	"	+1	Mission	Marck	"	1745	"	"	1850	1,05		122. (37)
907	Hintze	—	Bf 109	+1	Transfer Flight	Marck	2.9.40	1947	Denain	2.9.40	2016	-,29		
908	"	—	"	+1	Practise Flight	Denain	4.9.40	1443	"	4.9.40	1531	-,48		
909	"	—	"	+1	Bombing Practise	"	5.9.40	1424	"	5.9.40	1435	-,11		
910	"	—	"	+1	"	"	"	1450	"	"	1508	-,18		
911	"	—	"	+1	"	"	"	1520	"	"	1540	-,20		
912	"	—	"	+1	Transfer Flight	"	7.9.40	1132	Marck	7.9.40	1201	-,29		
913	"	—	"	+1	Mission	Marck	"	1806	"	"	1923	1,17		123. (38)
914	"	—	"	+1	Transfer Flight	"	"	1958	Denain	"	2028	-,30		
915	"	—	"	+1	"	Denain	8.9.40	0905	Cherbourg-Ost	8.9.40	1010	1,05		
916	"	—	"	+1	"	Cherbourg-Ost	"	1805	Dinard	"	1835	-,30		
917	"	—	"	+1	"	Dinard	9.9.40	1005	Cherbourg-Ost	9.9.40	1045	-,40		
918	"	—	"	+1	"	Cherbourg-Ost	"	1825	~~Jersey~~ Guernsey	"	1950	1,25		
919	Hintze	—	Bf 109	+1	Transfer Flight	~~Jersey~~ Guernsey	11.9.40	1430	Cherbourg-Ost	11.9.40	1450	-,20		
920	"	—	"	+1	Mission	Cherbourg-Ost	"	1630	"	"	1745	1,15		124. (39)
921	"	—	"	+1	Transfer Flight	"	"	1905	Denain	"	2005	1,-		
922	"	—	"	+13	"	Denain	18.9.40	1443	Cherbourg-Ost	18.9.40	1550	1,07		
923	"	—	"	+1	"	Cherbourg-Ost	"	1713	Denain	"	1820	1,07		
924	"	—	"	+1	"	Denain	20.9.40	1315	Cherbourg-Ost	20.9.40	1425	1,10		
925	"	—	"	+1	"	Cherbourg-Ost	22.9.40	1735	Denain	22.9.40	1840	1,05		
926	"	—	"	+1	Overland Flight	München	1.10.40	0920	Sandhofen	1.10.40	1035	1,15		
927	"	—	"	+1	"	Sandhofen	"	1118	Denain	"	1219	1,01		
928	"	—	"	+1	"	Denain	"	1445	Marck	"	1513	-,28		
929	"	—	"	+1	"	Marck	"	1647	Denain	"	1715	-,28		
930	"	—	"	+1	Practise Flight	Denain	11.10.40	1451	"	11.10.40	1539	-,48		
931	Hintze	—	Bf 109	+1	Practise Flight	Denain	11.10.40	1542	Denain	11.10.40	1549	-,07		
932	"	—	"	+1	"	"	13.10.40	1429	"	13.10.40	1511	-,42		
933	"	—	"	+1	Transfer Flight	"	15.10.40	1117	Marck	15.10.40	1145	-,28		
934	"	—	"	+1	Mission	Marck	15.10.40	1625	"	"	1730	1,05		
935	"	—	"	+1	Transfer Flight	"	"	1820	Denain	"	1845	-,25		

Flight No.	Pilot	Crew	Type	Code	Type of Flight	Take-off place	Take-off day	Take-off time	Landing place	Landing day	Landing time	Flight time	Kms.	Remarks
936	"	—	"	+1	Overland Flight	Denain	16.10.40	1445	Beauvais	16.10.40	1528	-,43		
937	"	—	"	+1	"	Beauvais	"	1735	Denain	"	1810	-,35		
938	"	—	"	+1	Transfer Flight	Denain	17.10.40	0913	Marck	17.10.40	0941	-,28		
939	"	—	"	+1	Mission	Marck	"	1350	"	"	1440	-,50		
940	"	—	"	+1	"	"	"	1650	"	"	1800	1,10		
941	"	—	"	+1	Transfer Flight	"	"	1845	Denain	"	1912	-,27		
942	"	—	"	+8	"	Denain	20.10.40	1254	Marck	20.10.40	1322	-,28		
943	Hintze	—	Bf 109	+8	Mission	Marck	20.10.40	1355	Marck	20.10.40	1410	-,15		
944	"	—	"	+8	Transfer Flight	"	"	1635	Denain	"	1703	-,28		
945	"	—	"	+7	"	Denain	21.10.40	1235	Marck	21.10.40	1303	-,28		
946	"	—	"	+7	"	Marck	"	1505	Denain	"	1535	-,30		
947	"	—	"	+11	"	Denain	25.10.40	0916	Marck	25.10.40	0945	-,29		
948	"	—	"	+11	Mission	Marck	"	1010	"	"	1120	1,10		
949	"	—	"	+11	"	"	"	1340	"	"	1400	-,20		
950	"	—	"	+11	"	"	"	1632	"	"	1652	-,20		
951	"	—	"	+11	Transfer Flight	"	"	1803	Denain	"	1833	-,30		
952	"	—	"	+6	"	Denain	26.10.40	0814	Marck	26.10.40	0844	-,30		
953	"	—	"	+6	Mission	Marck	"	1710	"	"	1805	-,55		
954	"	—	"	+6	Transfer Flight	"	"	1810	Denain	"	1840	-,30		
955	Hintze	—	Bf 109	+6	Transfer Flight	Denain	27.10.40	0829	Marck	27.10.40	0859	-,30		
956	"	—	"	+6	Mission	Marck	"	0940	"	"	1045	1,05		
957	"	—	"	+6	"	"	"	1410	"	"	1425	-,15		
958	"	—	"	+6	"	"	"	1715	"	"	1730	-,15		
959	"	—	"	+6	"	"	28.10.40	1710	"	28.10.40	1805	-,55		137. (52)
960	"	—	"	+6	"	"	29.10.40	1340						

Appendix 5
Combat victory report (Abschußmeldung) of an Erprobungsgruppe 210 pilot during the Battle of Britain

Extant combat report copies of Luftwaffe fighter pilots are comparatively rare, so the translations of the documents in this appendix are of interest for that fact, and also because this records the first claim of 3rd Staffel, Erprobungsgruppe 210 during the Battle of Britain.
The report of the 'claimant' is the 'Abschußmeldung', and those of the witnesses are shown as 'Luftzeugenkampfbericht'.
The reports gives a good overall picture of the combat which took place on 27th July 1940 following a successful attack on Dover harbour, the unfortunate Hurricane pilot almost certainly being Flying Officer P.A.N. Cox of 501 Squadron.
It should be noted that the reports consist of questions, and the replies given by the pilots of 3rd Staffel.

Marx Lt. 4.8.1940
3./Staffel of Erp. Gruppe 210

COMBAT VICTORY REPORT (Abschußmeldung)

1.) Time (Day, Hour, Minute) and Place: 27.*7.40, 18,50 Hours Channel*
Height: 300m.
2.) Type of shot-down aircraft: Hu*rricane*
3.) Nationality of aircraft: English
4.) Manner of destruction: B*urning, crashed into sea, black smoke.*
a) burning (white streams of fuel, dark smoke trails, light flames).
b) How crashed (Complete, in pieces).
c) forced landing (This side or other side of the front, complete or broken up).
d) after emergency landing on the other side of the front, burning on the ground.
5.) Manner of impact: first flat, then perpendicular dive.
a) this side or other side of the front.
b) perpendicular, flat trajectory, burst into flames on impact, clouds of dust.
c) not observed, why not.
6.) Fate of occupants (dead bailed out, not observed)
Not observed.
7.) Combat Report:

After a bombing attack on a relief cruiser in Dover harbour, the Staffel were returning in the direction of Calais. Concerning the report: The last machine was engaged in combat (and) the whole Staffel turned. The English machine veered away, but was however caught up by us. After two other aircraft had already fired at it, I managed to get within 40 m. and my first burst from behind and below set it on fire. It immediately dived blazing into the Channel.

Hintze Obltn. u. Staffelkapitän 4.8.1940
3./Staffel of Erp. Gruppe 210

AIR COMBAT REPORT (Luftzeugenkampfbericht)

1.) Time (Day, Hour, Minute): 27.*7.40, 18,50 Hours Channel*
Height at the beginning: 300m.
2.) How many friendly and enemy aircraft were definitely recognised: 8 *enemy, 7 friendly.*
3.) How many friendly and enemy aircraft were definitely known to have been shot down: 1 enemy
4.) How was the claim seen: bu*rning, dived into the water, black smoke.*
a) Crashed (Complete or in pieces)
b) through a perpendicular crash and burning on impact or clouds of dust.
c) through shooting down and burning in the air (white or black trails, light flames)
d) by an emergency landing on the other side of the front (complete or in pieces).
e) by an emergency landing on the other side of the front in flames.
f) Place and time of crash, emergency landing.
5.) To whom is the victory credited. Aircraft identify. First flat then perpendicular dive (Machine Nr. 3 Lt. Marx)
6.) Report of witness:

On the return flight from a mission against Dover harbour, the last aircraft was attacked by an English fighter shortly before reaching the French coast. After giving warning over the R/T that the last aircraft was in combat, I immediately turned towards the two machines, whereupon the English fighter, a Hurricane, sought to escape in the direction of Dover. After a short burst, I had to pull away to the left due to my greater speed. After completing the left turn, I saw that the Hurricane was hit by the third machine, and shortly afterwards fell burning into the sea.

Büttner, Feldwebel 4.8.1940
3./Staffel of Erp. Gruppe 210

AIR COMBAT REPORT (Luftzeugenkampfbericht)

1.) Time (Day, Hour, Minute): 27.7.40, *18,50 Hours Channel*
Height at the beginning: 300m.
2.) How many friendly and enemy aircraft were definitely recognised: 8 *enemy, 7 friendly.*

3.) How many friendly and enemy aircraft were definitely known to have been shot down: 1 enemy

4.) How was the claim seen: bu*rning, dived into the water, black smoke.*

a) Crashed (Complete or in pieces)

b) through a perpendicular crash and burning on impact or clouds of dust.

c) through shooting down and burning in the air (white or black trails, light flames)

d) by an emergency landing on the other side of the front (complete or in pieces).

e) by an emergency landing on the other side of the front in flames.

f) Place and time of crash, emergency landing.

5.) To whom is the victory credited. Aircraft identify. First flat then perpendicular dive (Machine Nr. 3 Lt. Marx)

6.) Report of witness:

After completion of the mission, on 27 July 1940, 18,30 hours, the first Schwarm, in which I flew as Nr. 2, with the Bf 109 E Nr. 11, was on the return flight. After being told over the R/T to turn back for combat, we saw an enemy aircraft (Hurricane), which, as we drew close, sought to escape in low flight. The Staffelkapitän, behind whom I flew closely, reached the enemy aircraft, which tried to avoid the bursts of fire by turning, whereupon I was able to give 2 short bursts to the enemy. With the enemy aircraft suddenly pulling upwards, No. 1 + 2 passed by it, due to greater speed. I then saw one of the following machines fire a heavy burst into the opponent, and the machine crashed into the water.

Appendix 6
Commanding Officers of Erprobungsgruppe 210 - 1940

Date	Gruppenkommandeur	Staffelkapitän, 1st Staffel	Staffelkapitän, 2nd Staffel	Staffelkapitän, 3rd Staffel	Adjutant
01-07-40	Hptm. Walter Rubensdörffer	Oberleutnant Martin Lutz	Oberleutnant Wilhelm-Richard Rößiger	Oberleutnant Otto Hintze	Oberleutnant Alfred Habisch
27-07-40	Hptm. Walter Rubensdörffer	Oberleutnant Martin Lutz	Oberleutnant Wilhelm-Richard Rößiger	Oberleutnant Otto Hintze	Oberleutnant Horst Fiedler
16-08-40	Oberleutnant Martin Lutz (acting)	Leutnant Ulrich Freiherr von der Horst (acting)	Oberleutnant Wilhelm-Richard Rößiger	Oberleutnant Otto Hintze	Oberleutnant Werner Weymann (acting)
26-08-40	Hptm. Hans von Boltenstern	Oberleutnant Martin Lutz	Oberleutnant Wilhelm-Richard Rößiger	Oberleutnant Otto Hintze	Oberleutnant Werner Weymann (acting)
05-09-40	Oberleutnant Martin Lutz (acting)	Oberleutnant Werner Weymann (acting)	Oberleutnant Wilhelm-Richard Rößiger	Oberleutnant Otto Hintze	Leutnant Wolfgang Schenck
07-09-40	Oberleutnant Martin Lutz	Oberleutnant Werner Weymann	Oberleutnant Wilhelm-Richard Rößiger	Oberleutnant Otto Hintze	Leutnant Wolfgang Schenck
28-09-40	Oberleutnant Werner Weymann (acting)			Oberleutnant Otto Hintze	Leutnant Wolfgang Schenck
05-10-40	Oberleutnant Werner Weymann (acting)		Hptm Knappe	Oberleutnant Otto Hintze	Oberleutnant Wolfgang Schenck
06-10-40		Oberleutnant Wolfgang Schenck	Hptm Knappe	Oberleutnant Otto Hintze	Leutnant Herrmann
30-10-40		Leutnant Wolfgang Schenck	Hptm Knappe	Oberleutnant Peter Emmerich	Leutnant Herrmann
01-11-40	Major Karl-Heinz Lessmann	Leutnant Wolfgang Schenck	Hptm Knappe	Oberleutnant Peter Emmerich	Leutnant Herrmann

Erprobungsgruppe 210 Aircraft in Color

2N+RH, Bf 110 C-6, 1st Staffel
Pilot - Leutnant Erich Beudel
Bordfunker - Obergefreiter Heinrich Diemer
This aircraft was damaged in combat with Hurricanes of 151 Squadron on 29th July 1940.
Leutnant Beudel force-landed the aircraft in France.

S9+CB, Bf 110 D, Gruppenstab
Pilot - Leutnant Karl-Heinz Koch
Bordfunker - Unteroffizier Rolf Kahl
Shot down following the raid on Croydon on 15th August 1940. Both crew survived into captivity.

S9+TH, Bf 110 C-6, 1st Staffel
Pilot - Leutnant Erich Beudel
Bordfunker - Obergefreiter Otto Jordan
Shot down following the raid on Croydon on 15th August 1940. Both crew killed.

S9+CK, Bf 110 D, 2nd Staffel
Pilot - Oberleutnant Alfred Habisch
Bordfunker - Unteroffizier Ernst Elfner
Force-landed following damage over Croydon on 15th August 1940. Both crew survived into captivity.

Yellow 3, Bf 109 E-4/B, 3rd Staffel
Pilot - Leutnant Horst Marx
Shot down following raid on Croydon on 15th August 1940. Horst Marx bailed out into captivity.

S9+EK, Bf 110 D, 2nd Staffel
Pilot - Unteroffizier Balthasar Aretz
Bordfunker - Gefreiter Rolf Schilleng
This aircraft, the 'E', W.Nr.3377, was flown extensively by Aretz and Schilleng in the second half of August 1940.

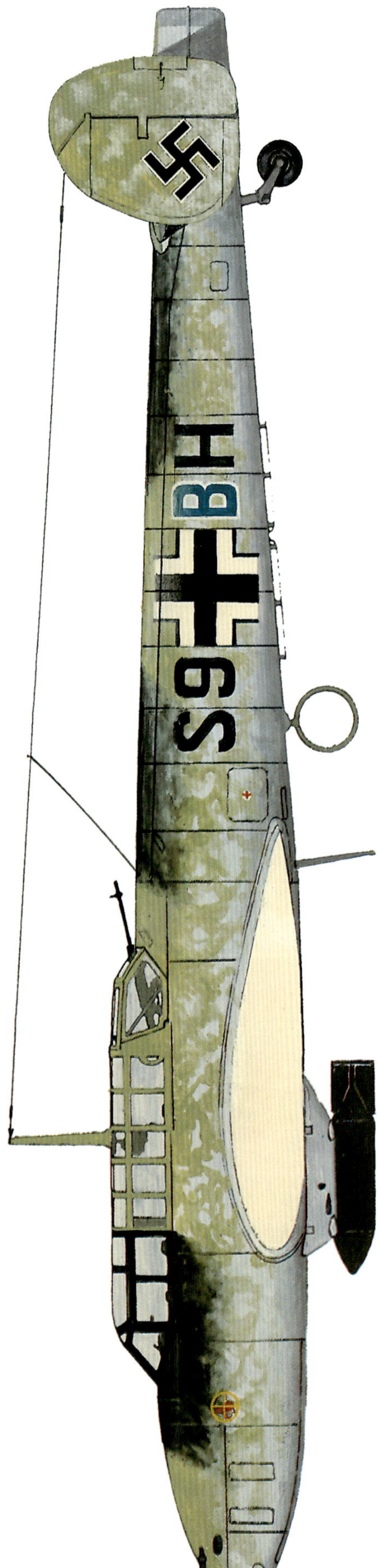

S9+BH, Bf 110 D-0, 1st Staffel
Pilot - Unteroffizier Gerhard Rüger
Bordfunker - Gefreiter Edmund Ernst
Shot down on 6th September 1940 en route to bomb Brooklands. Rüger was killed in action; Ernst bailed out into captivity.

S9+DH, Bf 110 D, 1st Staffel
Shown during the Battle of Britain with a distinctive camouflage pattern on the fuselage top surface.

S9+AH, Bf 110 D, 1st Staffel
Shown after a forced-landing. Date and crew not known.

Yellow 1, Bf 109 E-4/B, 3rd Staffel
Pilot - Oberleutnant Otto Hintze
Flown by Hintze from early July 1940 to 17th October 1940, thus participating in all the major raids undertaken by 3rd Staffel in the main period of the Battle of Britain.

S9+GK, Bf 110 E, 2nd Staffel
Shown in spring 1941

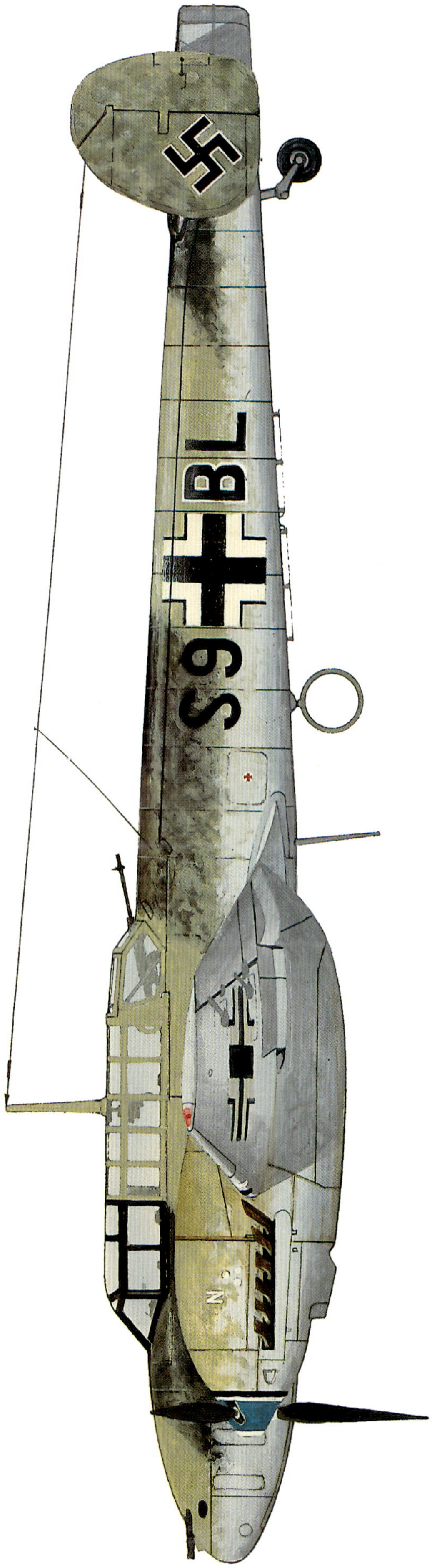

S9+BL, Bf 110 E-1, 3rd Staffel
On charge with 3rd Staffel, and lost in action with Schnellkampfgeschwader 210 on 19th May 1941.

Also from the Publisher

The Sting of the Luftwaffe

Schnellkampfgeschwader 210 and Zerstörergeschwader 1
"Wespengeschwader" in World War II

John Vasco

This photo-history of Schnellkampfgeschwader 210 and Zerstörergeschwader 1 "*Wespengeschwader*" in the years 1941-1944 shows for the first time in a single volume the many personalities, and the varied Messerschmitt and Junkers aircraft types flown by these units. Between the two units, they flew in more theatres of operations than any other unit. The work also contains a comprehensive loss/damage list for personnel and aircraft, drawn from the Deutsche Dienststelle records and the Quartermaster loss returns, and appendices covering reports on several combats by the actual participants, and extracts from three Flight Log books outlining the many tasks undertaken by the flying personnel of the unit. Drawing photographic content from mainly private sources, this work fills a gap in the overall documented history of the Luftwaffe in World War II.
Size: 9"x12", over 270 b/w photographs
160 pages, hard cover
ISBN: 0-7643-1305-3 $49.95